44321

W9-CIG-956

THE

WORLD

OF

BALLET

Oleg Kerensky

COWARD-McCANN, INC.

NEW YORK

Copyright © 1970 by Oleg Kerensky

First American Edition 1970

All rights reserved. This book, or parts thereof, may not be reproduced in any form without permission in writing from the Publisher.

Library of Congress Catalog Card Number: 75-113534
Printed in the United States of America

THE WORLD OF BALLET

IN MEMORY OF MY MOTHER

And with lasting gratitude to her for introducing me to
the ballet, for giving me my first critical standards, for
sharing her delights with me at so many performances,
especially those of Margot Fonteyn and Rudolf Nureyev,
and for everything. I hope she would have liked this book.

Contents

Part Three: THE APPEAL OF BALLET

Preface

ANYONE WHO WRITES about ballet is conscious of the excellent books which have already been written, and of an enormous debt to their authors. Cyril Beaumont's detailed accounts of so many ballets, classical and more recent, and G. B. L. Wilson's *Dictionary of Ballet* have been invaluable to me, as they must be to everyone interested in the subject. Arnold Haskell probably did more than anyone else to make ballet intellectually respectable in Britain and his books were its main guides for a whole generation. But there is now yet another new generation of dancers, choreographers, audiences—and critics; attitudes to ballet have altered as radically as the rest of our artistic and moral environment. The classics are produced in new ways and we expect different things from them, as we do from new ballets. We are more conscious of the erotic appeal of dance and dancers, discreetly ignored in most earlier writing, and choreographers now compete with each other in exploiting it.

Ballet is now so well-established that we no longer feel the need to be on the defensive about it. Nor should we any longer want to make rules about what ballet can or cannot do, or how it must be divided from the rest of the theater. This is a guide to the world of ballet as it is today, and as it may develop in the future. It is not a history or a technical handbook, though some history is inevitably included at the beginning and some technical terms are explained at the end. I hope it will be useful to those who have not yet seen any ballet and also that it will interest and stimulate even those who have seen a great deal.

In writing it, I have, of course, been influenced and helped by every ballet book I have read, by conversations with choreographers, dancers, fellow critics and regular balletgoers, and by all the ballets I have seen. Many articles in the British and American ballet magazines have been particularly valuable; and I must acknowledge that some of the material in this book is based on earlier articles of my own. In particular, some of the comments by dancers on their work originally appeared in *Ballet Today* as part of a series on "Ballet as a Career," some of the information about Dame Margot Fonteyn was obtained when writing a profile of her for the *New Statesman*, and my attack on Fokine's principles was first launched in the *London Magazine*. Many of my views on ballets and dancers have appeared in the *Listener*, the *Dancing Times* and, most recently, in the *New Statesman*. I am grateful to the editors of those magazines, and of all the other newspapers and magazines in which I have written, for the opportunities they gave me. More specifically in connection with this book, I am most grateful to my colleague Malcolm Stewart for reading the entire manuscript, making constructive suggestions and saving me from some mistakes; Roger Scales for doing the same thing with the proofs; Mary Clarke, the editor of the *Dancing Times,* and David Ellenberg, the conductor, for detailed and helpful advice on certain sections; Patricia Entract, my former colleague on the *Listener,* for obtaining and helping to select the photographs; and everyone in the world of ballet who has patiently answered my questions. Mary Clarke kindly allowed me to borrow and use photos from the *Dancing Times* collection. I also want to thank Richard Timmins for encouraging me to write the book in the first place, for sustaining my confidence when it flagged, and for providing valuable help, with Eddie Ruhier and Roy Stanbridge, with the arduous task of translating my scribbled corrections into legible writing. I am grateful to Roy Stanbridge also for suggesting the title and to Hilary Rubinstein, my agent, for his enthusiasm and for arranging the book's publication. Finally, the book would never have been printed but for the endless patience of my editor, Roger Machell, who coped valiantly with an extremely untidy manuscript. Despite all this help, the responsibility for any factual errors and for the opinions expressed is of course entirely mine.

OLEG KERENSKY

January 26, 1970

Preface to the American Edition

SINCE WRITING the British edition of this book, I have been able to spend nearly two months seeing ballet in the United States and Canada. I was tremendously surprised and impressed by the extent to which ballet is now flourishing there. The New York *Times,* for example, gives more space to dance reviews than any other national daily paper; New York, rather than London or Paris, is undoubtedly today's world capital of the dance. The sheer quantity of the performances is breathtaking, and intimidating, for the visitor. Apparently there is an enthusiastic audience for them all. I was delighted by the way in which ballet is widely accepted as a leading contemporary art and as a vital part of the theater. Wherever I traveled, people were interested in ballet and there was always some local dance activity. For this edition I have therefore written two extra chapters and I have also added further references to American ballet throughout the text. Correspondingly, I have reduced some of the British references. But the book of course remains the work of a British critic and the world of ballet is seen from an essentially British point of view.

I would like to express my gratitude to my American publishers, the U.S. Embassy in London, and the Council on Leaders and Specialists in Washington, who all did so much to make my visit practical and enjoyable; to Mrs. Helen Simpson for making me at home in New York; and to a large number of people who gave me their time, help and advice. In particular I must thank Mr. Clive Barnes of the New York *Times,* Mr. Nathan Cohen of the Toronto *Star,* Miss Arlene Croce of *Ballet Review,* Miss Doris Hering and Mr. Jack Anderson of *Dance Magazine,* Miss P. W. Manchester of the University of Cincinnati, and all the directors and press officers who took the trouble to explain their companies' problems and to enlighten me about the American ballet scene. Mr. Anderson gave me the benefit of detailed comments on the American sections of this edition. Miss Elizabeth Forbes, Dame Ninette de Valois, Mr. Clement Crisp, Herr Horst Koegler, and Mr. Keith Money have kindly drawn my attention to a few factual slips, which I have corrected. As with the British edition, however, the responsibility for the opinions expressed, and for any remaining mistakes, is entirely mine.

OLEG KERENSKY

March 16, 1970

Part One

WHAT IS BALLET?

CHAPTER I

The Classics

BALLET IS PRETTY GIRLS IN WHITE DRESSES, mooning around to music by Chopin, or in very brief tutus, balancing on the point of one foot to the music of Tchaikovsky. It is narcissistic, possibly effeminate, boys in tights, leaping in the air or gazing wanly at the ballerina. It is fairies, and Wilis, and peasant high jinks. It is exotic and Russian. It is sexy and French. It is cold and American. It is Pavlova and Nijinsky, Fonteyn and Nureyev. These are just some of the popular images of ballet, and they are all partly true. But ballet is also a high art form, attracting the talents of leading painters, composers, poets and writers. It can be "classical," "romantic," or "modern." It can include speech or song, or be performed in total silence. It can also be staged without scenery or costumes. It can be a mimed drama about Sex, Drugs, the Bomb, or God, to electronic music, just as easily as it can be waltzes and feats of technical skill. Nowadays it can even avoid anything that would normally be recognized as dancing. What have all these things in common, that they can all be classified as "ballet"? What is ballet?

Different theories about the nature of ballet have been current at different times, and still are. And ballet has served varying functions in its comparatively short history. Of course there has always been dancing, as long as there has been human society. Even the most primitive tribes have their folk dances. Dance formed an essential part of ancient Greek comedy, and featured in many early religious rituals. But ballet, as distinct from folk dancing, religious dancing, or social dancing, is fairly recent. Dance as a theatrical art in its own right is generally said to have developed in Italy from the traditional commedia dell'arte or harlequinade and to have been transported to France as an entertainment for the court of Louis XIV. Molière incorporated ballets in his comedies written for the court as Lully did in his operas. The Sun King used to dance in some of these spectacles himself; he appointed a royal dancing master, and he set up the National Academy of Music and Dance which still exists, at present as part of the Paris Opéra. Recently historians have reminded us that ballet was also developed in England at about the same time, having its origin in the Elizabethan masque. As early as 1717, John Weaver staged *The Loves of Mars and Venus* at Drury Lane Theatre and it seems likely that this story without spoken words, with mime and pure-dance interludes, was the first true ballet in anything like the sense we use the word today.

But ballet did not maintain a continuous tradition in England, and it is from France, through Denmark and Russia, that we know it today. The early development of classical ballet occurred there. From the beginning, the National Academy taught the five positions of the feet and the importance of turning out the leg from the thigh—which remain basic elements of classical ballet technique. It was the eighteenth-century French ballerina Camargo who first shortened her skirts to make possible delicate beaten steps and little jumps off the ground. And the first of the great theorists of ballet was also French.

Jean Georges Noverre's *Letters on Dancing,* published in

Stuttgart in 1760, laid down principles intended to make ballets more coherent and artistic. He himself created many ballets, in Stuttgart and in Paris, and his *Les Petits Riens* to music which he specially commissioned from Mozart is thought to have had a direct influence on Bournonville and Petipa, the two great choreographers who brought ballet from France to Denmark and Russia. But Noverre's principles were largely ignored in practice and forgotten in theory until they came into fashion again in this century when they were reformulated by the Russian choreographer Michel Fokine. Fokine ensured that for the first half of this century, lip service at least should be paid to those principles by all writers on ballet. Even now most of us have been brought up to believe that ballets must have a definite theme and that the various ingredients—music, dancing and decor—should all be appropriately matched to it.

No doubt this approach to ballet has much to be said for it. It raises ballet from mere acrobatics or circus to the level of a serious art. It is quite true that the sheer display of difficult steps does not in itself constitute a ballet. It is also true that good choreography—the actual steps being danced—can be diminished by ugly or inappropriate costumes and scenery, or by vulgar or characterless music. But it does not follow, as Fokine appeared to think, that every ballet must be a perfect blend of story, dance, music and decor. It is not even true, as Noverre claimed, that ballet must express a dramatic idea. This must be particularly evident to present-day American balletgoers, trained on Balanchine's mainly abstract repertoire. Before considering the theory of ballet any further, it will be more useful to consider the ballets which have actually been most successful in practice.

The nineteenth century, when ballet first became well known and widely popular, was above all the period of so-called romantic ballet, which had little to do with Noverre's urge for drama and his belief in ballet as a rational unity. The great romantic ballets, some of which survive today, were irrational and escapist. They were the ballets, immortalized in lithographs, in which Taglioni, Ellsler and Grisi floated among the clouds. These ballerinas specialized in lightness and ethereality; the most famous roles of this type were Giselle and La Sylphide.

Giselle is still regarded by many people as the greatest ballet. The story is simple but effective. Giselle, a peasant girl, falls in love with Albrecht, a nobleman, who presents himself to her as a peasant boy, Loys. The truth is revealed by the jealous Hilarion, who also loves Giselle. Albrecht admits that he must return to his fiancée, the Princess Bathilde. Giselle goes mad and dies, either of a broken heart or by stabbing herself, depending on the production and the ballerina's preference. In the second act, Giselle is transformed into a Wili, a spirit haunting the woods at night, obliged to lure men to dance till they are exhausted and die. The Wilis kill Hilarion in this way, and then Giselle is forced by the icy Myrtha, Queen of the Wilis, to attempt the same thing with Albrecht. But he is saved, first by sheltering under the cross on Giselle's grave and then by being sustained, dancing with Giselle, until dawn. Giselle returns to her grave, though in some productions Albrecht carries her to a separate grassy bank, presumably in an attempt to save her from her fate as an eternal Wili. Albrecht is left to mourn and repent.

The story, devised by Théophile Gautier from a book by Heine, will not bear close examination, though producers nowadays are constantly finding new ways of making it more plausible and coherent. How would a nobleman succeed in fooling a whole village, except the percipient Hilarion, into thinking him a peasant? Is he genuinely in love with Giselle or only trifling with her? What is to become of Giselle and Albrecht after the ballet is over? It is all ultraromanticism, the battle of love and faith against class distinctions, jealousy, the mystic forces of evil, and death itself. And it works superbly in the theater.

The title role of Giselle has been associated with nearly all the great ballerinas, from Grisi, who created it in Paris in 1841, and her contemporaries Grahn, Ellsler and Cerrito, through the Russians, Karsavina, Spessivtseva and Pavlova, to the twentieth-century British ballerinas Markova and Fonteyn. In recent years other outstanding interpreters have included Alicia Alonso in America, Yvette Chauviré in France and Galina Ulanova in the Soviet Union. The role calls for a combination of dramatic ability, charm, personality and dancing skill. In the first act the ballerina should suggest complete infatuation with Albrecht-Loys, and should ideally have the sort of nervous intensity or extreme sensitivity which makes madness and heart-break or suicide plausible. She must also be lively and rapid in leading the peasant girls in their dances and radiate the sheer physical joy of dancing, even while doing a difficult diagonal movement across the stage on the point of one foot. In the second act, she has mainly to dance, preferably jumping high and landing silently, like a spirit, while combining ghostliness with concern and devotion for Albrecht. The role has been called the Hamlet of the dance.

As with Hamlet, the problem is to find an artist young enough to look the part but mature enough to convey the emotions. Giselle is often danced quite successfully by a girl who has the right kind of face and dramatic ability but who would not attempt the other, more technically demanding, ballerina roles. But the full emotional effect of the ballet is more often achieved by a mature ballerina who has the art of simulating youth; sometimes these ballerinas, like Ulanova and Markova, go on scoring a dramatic success as Giselle even when they are no longer fully up to the technical demands. The ideal combination of youth, emotional range and technical assurance is rarely found; when it is, the result is a memorable Giselle. Among the outstanding exponents of this kind today are the Italian ballerina Carla Fracci, the Stuttgart ballerina Marcia Haydée, and the two Russians Ekaterina Maximova of the Bolshoi in Moscow and Natalia Makarova of the Kirov in Leningrad.

The principal male roles in the nineteenth-century ballets were subordinate to the ballerina's, but Albrecht is more than a

mere partner and porter. A skillful actor can suggest a youthful
flirtation with Giselle later converted into true love by her
death. In recent years, Nicolai Fadeyechev of the Bolshoi was
the first to show us that even Albrecht's walk to Giselle's grave
at the beginning of the second act can be a moment of extreme
beauty and emotion, while Fonteyn and Nureyev have achieved
a greater degree of togetherness, of mutual adoration and
empathy, than we had ever seen before in this ballet. Nureyev
excels too in the final moments, crushed and alone on stage
after Giselle has returned to her grave. Albrecht also, of course,
has to be a fine dancer, especially in the jumps and exhausted
falls of the second act. But given a great Giselle the ballet
works, even with an indifferent Albrecht. With an inadequate
Giselle, the ballet is scarcely worth doing, however well the
other parts are taken and however skillful the production. If a
great Giselle is supported by an equally great artist as Albrecht,
and if the smaller parts are also intelligently acted and well
danced or mimed, the total effect is naturally even more satisfying.

In recent years all sorts of attempts have been made to restore
"lost" passages of *Giselle* and to make the story more logical and
convincing. The Royal Ballet's revision in 1960 restored a long
mime passage for Giselle's mother, which was taught to Gerd
Larsen by the veteran ballerina Tamara Karsavina. The mother
warns Giselle of her fate as a Wili if she goes on dancing so
much, though how she knows Giselle will be betrayed by her
lover is not clear. The touring section of the Royal Ballet's
production in 1968, by Peter Wright, made Hilarion much
more sympathetic than before, as do the Bolshoi and David
Blair's version for American Ballet Theatre. Several of these
productions have Hilarion confirm his suspicions about his
rival's noble birth by comparing the crest on Albrecht's sword
with the crest carried by the hunting party, but again there is
no rational explanation for this unless Albrecht's marriage to
the aristocratic Bathilde is going to be incestuous! All these
glosses on the production, though they may be helpful and

effective in the theater, are only incidental to the success of the ballet.

The costumes for *Giselle* can be designed in various styles and colors but in any case they are not realistic. The peasant girls in the first act are sometimes dressed in a uniform color, or in matching shades, and no pretense is made of dressing them as real peasants. The music, by Adolphe Adam, was regarded as superior to the average ballet music of its day; it makes dramatic use of a theme associated with Giselle, which is repeated in a slower, broken way for her mad scenes, and of other recurring themes or leitmotivs. It is pretty music and ideally suited to dancing, and to the story of this ballet. But it is not the sort of music which a serious music lover would listen to alone, on disc or in the concert hall. In this it is typical of good ballet music, which is rarely good concert music. (It is tempting to make the generalization that good ballet music is *never* good concert music and vice versa; but there are exceptions to this, as to every generalization about ballet.)

These remarks about *Giselle* apply equally to its contemporary, Bournonville's *La Sylphide,* not to be confused with Fokine's *Les Sylphides.* The story is even slighter and less interesting. James, a young Scottish laird, is engaged to Effy but becomes infatuated with the Sylphide, who floats up chimneys and in through windows and finally persuades him to follow her to the forest. Meanwhile Madge the Witch, who was rebuffed by James when she visited his house, is plotting against him. She gives him a magic shawl for the Sylphide, whose wings drop off as soon as she wraps herself in it. Effy, thinking James lost, marries his friend and rival, Gurn. The ballet ends with her bridal procession and the Sylphide being wafted up into the heavens, leaving James alone, disconsolate.

The similarities with *Giselle* are obvious: again there are two acts, the first human and partly realistic, the second concerned with spirits, and ultraromantic in style. As in *Giselle,* the second act is an excuse for a chorus (corps de ballet) of girls in white. The role of the Sylphide is not as dramatic as that of Giselle and

the ballet's effect is less emotional. One cannot get deeply interested in the fate of any of the characters—the human ones are
too shallow and too fickle, and the Sylphide is too artificial.
Nevertheless a ballerina with the right combination of lightness
and a quizzical facial expression can make the Sylphide seem
amusing and touching, as Taglioni doubtless did, and as
Margrethe Schanne used to do with the Royal Danish Ballet,
and Lucette Aldous with the old Ballet Rambert. Carla Fracci
and the Danish ballerina Toni Lander have both been very
successful in this part with American Ballet Theatre. An outstanding mime can make much of the witch, as Gerda Karstens
and Niels Bjørn Larsen have done with the Danish Ballet. And
James is a fine part for a virile-looking male dancer with good
elevation; it is the part in which Erik Bruhn first attracted
attention in London and which he now dances so successfully
with Ballet Theatre, and one which the present Director of the
Royal Danish Ballet, Flemming Flindt, also takes to very good
effect.

There are two musical scores for *La Sylphide,* one by
Schneitzhoffer for the original French production in 1832 and
one by Løvenskjold for the Danes in 1836. Both are pretty and
appropriate, but like Adam's score for *Giselle,* they could not
stand up alone in the concert hall. Nor are they improved by
being reorchestrated and augmented as Adam's and Løvenskjold's have been by Ballet Theatre. The success of *La Sylphide*
and *Giselle,* and their continuous survival in the repertoire
until the present day, is not due to the intrinsic qualities of
their stories, decors, or musical scores. It is due to their qualities
as ballets.

What does this mean? It means in effect that there is just
enough of a story to provide an excuse for pretty scenery,
danceable music, various contrasting dances, and, above all, an
outstanding ballerina role. At the same time the story is not so
complicated that it needs a lot of elaborate mime, or would be
better told as a play. And none of the other ingredients—drama,

music, or decor—are allowed to distract attention from the principal one, the dance.

This formula was applied with perhaps even greater success to the so-called classics, the ballets created at the end of the nineteenth century for the Imperial Russian Ballet in St. Petersburg by Marius Petipa, a French balletmaster, and his assistant, Lev Ivanov. The Tchaikovsky ballets which they made remain the staples of the international repertory—*The Sleeping Beauty, Swan Lake (Le Lac des Cygnes)* and *The Nutcracker (Casse-Noisette)*. Petipa also created a vast number of other ballets, some of which did not survive at all while others remained in production in Russia but were unknown abroad. A few of these, like *Raymonda, Don Quixote,* and an act of *La Bayadère,* have recently been seen in the West as a result of foreign tours by Soviet ballet companies and of the enthusiasm and skill of the former Leningrad dancer Rudolf Nureyev, now dancing and producing in the West. These ballets seem to be just as rich in varied and exciting dancing as the Tchaikovsky works, but their stories are even more difficult to take seriously. Some of them also have the disadvantage of music by hack ballet composers like Minkus and Drigo, agreeable and appropriate as background music for dancing but obviously lacking the distinction of Tchaikovsky. *Raymonda* actually has a very beautiful score by Glazunov, and it is surprising that it has not yet been taken fully into the regular repertoire. The Royal Ballet performed Nureyev's production at the Spoleto and Baalbek festivals in 1964, but so far have done only the last act in London and New York. It has been left to the Australian Ballet to have the whole work in their permanent repertoire.

Petipa had a more or less stereotyped approach to the making of a ballet, an approach which easily lent itself to the sneers and criticisms of later purists and aesthetes. The story, of a fantasy or fairy-tale nature, with even less human interest than in the older "romantic" ballets, was used as an excuse for a whole series of dances in various styles. These would be designed to show off the varied talents of the chorus, soloists and, above all, the ballerina. There was usually a divertissement, a kind of danced variety show with many different specialty numbers and national dances, fitted into the action of the ballet as part of a celebration. There would be solos ("variations") for the principal dancers and at least one big formal duet ("pas de deux") for the ballerina and her partner. This pas de deux followed a standard pattern: the *entrée* and *adage,* a duet in which the ballerina is supported and lifted by her partner, solo variations for each of them, and the *coda,* in which they dance together again, performing various difficult technical feats at high speed. (Thus the pas de deux builds up to a climax of excitement; frequently these classical duets are performed on their own in concert and gala programs, or as interludes between short ballets.) Finally, after the divertissement and the big pas de deux, the Petipa ballet would normally have a happy ending, or at least the pretense of one.

The Sleeping Beauty is the most straightforward example of this style. The christening of the baby Princess Aurora is the occasion for a series of solos by the various fairies who bring her gifts, for ensemble dances by the fairies and their cavaliers, and for a piece of elaborate mime by Carabosse, the wicked fairy who comes uninvited and tries to put the spell of death on the Princess. The next act takes place on Aurora's sixteenth birthday. Four Princes come as her suitors and provide the cue for the famous Rose Adagio, in which Aurora dances with each of them in turn and holds an exciting and delicate balance on one foot while being passed from one to another. There is also a solo for Aurora, quick and light and bouncy, expressing her youthful joy of living, but ending with her pricking her finger on a spindle. Her dance becomes increasingly giddy and she collapses into her hundred-year sleep. The next act is an ethereal scene for the ballerina and corps de ballet, all in white, akin to the second act of *Giselle* or *La Sylphide,* a style which Petipa generally worked into his ballets on one pretext or another. In this particular case, the pretext is a vision for the Prince. He is out hunting with a party from the court, but he is moody and makes his entourage, including the attendant Countess who is evidently in love with him, leave him alone. Then the Lilac Fairy—the good fairy who has converted Carabosse's spell from death to prolonged sleep—comes and shows the Prince a vision of Aurora. And so Aurora and her attendants—fairies, spirits or her friends, it is not clear—dance for the Prince. Then the vision disappears and the Lilac Fairy guides the Prince through rivers and forests to the palace where Aurora is sleeping. This journey gives the producer opportunities to lay on lavish transformation scenes, culminating in the Prince finding Aurora, waking her with a kiss, and consequently waking the entire court and providing the excuse for the grand finale—the wedding celebrations. Here we have the standard Petipa divertissement, including a comic dance for Puss in Boots and a female cat, the famous Blue Bird pas de deux which gives a male dancer a chance to display his virtuosity, and the final "Aurora" pas de deux for the happy couple.

It will be seen that there is nothing particularly interesting or original about the dramatic treatment of the fairy tale. Various productions modify details of the story in different respects but it can never become very much more than an excuse for dancing. The wicked fairy Carabosse can be made into a strong character, either frightening or pathetic, and is often successfully played by a male character dancer. The original Carabosse was the famous Italian dancer and teacher Enrico Cecchetti, who also danced the Blue Bird. More recently, with the Royal Ballet, Robert Helpmann doubled the roles of Carabosse and the Prince, playing the wicked fairy as a frightening witch, while Frederick Ashton and Alexander Grant have also left a lasting impression with their impersonations, playing her rather as sour and jealous. The role usually makes less impact when danced by a woman, as was again found in the Royal Ballet's 1968 production. However, a female interpretation can be successful; Olga Adabache's incredible, bizarre makeup made a curiously hypnotic effect, as she marched about on her points in the spectacular fantasy production by the late Marquis de

Cuevas' company, and female Carabosses have also been fairly successful with London's Festival Ballet.

It is obvious that *The Sleeping Beauty* is capable of many different treatments. The decor can be in almost any style or period. Louis XIV period is usual, but the new Royal Ballet production, with decor by Henry Bardon and costumes by Lila de Nobili and Rostislav Doboujinsky, goes back to mock-medieval times. Kenneth MacMillan's production in Berlin is set in nineteenth-century Moscow, while the Cuevas version was in chic Parisian fantasyland. Professional critics tend to be shocked by each change of setting but there is no essential unity between the decor and this sort of choreography and music. What makes *The Sleeping Beauty* work, and survive, is the choreography, the music, and the ballerina role. The ballerina playing Aurora should be immature and girlish and radiantly happy at her first appearance, sylphlike and elusive in the vision, and radiant and more mature at her wedding. Margot Fonteyn has shown, as the famous Russian ballerinas doubtless did in earlier years, how Aurora can become a great ballerina role. It is the part in which she first appeared at Covent Garden, and in which she first conquered New York. It was at one time regarded by many experts as her greatest role.

Tchaikovsky's music is of course infinitely superior to the average run of ballet music. He is one of the only three composers who are equally famous for their symphonic and their ballet music. (The other two, also Russian, are Prokofiev and Stravinsky.) But although extracts from his ballet music are often performed at concerts, even a Tchaikovsky ballet score is not considered interesting enough to be played in its entirety on its own. The well-known Nutcracker Suite, for example, is mainly the music of the divertissement in the second act of *The Nutcracker,* while the music for the rest of the ballet remains virtually unknown outside the theater.

The Nutcracker is even less dramatic than *The Sleeping Beauty.* The original story is simply about a small girl whose toys, including a nutcracker doll, come to life and fight among themselves. The nutcracker, transformed into a victorious prince, takes her on a magic journey through the snowflakes to the Kingdom of Sweets. The appeal of the ballet is largely to children, especially as child dancers can be used in the opening party scene and to impersonate the toys as they come to life. The snowflakes scene provides the excuse for the inevitable "white" scene for the female corps de ballet, and the Kingdom of Sweets for the usual divertissement, culminating in a pas de deux for the Sugar Plum Fairy (the ballerina) and the Prince.

All sorts of attempts have been made to make this story more coherent or more interesting, and to enlarge the ballerina role. Originally all the ballerina had to do was the classical pas de deux at the end of the ballet. Many productions now give her a second role as well, as Queen of the Snow, and at least three producers—John Cranko, Yuri Grigorovitch and Rudolf Nureyev—have revised the plot so that the ballerina has a central role right through the ballet. Grigorovitch at the Bolshoi and Nureyev, in his productions at Stockholm, Covent Garden and La Scala, have the little girl, Clara, dream the whole journey, and she is seen waking up again at the end of the ballet. This device, which has also been used by other producers, has the advantage of giving the ballet some semblance of coherence. Grigorovitch and Nureyev also have the ballerina herself dance the part of Clara, then travel with the Prince, in her dream, through the snow, and finally dance the big pas de deux with him.

Cranko, for his production in Stuttgart, has invented an entirely new story, intended to have a more sophisticated and adult appeal. It becomes a ballet about a handsome soldier who flirts with all the girls except the one who loves him. Her fairy godmother contrives to make the other girls look ridiculous and whisks the girl and the soldier off to the usual kingdoms of snow and sweets. By the end, the soldier is converted to love of the girl. The heroine is a teenage girl, not a small child, and can therefore be more convincingly danced by a ballerina. (The snag about the Grigorovitch and Nureyev method is that only a certain physical type of dancer can even attempt to impersonate a small girl, and many people dislike adults pretending to be children.) The story may not be particularly subtle, but it works and provides Cranko with a convenient peg for his choreography, without his having to cope with any stage children.

In Europe, the dramatic weakness of *The Nutcracker* has prevented it becoming as popular, or as frequently performed, as the other Tchaikovsky-Petipa classics. But in the United States *The Nutcracker* has been adopted as the ideal Christmas entertainment; there are about 150 different productions every year. The inspiration for them doubtless comes from George Balanchine's production for New York City Ballet, a version which is surprisingly traditional. Balanchine has retained the original story, and has not expanded the ballerina's or the male dancer's roles. Indeed, the leading male dancer appears only for the final pas de deux, and does not even dance a solo variation. The success of this production is due largely to its nostalgic re-creation of a Victorian, family-Christmas atmosphere, with elaborate scenic effects which are themselves rare experiences for New York balletgoers.

The original choreography for *The Nutcracker* was not by Petipa, but by his assistant Lev Ivanov. It is possible that this style of ballet did not suit Ivanov as well as it did Petipa; that may be why the choreography does not seem as distinguished as that of *The Sleeping Beauty* and is more frequently altered by modern producers and choreographers. On the other hand it is now known that Ivanov also did the choreography for large sections of *Swan Lake,* all of which used to be credited to Petipa. The second act in particular, which is generally regarded as one of the choreographic masterpieces of all time, is now known to be Ivanov's work. *Swan Lake* provides one of the most difficult and rewarding ballerina roles. Whatever is done with the ballerina part in *The Nutcracker,* or even with Aurora in *The Sleeping Beauty,* neither of them begins to compare, either in dramatic complexity or in opportunities for technical virtuosity, with the dual role of Odette-Odile in *Swan Lake*. This is a personal view, not universally accepted, but I am fortified to find that it is also Margot Fonteyn's view. She regards *Swan Lake* as the most terrifying of all ballets but also as the one which, if properly performed, can give the greatest satisfaction to the ballerina and the audience. Despite the claims which can be made for *Giselle*, with its melodramatic and moving mad scene, I have long been convinced that *Swan Lake*—taken as a whole—remains the most remarkable and successful ballet in existence.

As in *The Sleeping Beauty* and the original version of *The Nutcracker*, the ballerina does not appear in the first act. The first act of *Swan Lake* takes place on Prince Siegfried's coming of age. Various folk and classical dances are performed as part of the entertainment and the Prince's mother, the reigning Queen or Princess, comes to tell him to grow out of constant pleasure-seeking and to choose a wife from various suitable candidates at the forthcoming ball. The Prince, depressed by his mother's reproaches, is diverted by the idea of hunting a flock of swans which fly overhead. They lead him to the lakeside, and to the famous second act of *Swan Lake,* which is often performed on its own in mixed programs with other ballets.

The swans, on landing at the lakeside, turn into young girls, in other words into the usual white-clad female corps de ballet. They are led by Odette, the ballerina Swan Queen. They have all been transformed into swans by Rotbart, an evil magician, and only resume their human form in the moonlight. The spell can be broken if someone swears true love to one of them, and remains faithful. (There is some uncertainty about the plot at this point. It is not clear how long the Prince must be faithful to Odette, or how her release would affect the other swan maidens.) Odette explains the situation to the Prince, who is immediately captivated by her. He swears eternal love, but as the moon fades, she is forced to rejoin the other maidens in their life as swans.

Odette's role in this act is the epitome of classical dancing.

She has a tender, loving pas de deux with the Prince, and a more energetic solo variation. There are fluttering arm movements and a gentle curving of the neck which suggest that the maiden is still part swan, or which at any rate remind us of her ambiguous status. There is a mime passage (now often omitted) in which she explains her plight to the Prince and throughout the act there are opportunities for her to convey her sorrow, her love for the Prince, her trust in him, and the tragic sense of doom at parting, when she is drawn back from him, as if by a hypnotic power. Even when dancing quick and difficult virtuoso steps, she should never look as if she is showing off, or dancing for applause. Everything is soft, poignant and lyrical.

In the third act, by contrast, the ballerina becomes a blatant show-off, a flashy, hard vamp. She is Odile, Rotbart's daughter, infatuating the Prince by impersonating Odette. Originally these roles were danced by two different ballerinas. This is still done sometimes, for example by the Royal Ballet on tour, as a way of giving two young dancers experience when neither of them is ready for the complete dual role. It was also done by the Bolshoi during their 1969 London season, when they had to rely on three overworked ballerinas. It showed remarkable lack of organizing ability by the Bolshoi, or remarkable contempt for London audiences, that they were reduced to such a humiliating situation.

Jack Carter's version for Festival Ballet uses two separate ballerinas for alleged dramatic effect but the confrontation between them is not developed to any purpose—when the same ballerina dances Odette and Odile she has the chance to show two completely contrasted sides of her personality and technique. Sometimes she does this to such an extent that it is difficult to believe it *is* the same ballerina, and impossible to understand how the Prince can be fooled. The subtle interpreter of Odile has just enough hardness and brilliance to be recognizably an impostor, but is constantly giving the Prince little reminders of Odette, by some of the same steps, arm and hand movements. Odette's warm and appealing smile, for example, can be transformed into a smile which might still captivate the Prince, but which, to the audience, is obviously insincere. Some Odiles wear a very flashy and vulgar costume, with streaks of red in the traditional black, but this is a mistake. The plot presupposes a certain credulity or blindness on the part of the Prince; it is made even less plausible if Odile is too obviously a fraud, and if, as in many productions, she is constantly seeking instructions from her sinister-looking father.

All that Odile actually has to dance is the celebrated and exciting pas de deux with the Prince known as the Black Swan pas de deux, often performed on its own in divertissements and mixed programs. This involves some difficult balances for the ballerina, and the notorious thirty-two fouettés. These are spins around on the point of one foot, whipping the other foot around at knee level. The spins are supposed to be executed on one spot on the stage, without traveling sideways or down toward the footlights. Originally this was a difficult stunt, a speciality of the Italian ballerina Legnani, but later it became a commonplace, performed not only by all ballerinas but also by many music-hall dancers. Some dancers have easily been able to do far more than thirty-two fouettés, and until recently it was assumed that almost any well-trained dancer could manage thirty-two. However in recent years British ballerinas seem to have found them difficult and there is now scarcely a single ballerina of the Royal Ballet who can be relied upon to do them impeccably. Some of them, and also some Soviet ballerinas, prefer to substitute a "manège," or series of quick turns around the stage, but audiences then tend to feel cheated, just as they do if an opera singer leaves out interpolated high notes which have become traditional. It is a far cry since the time in the mid-1930s when Vera Nemchinova, dancing Odile at the old Alhambra Theatre in London, was so embarrassed at muffing the fouettés that she ran off the stage, reappearing to start her whole variation again and execute the fouettés perfectly. It would be good to see more of that kind of determination today. Nevertheless a ballerina with the other qualities required to dance

Odette-Odile should not be deterred by her inability to do the fouettés; equally, of course, a dancer who can easily do an enormous number of fouettés is not thereby automatically qualified to dance Odette-Odile, a fact which some technically strong dancers find difficult to appreciate.

Obviously the interpreter of Odile cannot do any acting while she is actually dancing the most rapid and technically exacting parts of the Black Swan. But in the opening duet there are slow passages in which she parodies the love duet between Odette and the Prince, and after the pas de deux she has a moment of open triumph when the Prince swears his love, thus breaking his oath to Odette. The Black Swan can be a success even without any acting at all, just as a technical tour de force. If it is at all competently performed, it usually stops the show with a long round of applause and sometimes the dancing itself is punctuated with applause at the most sensational steps.

In the last act, the ballerina is Odette again, heartbroken by the Prince's unfaithfulness and realizing that she is now doomed to be a swan forever. First she dances with her fellow swan maidens, expressing her grief; then the Prince arrives, full of remorse, and they dance a gentle pas de deux. Odette then drowns herself, the Prince follows, and this proof of their deep love destroys Rotbart's power and leaves them reunited, in a final apotheosis, in a better world.

At least that is the ending to which western audiences are now most accustomed. But the story of *Swan Lake* is more tinkered with in different productions than that of any other classic ballet, in attempts to make it more logical or intelligible. In the original Petipa production, according to Cyril W. Beaumont, Odette and the Prince simply indicated their readiness to die and this in itself was sufficient to break Rotbart's spell and enable the swan maidens to be fully human again. Something like this is seen in Igor Belsky's production for the Dutch National Ballet, in which Odette and the Prince overcome Rotbart by the sheer force of their love. Asaf Messerer's production at the Bolshoi Theatre, Moscow, on the other hand, in accordance with the Soviet desire for realism and the triumph of virtue, has the Prince fight Rotbart, rip off his wings, and end happily united with Odette in the dawn. The trouble with these endings, apart from their banality, is that one wonders why they could not have happened earlier. If love, or a fight, are enough to defeat Rotbart, why not defeat him in the second act? Kenneth MacMillan tried to solve this problem in his Berlin production by presenting the whole story as the Prince's dream, with the hero awakening at the end to find his girl friend waiting for him in real life. In this version, Rotbart is the *Prince's* evil genius, not Odette's. A tragic ending, possibly more in keeping with the spirit of Tchaikovsky, is provided by John Cranko in his Stuttgart production and by Rudolf Nureyev in his Vienna one. In these, the Prince is drowned alone, leaving Odette to her fate as a swan.

It is not only the ending which is altered in various productions. Vladimir Bourmeister, in his production for the Stanislavsky Theatre, Moscow, and later for the Paris Opéra, introduced a prologue in which Odette is seen being kidnapped by Rotbart. London's Festival Ballet once adopted this idea, and an expanded version of it was used by Robert Helpmann in his production for the Royal Ballet. It was later dropped. This prologue, intended to clarify the story, does not really do so as it does not explain how the other swan maidens met their fates, and it has the disadvantage of introducing the ballerina, for practically nothing, at the beginning of the ballet and spoiling the effect of her normal first entrance in the second act. (The Helpmann production runs the first act straight into the second, without an interval, and calls the whole thing Act One. This is most confusing, as the lakeside scene is internationally known as Act Two, and performed under that title when it is done on its own.)

Various other alterations are frequently made in the first act, in the interests of clarity or liveliness. In many productions the Prince's mother presents him with a crossbow, thus giving him the idea of going shooting. Sometimes she does this instead of warning him that it is time to get married, so that an important dramatic point is lost. Igor Belsky told me, in connection with his production for the Dutch National Ballet, that audiences do not understand the mime anyway, so it might as well be omitted. But as the mime includes the mother pointing at her wedding ring, it is fairly clear to most audiences, and in any case it is so short that it cannot bore those who do not understand. The original version of this act also includes a drunken tutor, who attempts a clumsy dance with one of the peasant girls and is finally mocked and almost knocked over by her. This character is now frequently omitted, as in Helpmann's production, and his departure seems to be no great loss. Soviet versions, often imitated in the West, for example by the Danes and by Festival Ballet, usually replace him with a jester, which provides extra opportunities for virtuoso male dancing. But the jester's antics easily become intrusive and out of keeping with the mood of the ballet. Also, there are too many jesters in ballet already.

In the third act, Bourmeister introduced the very effective device of making all the dancers who provide the divertissement at the ball in the third act appear as part of Rotbart's entourage, so that their flashiness and occasional vulgarity (for example, the pseudo-Spanish dance) could be taken as typical of Rotbart's taste, and of his plan to captivate the Prince. This device too was included in Helpmann's production, but was not as consistently worked out, so that it seemed pointless.

In general, I am against attempts to clarify the story by enlarging the role of Rotbart. In Helpmann's production, for example, Odette protects Rotbart from the Prince's bow and arrow in the second act instead of, as in other productions, protecting her fellow swans. This simply mystifies the audience, unless they have read the curious explanation printed in the program that if the Prince shoots Rotbart, the spell can never be lifted. The usual version, in which Odette protects her fellow swans, makes immediate sense and also provides a much more attractive and appealing stage picture. Again, when Rotbart usurps the functions of the Chamberlain at the ball, one may well wonder why the Queen, the Prince, and the court permit him to do so. In Helpmann's production, Rotbart produces Odile out of the folds of his enormous batlike wings, and it is impossible to understand how the Prince can be fooled by an Odile presented in such suspicious circumstances. Since this production was first performed, Rotbart's role in this act has been reduced. But he still plays an active part in the last act, rushing around dominating the swans and finally being felled by the branch of a tree when the lovers drown themselves. Personally, I find all these antics for Rotbart make the fairy tale too literal and realistic. The plight of Odette and her fellow swan maidens is more moving if more mysterious.

For the strength of the story of *Swan Lake* is that it can be taken at many levels, allegorical as well as literal. It is about man's search for ideal love, about the ease with which he can be deceived, and about the fates which generally prevent the achievement of complete human happiness. A wicked magician dressed as an owl or a bat only distracts from these deeper meanings. I am not sure that there is really any need for Rotbart to appear on the stage at all; and surely it is sufficient for him to be a shadowy but sinister presence in the background, as he is in David Blair's production for American Ballet Theatre and as he was in the Royal Ballet's older version. The lyricism and allegorical significance of *Swan Lake* emerge more clearly if the ballet is not elaborated into a vulgar spectacle.

The other strengths of *Swan Lake*, apart from the story, are its choreographic variety, its musical score and its ballerina role. The dances in the third act include Spanish, Neapolitan and Russian folk dances, and balleticized versions of them, as well as the Black Swan pas de deux. The first act includes a smaller divertissement, with a waltz and a virtuoso dance performed by three or four dancers for the Prince's entertainment. All these dances are contrasted with the romantic and lyrical ones of the two "white" acts. The score similarly ranges from full-blooded and melodious waltzes, mazurkas and a polonaise to the famous swan theme and lakeside music. The ballerina role has been taken by nearly all the great ballerinas of this century.

Many of us who have seen Margot Fonteyn as Odette-Odile will always regard her as the ideal interpreter. Everything about her performance—the soft style of movement, the gentle, loving manner, the trust and affection in her face, the total musicality of her dancing, the precise small beats of her feet—made her the personification of the tragic and trusting Odette. Flashier dancers have made more of Odile's acrobatics but Fonteyn's Odile was always recognizably related to her Odette and had a sophisticated glitter which seemed entirely appropriate. With the Royal Ballet, the Canadian dancer Lynn Seymour was also a memorable recent Odette; even at the beginning of her career, her very individual rounded style of movement made her interpretation unusually poetic and moving. Antoinette Sibley is rapidly becoming a worthy successor to Fonteyn, not yet as touching but with a very musical and effortless lyric style.

Russian ballet has not recently shown us any great Odette-Odile. Maya Plisetskaya, who specializes in the role with the Bolshoi Ballet, seems to me to exaggerate the swan aspects of Odette and the vulgarity of Odile. Her enormous beating arm movements, with almost serpentine writhing, apparently suggest a swan to some people but they become monotonous after a time, while her spectacular Odile could not possibly be mistaken by even the most stupid Prince for any conceivable Odette. Natalia Bessmertnova is less exaggerated but also rather mannered, and her admirable dancing remains curiously unemotional. Natalia Makarova's Odette, with the Kirov, is admirably danced but not, to my mind, particularly moving.

American ballet has produced several outstanding Odiles, including Rosella Hightower, Alicia Alonso and Nora Kaye. All these dancers made a speciality of the Black Swan pas de deux, performing it in isolation with various partners, as a technical and semiacrobatic stunt. They achieved breathtaking feats of balance, speed, and virtuosity. Maria Tallchief also scored a

success in New York as Odette, in Balanchine's rather unsatisfactory version of the second act. (For some reason this ballerina
never found her best form on her visits to London.) Recently
Melissa Hayden has been highly praised in this production.

Like *Swan Lake, Giselle, The Nutcracker* and *The Sleeping
Beauty,* one other major classic—*Coppélia*—is found in the
repertory of most big companies. It was originally produced in
Paris in 1870, with choreography by Arthur Saint-Léon, but the
best-known versions today are based on the revision done in St.
Petersburg by Ivanov and Cecchetti. There is also a well-established Danish version, handed down from the nineteenth century and revised in the twentieth by Harald Lander. The story
is slight but very suitable for children, with plenty of opportunities for humor. There is no romantic "white scene" and
the plot has no allegorical significance. It is a straightforward
tale of a peasant girl, Swanilda, and her boy friend, Franz. Franz
is blowing kisses to Coppélia, who appears to be a curiously
impassive girl sitting up on the balcony of old Dr. Coppelius'
house; she is actually a life-size doll. Swanilda is jealous, especially as in many productions Franz dances some national
dances with another peasant girl. Dr. Coppelius crosses the
square to the inn, is jostled and mocked by the village boys, and
drops his key in the confusion. Swanilda finds the key and leads
her girl friends into his house to explore. Dr. Coppelius, having
missed his key, also returns, and Franz enters the house by
climbing up a ladder to the window. In the second act, the girls
are startled by Dr. Coppelius. They all escape, except Swanilda
who hides in the doll cupboard and pretends to be Coppélia.
Dr. Coppelius persuades Franz to drink some drugged wine and
then tries to transfer Franz's bodily movements, and also his
soul, to what he thinks is the doll Coppélia. Swanilda pretends
to respond to this magical treatment—she first dances like a
robot doll, gradually thaws into life, and then dances Spanish
and Scottish variations suggested by the presence of Spanish and
Scottish dolls. She then succeeds in waking Franz from his
drugged sleep, shows Dr. Coppelius the lifeless doll Coppélia,

and makes her escape with Franz. The last act is simply a wedding celebration for Swanilda and Franz, which provides the excuse for a little divertissement—two female solos, a few group dances, and a pas de deux for the hero and heroine.

The part of Dr. Coppelius is a gift for a talented mime. It can be made very comical; indeed the comic business can be so elaborate that Coppelius steals the show, as he tended to do when Robert Helpmann played the part. He can also be played as a sinister, wicked magician. If he is too likable it makes Swanilda's behavior seem callous; if he is too unsympathetic, he may seem out of tune with the cheerful nature of the production as a whole, and of Delibes' music. Clearly he must be the kind of ludicrous or sour eccentric who is liable to be mocked by younger people. Swanilda is often played by young and pretty dancers who are not yet ready, emotionally or technically, for the more demanding ballerina roles. Ideally Swanilda needs to be high-spirited and charming, and to dance with lightness, speed, and precise musicality. There is plenty of scope for acting—mock or real indignation with Franz, mockery of Coppelius, impersonation of a doll, and then of a doll coming to life. An outstanding interpreter can present a girl pretending to be a doll and can combine a convincing act for Coppelius with reminders to the audience behind his back that she is really a girl. Franz does not have much to do; if he is good-looking and can flash a convincingly roving eye it helps. The last act pas de deux is not as difficult or as interesting as the big pas de deux in *The Sleeping Beauty, The Nutcracker,* or *Swan Lake.*

Perhaps the biggest single factor in the constant popularity of *Coppélia* is Delibes' score, which is full of bright, catchy melodies, including some rousing national dances. Once again, it is not a score that would be played complete in a concert hall, but it does send audiences out of a theater humming happily. It is preeminently music for dancing.

It is clear that all these old-established ballets have a great deal in common. There is a distinction between the earlier "romantic" ballets and the later "classic" ones, but they can all for convenience be bracketed together as classics, in the wider sense of that word, having become such by surviving over many years. Indeed there are a number of twentieth-century ballets which were intended to be revolutionary, anticlassical works but which are also sometimes described as classics, because they have become standard works in the international repertoire. And many choreographers are once again creating full-length ballets which in many ways resume the old classical tradition. What the classics, in the sense we have been discussing, have in common is that they are primarily excuses for dancing, in which the other ingredients—drama, decor, and music—are of secondary importance, and often of secondary quality. They can be altered and rearranged, yet the ballets live, because of their choreography.

CHAPTER II

The Diaghilev Revolution

BY THE BEGINNING OF THIS CENTURY, ballet in Russia had fallen into a rut. There was a host of marvelous dancers, possibly the most distinguished galaxy of classical ballerinas that has ever been assembled. But choreography in St. Petersburg was set in the ways of Petipa, who had held sway for half a century. A sort of revolt took place in Moscow, where Alexander Gorsky revised the classics and tried to make them more dramatic and more coherent. Gorsky had considerable influence, not only on later Soviet ballet but also on the young Léonide Massine and, through Gorsky's disciple Kasyan Goleizowsky, on the young George Balanchine, who later became two of the most important choreographers in the West. Gorsky's significance was not appreciated at the time, as Moscow was then a comparatively unimportant provincial city in relation to St. Petersburg. The revolution which was immediately important, and started the rebirth of ballet in western Europe, was the revolution associated with the name of Diaghilev.

Serge Diaghilev was a wealthy connoisseur of the arts who

became dissatisfied with the ossification of ballet in Russia. He founded a journal—*Mir Isskoustva* (*The World of Art*)—which became a forum for new ideas and brought him in touch with the leading young creative artists. After a quarrel with the director of the Imperial Theatre, he turned his attention abroad, starting with an exhibition of Russian painting in Paris in 1906. His excursions abroad were caused by two separate motives: to display Russian achievement and to escape from the rigid conservatism imposed on the arts in St. Petersburg.

Under the influence of a young choreographer, Michel Fokine, and of a young artist, Alexandre Benois, Diaghilev became more and more immersed in ballet. His first ballet season in Paris, in 1909, was a tremendous success, as was his first London one, in 1911. From then until his death, in 1929, the words ballet and Diaghilev were virtually synonymous outside Russia. And the ideal of ballet set up by Fokine, and practiced in one way or another by his successors with the Diaghilev ballet, continued to dominate thinking throughout the 1930's, the period of Colonel de Basil's Ballets Russes. The entire generation which was brought up on ballet between the wars tends to look at it through Diaghilev-Fokine eyes.

Fokine's main concern was dramatic strength and credibility. He was against acrobatic stunts, performed simply to gain applause, and against dancers playing to the audience for applause. He believed the dance must be exactly coordinated with the music, not as in the Imperial Russian Ballet, where the practice had arisen of stars performing their own favorite steps, regardless of choreography and music. And he believed that the dance, the music, and the decor must all be specially created to go together, so as to unite in expressing some dramatic idea, or at least some mood or theme. He found that full-length ballets, split into several acts and lasting a whole evening, inevitably diffused dramatic unity and coherence, so he concentrated on short, one-act ballets. In these, all the ingredients were supposed to be of equal importance: the dancers subordinated to their roles and the ballets regarded as works of art, not just theatrical entertainments or display pieces.

Fokine's most famous ballet, which has certainly attained the status of a classic, is *Les Sylphides*. It is performed by practically every company, it became the almost invariable curtain raiser to every mixed program of short ballets, and it sums up exactly what most nonballetgoers think ballet is all about. Essentially it is a very simple work—girls in long white dresses dancing to the music of Chopin. There is no story, only a romantic, moonlit atmosphere. There are three solo roles—waltz, mazurka and prelude—for ballerinas, and there is also a male soloist who dances a mazurka and a pas de deux with one of the ballerinas. This is not a pas de deux in the flashy, Petipa sense, but a lyrical waltz. The ending, when the music speeds up, the soloists join the ladies of the corps de ballet, and the male dancer leads the way back to the tableau which opened the ballet, is particularly effective. When the corps de ballet is not dancing, it forms various groupings around the soloists. The solos are light and lyrical, with soft footwork, gentle arm movements and quiet jumps. The whole effect should be dreamy and romantic, not athletic, rather like the "white" acts of the old romantic ballets, *Giselle* and *La Sylphide*.

The enormous success of *Les Sylphides*, which may well be the most frequently performed ballet in the world, is ironic: it is not a particularly good example of Fokine's own principles. The music by Chopin was not written for ballet; it is a series of piano pieces which have been orchestrated and reorchestrated by various people for different productions. The original decor by Alexandre Benois has also been frequently replaced by the work of other designers. Fokine himself was constantly changing the ballet, even inserting a completely different male solo, with different music. (His first version, created in Russia before he joined Diaghilev, was called *Chopiniana* and was very different. It began with the martial Polonaise in A-flat played as an overture, and the curtain rose on a ballroom, with Chopin seated at a piano. Soviet companies still retain this overture, but then go on incongruously to perform the later version of the ballet. The Kirov concealed this absurdity on their London visits by the sheer romanticism and style of their dancers; the Bolshoi emphasized it, as their dancers had little or no feeling for the appropriate atmosphere. They even flitted across the stage taking applause after solos, a practice Fokine abhorred.) So it can scarcely be said to be a completely coherent blend of dancing, music and decor, with all the ingredients of equal importance. As for the theme, it is true that although the ballet has no specific scenario it does express an elegiac, wistful, poetic mood. Or at least it should; all too many performances do not express anything at all.

Like all Fokine's ballets, *Les Sylphides* is very difficult to perform. In one sense, it is deceptively simple. The steps are not very demanding from the technical point of view; musicality, lightness and soft arm movements are the main requirements. Mechanical, routine performances even when the steps and groupings are correctly performed are sometimes the fault of the dancers who may have cold, blank faces, exaggerated or hard arm movements, or noisy blocked shoes. They are also sometimes the fault of harsh, unromantic lighting or bad orchestral playing. Another common error is to stage *Les Sylphides* as a vehicle for a ballerina and possibly also for her partner. The star's solo is then followed by applause and curtain calls, which shatter the atmosphere. There *is* room for stars in *Les Sylphides*: Diaghilev's original production included Anna Pavlova, Tamara Karsavina and Vaslav Nijinsky, who were among the biggest stars ballet has ever known. Indeed stars may be needed to create the rapt atmosphere which usually eludes lesser dancers. But no one role should be allowed to stand out above the others, and both stars and audience should understand the nature of the work, and not spoil it by showing off.

To some extent, the same problems affect the revival of all Fokine's works. He himself devoted endless pains to rehearsal and preparation of his dancers, and to supervision of every aspect of the productions. Success depended so much on detail, on feeling for character and atmosphere, on correct decor and lighting, that it is very difficult to re-create the success without him. Between the wars, Fokine's ballets were staple items in most repertoires; now they are comparatively rarely performed and in general they are no longer among the most popular works, either with dancers or with the public. One reason for this is that the performances they receive nowadays are seldom successful in recapturing the effect originally intended by the choreographer.

The best-known Fokine ballets, apart from *Les Sylphides,* are *Prince Igor, Carnaval, Scheherazade, The Firebird (L'Oiseau de Feu)* , *Specter of the Rose,* and *Petrouchka.* All of them are still performed; *The Firebird* and *Petrouchka* have been reasonably successful at Covent Garden but the Royal Ballet's attempt at *Prince Igor* was an immediate flop; *Carnaval* has been attempted without any great success by both the old Sadler's Wells Theatre Ballet and Western Theatre Ballet, and by Eliot Feld's new American Ballet Company. *Petrouchka* was staged by both Ballet Theatre and the Joffrey Ballet in 1970.

Prince Igor is actually the Polovtsian dances from Borodin's opera *Prince Igor.* Fokine's version of the dances is usually staged on its own, as a ballet, when a company has a male dancer with the personality and technique for the principal part, the Polovtsian warrior chief. The men have to do a lot of crouching, leaping, and ferocious handling of bows and arrows, and of their women. The primitive, sensual atmosphere of the soldiers' camp should be evoked, helped by Borodin's pulsating and exciting music. There have been innumerable productions, with different decors, even in Fokine's own time. To make its full effect the ballet needs a large stage, with skillful lighting, a large orchestra, and a singing chorus. It also needs an exceptionally virile and energetic male corps de ballet.

The atmosphere of *Carnaval* is even more elusive. The traditional harlequinade characters are seen through gently mocking Victorian eyes, with pathos provided by Pierrot and merry virtuoso dancing by Harlequin. Various moods and emotions are delicately conveyed, in a simple setting by Bakst to specially orchestrated piano music by Schumann. Or at least that is apparently what happened in Diaghilev's production of 1910, when Adolph Bolm mimed Pierrot, Nijinsky was the Harlequin, and Karsavina was his Columbine. We are told by Cyril Beaumont that even in the 1918 revival, the mood had changed, and in most recent revivals there has been little mood left. Neither dancers nor audiences any longer have much interest in, or feeling for, the harlequinade characters, and the roles have usually been danced without either the virtuosity or the style which alone might justify a revival.

Scheherazade, a voluptuous oriental orgy to music by Rimsky-Korsakov, has not fared any better. Revivals tend to look like dowdy excerpts from a corny musical comedy, and successive interpreters of the Golden Slave have lacked what must have been Nijinsky's erotic magnetism and sensational technique. It is doubtful whether any production, however authentic, could make *Scheherazade* seem a worthwhile ballet to modern audiences.

Specter of the Rose, The Firebird and *Petrouchka,* on the other hand, can all still be made to work in the theater. *Specter* is really a romantic pas de deux—a girl falls asleep and dreams that the spirit of a rose floats through her window and dances with her, to Weber's *Invitation to the Waltz.* It was originally danced by Karsavina and Nijinsky; his leap through the window became a legend. John Gilpin had considerable success in this part in various revivals by Festival Ballet though none of the girls created the dreamlike atmosphere as Karsavina must have done. There was a fascinating occasion, at a gala performance given by Festival Ballet, when the elderly Karsavina herself walked onto the stage and made a little speech to introduce the ballet. Many of us who were present felt that she created more of the right feeling, just standing there gazing through the window talking about the spirit of the rose, than any of the young dancers we had seen in the part!

Petrouchka and *The Firebird* are probably the most popular

of the Fokine ballets, after *Les Sylphides*. They both have the
appeal of Russian folk-tale atmosphere, and of scores by Stravinsky which were specially written for the ballets and which
incorporate traditional Russian folk melodies. *Petrouchka* also
has a dramatic story about a tragic puppet who comes to life,
falls in love with a ballerina puppet, and is chased away and
killed by the more primitive blackamoor puppet. The actual
steps to be danced by the interpreters of these three parts are
not particularly difficult, but the interpretation is. The
Petrouchka must suggest that he is half-sawdust, half-human,
and must be able to convey the pathos of his loneliness in his
cell and of his hopeless love, and then of the final scene in which
his ghost appears from a rooftop to frighten the Showman. The
Ballerina is pretty and fickle, easily seduced by the more obvious
animallike charms of the Blackamoor, who in turn alternates
between placid, almost imbecile contentment, playing with a
coconut, and lustful chasing after the Ballerina. Throughout,
the audience should never be quite sure whether these characters really have souls, or whether they are just dolls.

The opening and closing scenes of *Petrouchka* show Ad-
miralty Square, St. Petersburg, in carnival time, 1830, and
provide opportunities for various Russian folk dances and for
very realistic crowd scenes. There are dances for coachmen, wet
nurses, fairground ballerinas, and even a performing bear.
Fokine was determined that the crowd should look and behave
as much as possible like an actual carnival crowd, and not like a
corps de ballet, but this effect is not always achieved in modern
productions. Ideally, the ballet needs more older and weightier
dancers among the crowd than most western companies possess.
It also needs a very large number of dancers who can be carefully rehearsed so that they act all the varied parts Fokine
provided, while giving the impression of complete spontaneity.
Fokine himself could not see anything particularly difficult
about the principal roles, provided the dancers stuck to his
instructions, but he never found interpreters who satisfied him
as well as Nijinsky and Karsavina. He did not want dancers to

"interpret" or add their own expressions or gestures, but just to perform exactly what he prescribed. And he explains in his memoirs that the essential difference between Petrouchka and the Blackamoor should be expressed through their physical stance; Petrouchka is always "turned in," thus looking awkward and unathletic (and incidentally unlike a ballet dancer), the Blackamoor is "turned out," extrovert, self-assured. But even in his lifetime, Fokine complained, dancers were confusing the two roles.

The Firebird, based on Russian folk tales, is about a young prince who goes hunting, meets a magic firebird and is helped by her to rescue and marry a princess who is held captive by a wicked magician. (It is in a way a happy version of *Swan Lake*.) Again the actual steps danced are fairly simple, though the role of the firebird is an exotic and glittering one for a ballerina. Karsavina, who created it, taught it to Margot Fonteyn, who succeeded in combining commanding authority over the magician and his entourage with terror and then gentleness in her scenes with the prince. The prince has little to do except look young and handsome at the beginning, and suitably dignified and royal at the end. But the evil magician is a fine part for a character dancer or mime, and the princess, when danced by Svetlana Beriosova with the Royal Ballet, became a truly soulful and charming Slavonic maiden. There are lots of dances for the magician's entourage—monsters, dwarfs, and strange creatures of all kinds—which come as a striking contrast after the limpid, innocent dances for the princess and her attendant maidens.

But none of these ballets now draws as large a public, or arouses as much enthusiasm in the theater, as the older classics or some of the more modern works. The reason is partly the difficulty of staging them effectively and convincingly; it is also that they do not provide opportunities for obvious virtuosity on the part of the dancers. And it is *dancing* which ballet audiences primarily want to see. After seeing *The Firebird* for the first time, Nureyev was quoted as asking, "But where is the choreography?" That question is implicit in the attitude to Fokine of most modern audiences.

The other leading choreographers of the interwar period, first with Diaghilev and then with his successor Colonel de Basil, all more or less followed Fokine's principles. They all aimed to create works of art in which dance, decor, music and drama blended to form a coherent whole. These choreographers included the dancer Nijinsky, his sister, Bronislava Nijinska, Léonide Massine, Serge Lifar, David Lichine, and George Balanchine. Of these, Nijinsky's career as a choreographer was unfortunately very short, ending with his marriage and quarrel with Diaghilev and with his subsequent madness. Lifar became director of the ballet at the Paris Opéra, where he created an enormous number of ballets which have not, on the whole, found their way into the international repertoire. Lichine's *Graduation Ball,* on the other hand, is performed frequently in many countries as are numerous works by Massine. Balanchine has gone on to greater glories as founder and choreographer of New York City Ballet and Nijinska has recently been redis-covered in London.

Nijinsky's most famous ballet, which is still performed, was *The Afternoon of a Faun (L'Apres-Midi d'un Faune)* to music by Debussy, with decor by Léon Bakst. Nijinsky himself ap-peared as the faun, reclining on a rock, who tries to flirt with some passing maidens, dances with one of them, and is finally left erotically fondling her scarf. The ballet created a sensation in Paris in 1912 both because Nijinsky's costume, his handling of the scarf, and the whole theme were considered daring and because the choreography was strikingly unusual and original. The movements were all presented in profile, so that the effect was two-dimensional and intended to be like an ancient Greek bas-relief. There is some dispute whether the original idea for the theme and its treatment was Diaghilev's, Bakst's or Nijin-sky's; as they were all in close contact it probably evolved between them. But Dame Marie Rambert, who worked with Nijinsky, believes that he could have gone on to become a great and original choreographer and speaks highly of his version of Stravinsky's *Rite of Spring* (*Sacre du Printemps*) which is now forgotten. *Faun* is another of those ballets, like most with which Nijinsky was associated, which seem impossible to re-create completely successfully today. There have been many interesting revivals, especially by Ballet Rambert, but one misses what one feels must have been Nijinsky's magnetism and impact, and of course the work no longer seems revolutionary or daring.

Massine's most famous ballets are *La Boutique Fantasque, Three-Cornered Hat* (*Le Tricorne*), *Le Beau Danube, Gaieté Parisienne* and the three symphonic ballets, *Les Présages, Choreartium,* and *Symphonie Fantastique. Three-Cornered Hat* is a special case, a re-creation of a Spanish drama in ballet terms, complete with Spanish-style dances, decor by the Spanish-born artist Pablo Picasso and music by the Spanish composer Manuel de Falla. Massine himself created the part of the Miller in London in 1919 and was still dancing it, with the Royal Ballet, thirty years later! His part demanded some fiery acting and had several solos, including an exciting and difficult one based on the Spanish *farucca*. The ballet was subsequently performed with success by various other dancers, especially Harold Turner, and the Russian-born Violetta Elvin scored a great personal success as the Miller's Wife, a part created by Karsavina. It was revived by the Joffrey Ballet in 1969 for their Spanish dancer Luis Fuente but the dramatic atmosphere seemed elusive and the work looked dated.

The rest of Massine's successful ballets can be divided into two groups: the musical-comedy ballets or danced operettas, and the symphonic ballets. They are both genres which he may be said to have invented. The former are still performed with success, though they tend to be sneered at by highbrows and critics; the latter have passed completely out of favor though they may well return.

The most famous and most popular of the musical-comedy ballets is *La Boutique Fantasque*. Originally created in London in 1919, it has remained fairly constantly in one repertory

or another till now—a most recent revival, supervised by
Massine himself, was for the touring section of the Royal Ballet
in 1968. Part of *Boutique's* success is due to Rossini's music,
selected and orchestrated by Respighi. The slight story concerns
a toy shop, where the toys perform amusing dances for the assorted customers, two English old maids, an American family
with a horrid spoiled boy, and a Russian family with five children. The toys include a pair of tarantella dancers, poodles
(one of whom misbehaves on the American boy's trousers),
cossack soldiers, an elegant snob, and the famous cancan
dancers, originally played by Massine himself with Lydia Lopo-
khova. Massine also danced this part at Covent Garden in the
1948–49 season, with Moira Shearer.

The basic idea, toys coming to life and dancing, is obviously
derived from *Coppélia* and *Nutcracker*. But Massine made this
the whole point of his ballet. The climax comes when the two
cancan dancers are threatened with separation, one being
bought by the American family, the other by the Russian.
During the night the other toys get the cancan dancers out of
their wrappings and in the morning they drive the customers
out of the shop, finally belaboring the luckless proprietor and
his assistant.

Fokine criticized Massine for making the dolls and the human
characters too much alike and certainly it is true that the
humans, as in all Massine's comedy ballets, walk in an artificial
way and have very exaggerated gestures and facial makeup. But
this contributes to the very special fantasy feeling of these
ballets. There is always a great deal of humor and a lot of
inventive characterization for all the cast. Indeed there is so
much detailed acting, and so much going on all over the stage,
that it is impossible to take it all in at first viewing. Some people
like this style, others find it too fussy. In any case some of the
detail tends to get lost in a large opera house. Just as the old
classics look best there, and inevitably lose something on tour,
the Massine comedy ballets tend to look better in smaller
theaters up and down the country.

Massine's symphonic ballets were attempts to interpret great
musical works in movement, not just in an abstract sense but
with emotional and dramatic undertones. *Les Présages* was set
to Tchaikovsky's fifth symphony, *Choreartium* to Brahms'
fourth, and *Symphonie Fantastique* to the Berlioz symphony of
that name. The first two were much criticized when they were
new, in 1933, for daring to use such famous concert music for
the ballet, but they were enormously popular with the public.
We should not be inclined to make the same criticism nowadays; on the contrary, Balanchine is widely praised for his
choreography to a wide range of concert music. But "symphonic
ballet" seems to be a term of abuse in most circles where ballet
is discussed, apparently because Massine's work was not abstract
like Balanchine's but contained such things as figures of Fate,
struggles between Good and Evil, and religious processions.
Now that avant-garde artists rejoice in mixing all the media,
and that the main concern of young audiences seems to be
aesthetic and emotional experience irrespective of plot or logic,
there might surely be a public once again for works in this style.
It would not surprise me if Massine's early attempts had a successful revival, or if someone made a new attempt. Indeed,
some modern works, for example Kenneth MacMillan's *Song
of the Earth,* to Mahler's song cycle, or Igor Belsky's *Leningrad Symphony,* to music from Shostakovich's seventh symphony, are not all that dissimilar.

Two of Nijinska's most famous works, *Les Noces* and *Les
Biches,* have recently been revived by the Royal Ballet. Originally created in 1923 and 1924 respectively, they were in some
ways ahead of their time. *Les Noces* is a stylized staging of traditional Russian peasant wedding ceremonies; Nijinska and her
designer, Natalia Gontcharova, had the idea of presenting the
dancers in somber brown and white uniform costumes, and the
choreography is formal and ritualistic. Stravinsky's score for
four singers, chorus, four pianos and percussion seemed extremely modern at the time and even now seems to me to
succeed by its hypnotic power rather than its beauty. The whole

work, with its sculptured groupings, is unusual and strangely effective, though not one which audiences are likely to want to see very often. *Les Noces* has also been staged for Ballet Theatre with entirely new, though equally effective, choreography by Jerome Robbins.

Les Biches is a lighthearted period piece, a comment on the social functions and permissive sexual habits of the twenties. To Poulenc's delightful and evocative music, it shows various flirtations at a house party and includes a notorious dance for two girls, ending with a kiss on the lips, an ambiguous solo for a boyish girl in blue velvet, and a bored, sophisticated hostess with a long cigarette holder and pearl necklace. Some people who remember the original production say that a lot was lost in the recent Covent Garden revival, though both it and *Les Noces* were supervised by Nijinska herself. Certainly the Lesbian pas de deux was toned down, with only a chaste kiss on the cheek, which seems odd in our very permissive age. Though delightful when subtly and delicately performed, *Les Biches*—like *Les Noces*—seems unlikely to become anything more than an occasional curiosity in the repertoire.

CHAPTER III

The Revolution and Counterrevolution in Britain

ALTHOUGH THERE HAD BEEN a British ballet in London as early as the eighteenth century and although the great nineteenth-century ballerinas like Taglioni and Grisi danced in London regularly, the renaissance of British ballet in modern times owes its inspiration to Diaghilev and the Russians. It was Diaghilev and his successor Colonel de Basil who stimulated the demand for ballet in London, and ballet was generally thought of in Britain, at least until the 1939–45 war, as being an exclusively Russian art. The two great founding mothers of British ballet, Dame Marie Rambert and Dame Ninette de Valois, both had much of their early experience and training with Diaghilev and the first star dancers of British ballet, Alicia Markova and Anton Dolin, both started their careers in his company. It is not surprising, therefore, that the ballets created in the first decade of modern British ballet were similar in style and aim to those associated with Diaghilev.

The principal British choreographers in those early days, and the ones whose works have survived, were Frederick Ashton, Antony Tudor and Ninette de Valois. The most prolific of them was Ashton, whose ballets now form the basis of the Royal Ballet's repertoire. De Valois' works have also been performed regularly at Covent Garden but, like Massine's, they seem less effective there than in the smaller theaters because of their wealth of detailed characterizations. Tudor emigrated to the United States, where he worked with American Ballet Theatre, but has recently returned to Britain to create two new works for the Royal Ballet. Another choreographer who emerged during the 1939–45 war was the Australian dancer Robert Helpmann, who created several highly dramatic works which were very popular but which do not seem to have stood the test of time.

De Valois' best-known ballet is *The Rake's Progress,* created in 1935. With scenery and costumes by Rex Whistler, it was a translation into ballet of a series of eight paintings by William Hogarth. There are six scenes depicting the incidents on the rake's journey from inheritance, new clothes, dancing and fencing lessons to his death in a madhouse. Each scene looks like Hogarth come to life, and the specially written music by Gavin Gordon acts as an appropriate background. The choreography does not include very much pure classical dancing, except for the dancing master, but the girl who befriends the rake and is then abandoned by him dances on point. Her scenes with the rake can be very touching, as they were when danced by Margot Fonteyn and Robert Helpmann. Helpmann was a very theatrical and dramatic rake, especially in the mad scene; in recent years David Wall has danced the part with a greater sense of period style, more elegance, and perhaps almost as much dramatic force.

Job and *Checkmate,* Ninette de Valois' other most successful ballets, have not been performed so much recently but were seen regularly at Covent Garden in the years just after the war.

Dating from 1931, and thus being one of the very first works created for the British ballet, *Job* was called a masque and did not use classical footwork. It always made a strong religious impact and in Satan it provided a strong male role which was seized to full effect by both Anton Dolin and Robert Helpmann. The music of Vaughan Williams played an important part in the success of *Job,* which was originally inspired by Blake's drawings.

Checkmate (1937) treated the pieces in a game of chess as live human beings and presented a drama in which a weak and doddery Red King is destroyed by a cruel and ruthless Black Queen. She seduces a Red Knight, who could have defended the King, and then kills him. The action is intelligible even to those who do not understand chess and the choreographer has been very successful in differentiating the various pieces. The pawns are soft and weak (the female corps de ballet), the Red Knight has opportunities to show off his classical dancing technique, the Black Queen marches about aggressively on her points, wielding her sword in an almost masculine manner, while the Red King is a good part for a character dancer who can suggest fear and pathos. The Black Queen and the Red King were created by June Brae and Robert Helpmann; Beryl Grey and Ray Powell have also been very successful in these parts since the war. A large part of the success of *Checkmate* was also due to the specially written music by Arthur Bliss, who wrote the scenario for the ballet as well. The settings by McKnight Kauffer were regarded as very effective when the ballet was new, but seemed rather dated by the time they were reproduced at Covent Garden. It may be that *Checkmate* could enjoy a new lease of life with new decor.

All these ballets by de Valois, in their different ways, seem admirable examples of Fokine's principles in practice. So were Frederick Ashton's early ballets, although his work always owed more than hers to the actual quality of the movement, and less to the dramatic idea. One of his earliest works, *Façade* (1931) has always retained its popularity and has been performed in recent years by the Royal Ballet, Ballet Rambert and the Joffrey Ballet. It tends to make more effect in a smaller theater than it does at Covent Garden. It is a lighthearted divertissement, including several parodies of popular dances of the twenties, such as "Popular Song," a music-hall shuffle for two men in boaters and deadpan expressions, and the pseudo-Spanish "Tango" which always brings down the house at the end. The choreography is perfectly fitted to William Walton's concert suite and has pleasant, unobtrusive settings and costumes by John Armstrong.

Les Rendezvous (1933), like *Façade,* is most effective in intimate theaters like Sadler's Wells, where it was first performed. It is a slight suite of dances to music by Auber with designs by William Chappell. The dances are gently linked by the idea expressed in the title: the ballet starts with assorted couples shaking hands as they meet, and it ends with several couples disappearing through the gates at the back of the stage. The ballerina role, created by Markova, requires great charm and delicacy, and there is also quite a virtuoso male role, created by Idzikowsky. Already in *Les Rendezvous* Ashton showed his choreographic invention and taste: particularly in the amusing pas de trois for two boys and a girl in which their arms bob up and down, almost like clockwork, in time to the music, while the girl is twisted quickly from side to side in the manner Ashton used again later in his Neapolitan Dance for *Swan Lake,* and in the pas de quatre for boys, which ends with them half-lying on the stage, supported on their right hands, waiting for the girls to come and join them.

Perhaps the most successful of all Ashton's early ballets, and one of the most successful of all ballets, is *Les Patineurs.* Created in 1937, it might be called the English answer to *Les Sylphides.* Set to lilting music by Meyerbeer and with very pretty decor and costumes by William Chappell, it did for a skating rink what Fokine's ballet did for moonlit glades. A charming suite of dances, including a virtuoso role for the principal male soloist ending with a seemingly endless series of spins on one leg, some pyrotechnics, including very quick turns and spins, for two girls, and a few comic mishaps, like simulated falls on the ice, it has proved a constantly popular curtain raiser, both in the old days at Sadler's Wells and now at Covent Garden, and in the repertoire of American Ballet Theatre which it entered in 1946, with new decor by Cecil Beaton.

Antony Tudor's most famous ballet is still *Jardin aux Lilas* (*Lilac Garden*), which he created in 1936. It is a deceptively simple work, conveying a whole range of emotional conflict and involvement with extreme economy. At a party in an Edwardian, lilac-drenched garden, a bridegroom and his intended bride each meet their former lovers. The ballet consists of dances for various combinations of these four characters, with eloquent glances over the shoulder and a famous tableau in which all four characters together are frozen exchanging significant looks of longing and despair. The ballet works best in a small theater and has long been in the repertoire of Ballet Rambert. But it can also "carry" on the larger stage of an opera house, as was proved when the American ballerina Nora Kaye danced it at Covent Garden with Ballet Theatre. The Royal Ballet danced it for the first time in 1968, under Tudor's personal supervision, but the first performances did not recapture the mood and atmosphere of the piece. When they are captured, it is remarkably touching and poetic. The music by Chausson and the original decor by Hugh Stevenson fitted the ballet perfectly. *Jardin aux Lilas* (Tudor himself insists on the French version of the title) is a true modern classic.

Tudor's *Gala Performance* (1938) has also passed into the repertoires of many companies; it has been performed regularly by both Ballet Rambert and Ballet Theatre. It is a parody of the mannerisms and technical exaggerations of the pre-Diaghilev ballerinas, which are by no means unknown today. Three ballerinas, from Paris, Milan and Moscow, compete for attention at the gala of the title, but first we see them bickering and warming up in a brief backstage scene. The mock gala can be very funny, with the French ballerina being fluffy and flirtatious, the Italian holding endless balances, and the Russian adopting the overdignified "grand" ballerina manner. It has to be very well danced, so that one can be sure that any mistakes are deliberate, and the audience really needs to be familiar with classical ballet to appreciate the jokes. Tudor's choice of music, mostly from Prokofiev's Classical Symphony, was criticized at first as being too modern for the theme, but it now seems just sufficiently classical, with the right hint of mockery.

His more recent works have shown Tudor still creating in a style which Fokine and Diaghilev would certainly have approved. And indeed most choreographers still create some ballets in this style, though they have developed it in various ways and the choreography now tends to be the dominant ingredient.

But this style is by no means the only one, or even the most popular one, in ballet today. In fact the leading trends in Britain, the United States, and the Soviet Union—the three countries which dominate the world of choreography—are entirely opposed to the principles of Diaghilev and Fokine. There has been, albeit unconsciously, a counterrevolution, which has taken a somewhat different course in each country but which has led to a wealth of new ballets and a wealth of new theories justifying them.

Perhaps the counterrevolution in England may be said to have started during the 1939–45 war, with its shortage of male dancers. It was during this period that the Australian dancer Robert Helpmann emerged as a choreographer. Partly because of the circumstances, partly because of his natural inclinations, Helpmann created highly theatrical dance dramas in which the emphasis was more on drama, and on music and decor, than on dance. They were very successful, having a powerful effect on audiences, and many people thought Helpmann was showing the way ballet should go. He certainly showed the way some ballet *has* gone, though his own later works, made for the Australian Ballet, have involved far more actual dancing.

Helpmann's two biggest successes during the war were *Hamlet* (1942) and *Miracle in the Gorbals* (1944). His postwar works with the Royal Ballet had shorter lives, though *Adam Zero* (1946), which took full advantage of the large Covent Garden stage and its machinery, has been revived and might perhaps be seen again. *Hamlet,* to Tchaikovsky's fantasy overture of the same name, was an impressionistic flashback of the main events in Hamlet's life, as seen by him on his deathbed. It presupposed knowledge of the play, a fairly reasonable presupposition for an educated audience though some purists would say that a ballet or any other work of art must stand entirely on its own feet. And it made use of the Freudian theory that Hamlet identified Ophelia with his mother: there was a very effective pas de trois in which the two ladies alternated around him, so that he was confused about their identity. The costumes and scenery by Leslie Hurry were suitably elaborate and fantastic, making the work spectacular as well as dramatic.

Miracle in the Gorbals had a scenario by Michael Benthall, an atmospheric score by Arthur Bliss, and realistic scenery and costumes by Edward Burra. Set in the slums of Glasgow, it told of a mysterious Stranger, a second Christ, who restored a suicide girl to life, was tricked by a hypocritical Official into visiting a prostitute, and redeemed her but only to be lynched and killed by the outraged mob. It had enormous impact and in many ways anticipated the theater of cruelty and the real-life ballets which have come since. Its story was more gripping than the very similar scenario of Bartók's *The Miraculous Mandarin* and it was more credible and emotionally stirring than various recent efforts in the same style. Now that the Royal Ballet has moved away from this type of work, one of the more "modern" companies might well think of acquiring it.

Although both *Hamlet* and *Miracle in the Gorbals* were performed at Covent Garden in the first years after the war, and have been revived since, they never really caught on there as essential parts of the repertoire. This is partly because, like most dramatic ballets, they work less well in an opera house than in the smaller theaters where they were first staged. It is also partly because the Royal Ballet no longer boasts such powerful actor-

dancers as Helpmann himself, Gordon Hamilton, David Pal-
tenghi, and the others who appeared in Helpmann's works. But
it is mainly because the taste of Covent Garden audiences has
moved away from drama toward pure dance.

This in its turn may have started as a reaction against the war
years, when pure dance and good dancers were so hard to find.
But it is also a realization that in ballet it is fundamentally the
dancing which counts, just as in opera it is the singing. It is
notable, for example, that no matter how good a modern
dramatic ballet may be, it is not likely to attract the same
audience time after time. Once people know the plot, they are
no more likely to want to see it several times than they are to
keep going to the same film, or rereading the same novel. If
anything, the impact becomes weakened at each viewing. The
appeal of pure dance, on the other hand, is aesthetic and emotional, not intellectual and certainly not lessened by repeated
viewing. On the contrary, there is constant interest for the regular balletgoer in comparing performances by different casts in
the same ballets, and even in comparing the same dancers on
different occasions.

The fact that since the war the Royal Ballet's London home
has been the Royal Opera House, Covent Garden, rather than
Sadler's Wells Theatre as it was before the war or the New
Theatre during the war, has inevitably influenced the repertoire. From the foundation of the company, Ninette de Valois
insisted on the classics as training for both dancers and audiences. As these ballets were originally made for large opera-
house stages, it is not surprising that they blossomed and seemed
at their best at Covent Garden, just as the more intimate
modern ballets lost something in the transfer. As we have seen,
the classics are essentially showpieces for ballerinas, and the
Royal Ballet since the war has been lucky or skillful in producing a large number of classical ballerinas, apart from the unrivaled *assoluta*, Margot Fonteyn. And the expense-account,
snobbish element of the audience, which exists at Covent
Garden as at every national opera house, is more interested in

seeing famous stars in famous ballets than in experimenting with new works. It is easier to fill Covent Garden with any full-length classic, with almost any cast, than with even the most interesting triple bill of twentieth-century works. And so, despite Fokine and his revolution, the sprawling full-evening ballet rather than the integrated short work has recently dominated the British ballet scene.

The number of standard full-length classics is ridiculously small: *Giselle, Coppélia, Swan Lake, The Sleeping Beauty*. For some reason *The Nutcracker* was not staged at Covent Garden till Nureyev's production in 1968 and *La Sylphide* has not yet been mounted by the Royal Ballet, although it suits Fonteyn and Nureyev perfectly. Nureyev's arrival brought the possibility of staging some of the lesser-known Russian classics. He mounted Petipa's *Raymonda* for the touring section of the company but only the last act of this invigorating and tuneful work has yet been seen at the Garden. And his version of Petipa's *Don Quixote* has been staged only at the Vienna Staatsoper and by the Australian Ballet. But at least his staging of one act of Petipa's *La Bayadère* now provides Covent Garden with a romantic and exciting alternative to the second act of *Swan Lake* and to *Les Sylphides*.

The main work of extending the Royal Ballet's range of full-length classic ballets has been undertaken by Sir Frederick Ashton, who has remained with the company through the years, becoming its director in 1964. He has produced every kind of ballet for the company, never falling beneath a highly acceptable professional level and often reaching heights which have established him as one of the two leading choreographers of our day. Those who dislike George Balanchine's choreography for New York City Ballet would call Ashton *the* choreographer of our day, but Balanchine also has his followers who dislike Ashton's work and give the Russo-American the supreme accolade. As an admirer of both of them, I prefer to bracket them together in importance and talent, while noting the crucial differences between their styles.

Ashton has many styles but they all have something in common, something specifically Ashtonian. This is extremely hard
to define; it might be called a romantic approach to classicism.
There is always a touch of feeling, sometimes of sentiment, even
sometimes of sentimentality, in his work. He creates glorious
lyrical dances, especially pas de deux for the ballerina and her
partner, but the dance always expresses something, even if it is
only a mood or an emotion. In this respect he is true to the
principles of Noverre and Fokine. But at least two categories of
his ballets are among those which Fokine condemned.

First, the full-length classics. Ashton has made virtually new
full-length ballets to three scores originally used by eighteenth-
and nineteenth-century French ballet masters, and three more
in the classical style to full-length modern scores. Between the
wars it was taken for granted, outside Russia, that the day of the
full-length ballet was over, apart from the occasional special
revival, like Diaghilev's star-studded but financially disastrous
staging of *The Sleeping Beauty* in London in 1921. The Soviet
Union, which continued to stage new full-length works, seemed
as hopelessly reactionary from the point of view of ballet as it
was in politics. Then the Vic-Wells Ballet revived the classics
and found, on arrival at Covent Garden, that it needed more
spectacular full-length works, to attract the public and to provide adequate variety for the ballerinas and dancers of the
company.

Ashton's first full-length ballet, *Cinderella* to Prokofiev's
music, seemed in 1948 a daring experiment. We still thought of
full-length ballets as a Russian prerogative; even the Prokofiev
score underlined this, having been written for a production at
the Bolshoi in 1945. It is not Prokofiev's best ballet score; that is
Romeo and Juliet, which has now been choreographed by many
western choreographers, including Ashton. But *Cinderella* is
attractive enough, and not too cloying, with a hint of fantasy
and tongue-in-cheek humor in the music which was admirably
matched in Ashton's original production by the chic fantasy
costumes and scenery by Jean-Denis Malclès. (This decor was

replaced in 1965 by much more realistic and less interesting designs by Henry Bardon and David Walker.) And of course the story had the advantage in England of already being the most popular subject of traditional Christmas pantomimes.

Ashton incorporated part of the British pantomime tradition in his ballet by having Cinderella's two ugly stepsisters mimed by himself and Robert Helpmann. Their performances, repeated at intervals over the next twenty years, have become classics in themselves: Ashton as the shy, ridiculous sister that one grows to love and pity, Helpmann as the horrid, bullying one. Some of their business, when trying on their clothes at the beginning, and Cinderella's slipper at the end, is pure slapstick, transmuted into something more by their personalities and their art. In the ballroom scene, they developed their parody of classical ballet over the years, so that it eventually became another highlight of the ballet. Fonteyn was ill when the ballet was created, so that the honor of being the first ballerina in a full-length British ballet fell to the glamorous and popular Moira Shearer. At later performances Fonteyn made the part very much her own, investing it with her special brand of pathos in the first act and with her equally special surprise and joy on arrival at the Ball. Ashton created one of his most radiant and lovely pas de deux for Cinderella and the prince, which has been danced with supreme distinction by Fonteyn, first with Michael Somes, later with David Blair, and later still with Donald MacLeary. But, as in the old Petipa ballets, the prince has virtually nothing to do apart from this pas de deux, except to look noble and romantic. Ashton eliminated the prince's journey through various lands in search of Cinderella, which in the Soviet version gives the prince more to dance and also provides an excuse for some regrettably uninteresting national dances. There is an energetic jester at court, brilliantly danced for many years by Alexander Grant, but in the main Ashton's version concentrates on female dancing: Cinderella herself, the fairy godmother and four attendant fairies, who all have solos, and the female corps de ballet. The story line is not particularly

strong, though stronger than *The Nutcracker* and as strong as
The Sleeping Beauty. But Ashton found more dramatic interest
in his later full-length ballets, *La Fille Mal Gardée*, *The Two
Pigeons*, *Romeo and Juliet*, and even *Sylvia*.

Sylvia, to the charming music written by Delibes for the
original production in Paris in 1876, never really caught on at
Covent Garden and has now been reduced to a rather unsatisfactory one-act version. But Ashton's first version, in 1952, had
much to be said for it, especially a ballerina role which showed
an unusual side of Fonteyn's personality and was later splen-
didly danced by the athletic, high-jumping Nadia Nerina. It
was a change to see Fonteyn bounding on as the leader of
Diana's Amazonian huntresses; since jumping has never been
her strong suit, she was more at home in the later parts of the
ballet, craftily dancing and drinking her captor Khan to sleep,
and then rejoicing in a final pas de deux with her lover. This
pas de deux, in which the ballerina is carried onto the stage
standing upright in her partner's arms, is a particularly memorable Ashton invention, as is her solo to the *pizzicato* polka.
The plot is rather a musical-comedy one; nobody could take the
kidnapping or Sylvia's rescue by the divine intervention of Eros
seriously. Ashton did not pretend to, and established Eros at the
beginning as a comic character, mincing delicately about when
disguised as a human before revealing himself as a god. This was
another of the gallery of remarkable character parts devised by
Ashton for Alexander Grant. The last act contained a long and
elaborate divertissement, in classical style, which gave opportunities to a large number of good dancers.

Ashton's *Romeo and Juliet*, to the Prokofiev score, was staged
for the Royal Danish Ballet in 1955. It is a fine work, with some
magnificent pas de deux, but it has been eclipsed in fame, at
least for American audiences, by Lavrovsky's Bolshoi production, by Kenneth MacMillan's for the Royal Ballet, and by
John Cranko's version for the Stuttgart company. So Ashton's
most successful full-length ballets have been two more re-
creations of early French works—*La Fille Mal Gardée* and

The Two Pigeons. The former is the most popular of all, and has been regularly performed by both the Covent Garden and the touring sections of the Royal Ballet, with innumerable different casts and always with great success; it has also been reproduced by Ashton, with rather less success, for the Royal Danish Ballet.

The original *Fille Mal Gardée* was produced in Bordeaux in 1789, the year of the French Revolution. It is therefore one of the oldest ballets in existence, though there is really not much connection between the original and modern versions. Even the music was newly written in 1828 by Ferdinand Hérold and again in 1864 by Peter Ludwig Hertel. Petipa staged the ballet in 1885, with Hertel's music plus bits and pieces by other composers. Various companies, including Ballet Theatre, the Cuevas Ballet and the Strasbourg ballet, have danced versions of it. But Ashton has choreographed it afresh, incorporating some of the traditional mime and comic business, with a score based on Hérold but arranged by John Lanchbery with some additions from Rossini, Donizetti and the original Bordeaux score.

The ballet's first choreographer was Jean Dauberval, a pupil of Noverre, and Ashton in his turn has been remarkably successful in integrating action and dancing so that one scarcely notices what is mimed and what is danced. There are no formal divertissements in the Petipa sense, and even the pas de deux and other dances arise as logical parts of the story.

La Fille Mal Gardée opens in a farmyard, with a delightful comic dance for four hens and a cockerel. It is dawn, and soon we see Lise and her handsome lover Colas, a young farmer. But Lise's mother, the Widow Simone, is arranging her engagement to Alain, the simpleton son of a rich vineyard owner. In the second scene, sometimes played as a separate act, there are harvest festivities; Alain makes a fool of himself trying to dance with Lise, who dances a joyous pas de deux with Colas. The Widow enters into the spirit of the proceedings and dances a lively and amusing clog dance. Then, during a general dance around the maypole, a storm breaks out, Colas protects Lise, and Alain is swept up into the air by his umbrella. In the last act, which takes place inside the Widow's farmhouse, Lise tries to steal a key from her sleeping mother to let Colas in or herself out: Colas eventually gets in hidden in a bale of corn and he hides in Lise's bedroom when the Widow returns. Alain and his father arrive to sign the wedding contract, the Widow gives Alain the key of Lise's bedroom but when he opens the door, she and Colas are revealed, kissing. In the end the Widow forgives them and everyone lives happily ever after—even Alain seems happy when he is reunited with his umbrella.

This ballet could easily have been too coy and cloying, and I remember fearing this during the first ten minutes on the first night. But Ashton has been extraordinarily inventive, both as choreographer and as producer. The Widow Simone is another travesty part, less exaggerated and pantomimelike than the Ugly Sisters in *Cinderella* but at least as funny, especially when danced by the original interpreter, Stanley Holden. (The part was first intended for Robert Helpmann, but he never performed it.) Holden's masculinity always showed through his female impersonation, in a way which has been compared to the cabaret entertainer Danny La Rue. Ronald Emblen has made the part almost as much his own, in a slightly more conventional way, and many other dancers have also succeeded with it. The clog dance is the highlight; I think it was Holden who introduced a trip over an imaginary lump on the stage followed by a long slide which is particularly funny. The last scene, in which the Widow slumbers at the spinning wheel but is just sufficiently awake to stop Lise taking her key, also provides many opportunities for closely observed and humorous mime.

The part of Alain, created for and by Alexander Grant, became one of that great character dancer's most detailed and touching portraits. He combined idiocy with a heart-warming pathos. Alain's symbol is his enormous red umbrella: he hides under it at his first bashful entrance, rides it like a hobbyhorse, flies up into the air on it at the end of the second scene, and finishes off the ballet by climbing through the window, after everyone else has gone to celebrate the engagement of Lise and Colas, to search for it. Throughout the ballet, Alain makes clumsy but strangely appealing attempts to do classical ballet steps. In the last scene, when he is given the key to Lise's bedroom, he goes through an agony of embarrassment, squirming and falling downstairs, before he finally unlocks the door and reveals the lovers' embrace.

For the hero and heroine, Ashton devised a lot of business, possibly a bit too much, with ribbons. At Lise's first entrance, she ties a ribbon into a lovers' knot as a signal for Colas; when he finds it he ties it to his staff. When they dance together, there is a lot of play with ribbons, and they make a cat's cradle which usually wins a round of applause. There are more ribbons, of course, on the maypole in the harvest scene. And in the last act, Simone and Lise wear different-colored ribbon scarves; Lise swaps hers with Colas, which in due course reveals to Simone that he has got in. All this ribbon work emphasizes the folksy nature of the ballet, and indeed a lot of the dancing, especially for Widow Simone and the corps de ballet, is based on traditional English folk dance.

But there is also a great deal of difficult classical dancing for Lise and Colas. When Nadia Nerina and David Blair created these parts, at the height of their very considerable technical powers, everyone thought they would retain exclusive command of the roles, which seemed so difficult. But dancers rise to the heights which confront them, and over the years almost every young ballerina and would-be ballerina of both sections of the Royal Ballet has danced Lise, and innumerable boys have danced Colas. They have nearly all been successful, even in the fast and intricate footwork of the solos and pas de deux in the harvest scene, in which the girl requires speed, good balances and jumps, the boy must do some very rapid jumps and quick spins, and both of them must move precisely to the music. Since the first performance, Christopher Gable has also introduced a more spectacular Soviet-style walk while holding the ballerina in a one-handed lift. This is now accepted as an essential part of the choreography.

As far as acting is concerned, for most of the ballet Lise and Colas just have to be young and charming, like Swanilda and Franz in *Coppélia,* a ballet in much the same genre. But in the last scene, Lise has quite a lot of acting to do. She is fumbling in the Widow's lap for the key; when the Widow wakes, she hastily pretends that she has found an insect on her mother's dress, and enthusiastically kills it with her foot on the ground. Next time the Widow wakes, Lise is at the door, kissing Colas through a trap. This time she pretends to be doing a high-spirited, almost lunatic dance around the room, which makes her mother think she is ill. When she is eventually left alone in the house, she imagines she is married. In a charming mime passage, she indicates a bridal veil, pregnancy, and children of different heights, one of whom has to be spanked, another gently cuddled. She is just rocking an imaginary baby in her arms and is about to lay it on a pile of corn when Colas leaps out of the pile, giving her the fright of her life. She is acutely embarrassed, and he comforts her, wiping her eyes. And when the Widow returns, the flustered Lise is pretending again, this time to be sweeping the floor.

There are many other touching and amusing bits of business in *Fille,* Lanchbery's arrangement of the score is very tuneful, danceable and well-suited to the action, and Osbert Lancaster's scenery and costumes are quite adequate though sometimes the scenery hovers a little uncertainly between realism and caricature. The ballet could be redesigned without any great sense of loss.

The Two Pigeons has not become such an enormous popular success as *Fille* but it is an equally delightful work and one which I personally find stands the test of repeated viewing even better. To music by Messager, it was first staged in Paris in 1866 with choreography by Louis Mérante, who also did the original version of *Sylvia.* The story is based on a fable by La Fontaine, but Ashton has altered the scenario from that used by Mérante while of course his choreography is entirely new. In Ashton's version, the story opens in a young artist's attic studio in late nineteenth-century Paris. He is painting his girl friend, who keeps wriggling about in the chair, making faces and generally exasperating him. A band of gypsies is heard passing in the street below and money is thrown down to them to come up. They dance, and the artist is increasingly attracted by the leading gypsy girl. Ashton has devised nicely contrasted solos for the two girls, with the gypsy doing dynamic, slightly vulgar steps and the more innocent girl imitating them but in a softer style. Eventually the heroine gets fed up, and drives the gypsies out of the house. But the artist is hypnotized, and insists on following the gypsies. The second act opens in the gypsy camp, with a little gypsy boy picking the pockets of rich sightseers. The artist dances with the gypsy girl, then has a trial of strength with her gypsy boy friend and finally is beaten and tied up by the gang. He limps his way home, and is happily reunited with his girl, who has watched for him patiently at the attic window.

Ashton has ingeniously used two live pigeons—actually, the French word "pigeons" in the title might be more appropriately translated as "doves"—to link the scenes of the ballet and his two human doves. In the first scene, the lovers see the birds flying outside the window and then imitate the birds in a playful dance together. When the artist departs, a bird flies after him, and when he is beaten up and staggers out of the gypsy camp, the bird lights on his hand and guides him home. Finally when the lovers are reunited, a second bird comes fluttering in, so that two real birds are nestling on the chair behind the lovers. Usually the birds give just as skillful performances as the dancers though they have been known to misbehave, even on one occasion flying out into the stalls and settling on a member of the audience.

In the original Paris version of the ballet, the ballerina role was a dual one, rather like Odette-Odile in *Swan Lake*. The heroine followed her lover to the gypsy camp and impersonated a gypsy girl. This gave her the chance to be both softly lyrical *and* dashingly flamboyant. Ashton discarded this idea, so that his ballet has two ballerinas. The innocent heroine was created by Lynn Seymour, who brought to the part her highly individual, rounded style of movement and strong humorous personality. She conveyed her great love for the artist, even when mocking and infuriating him. She also managed the imitation of the doves naturally and convincingly. Among her most satisfying successors have been Merle Park, Doreen Wells and Alfreda Thorogood; none of them has yet fully equaled Seymour, though Thorogood is well on the way to doing so. Nor has anyone fully equaled Christopher Gable, the first young artist. Although the role was originally intended for Donald Britton, a very different type of dancer who was prevented by injury from taking the part until later, Gable at once made it very much his own. His combination of sensitive natural acting and virile, technically assured dancing was a rarity in British ballet, and indeed in ballet of any nationality. He has been very much missed since he decided to abandon ballet, though he is now beginning to make a mark as a straight actor in the theater, cinema and television. His best successors in *Pigeons* have been David Wall and Paul Clarke. Wall is a bit more earthy than Gable, and therefore a bit more credible as a follower of gypsies, and perhaps closer to Ashton's original vision of the part, but he lacks the elegance which made Gable's dancing so memorable in the gypsy scene. Clarke, who is very similar to Gable physically, is untidy at times, and tends to overdo the comedy and the mocking of the heroine, but at best he can give a very touching and exciting performance. Elizabeth Anderton, the original gypsy girl, combined glamor and technical strength in a way which has only been equaled since by the young South African Margaret Barbieri. Georgina Parkinson is very glamorous but looks too delicate to be a gypsy, while Monica Mason, on the other hand, is a very convincing gypsy but scarcely seems sufficiently feminine and seductive.

One of Ashton's problems in making *The Two Pigeons* was the large number of gypsy dances, first in the studio and then at the camp. The music for these dances is catchy and lively, but essentially a French operetta composer's idea of gypsy music. The dances must therefore also be rather an operetta version of gypsy dances (what are real gypsy dances anyway?) but Ashton has succeeded in making them all different; they give the corps de ballet a good chance to show off, a chance particularly well taken by the touring section of the Royal Ballet, which often had more vivacity and gusto than the Covent Garden section.

Of course these dances, unauthentic and theatrical as they are, and designed to display dancers and win applause, are exactly the sort of thing which Fokine and Diaghilev were reacting against. We can afford to enjoy them again now, without feeling guilty about the betrayal of art.

And audiences always do in fact seem to enjoy *The Two Pigeons,* once they are in the theater. The difficulty is that the title does not attract them, and the Royal Ballet has found difficulty, both in Britain and the States, in filling the theater when this delightful work is being performed. The people who "only like the classics" often have not heard of it, and those who want modern works fear it may be too old-fashioned.

Ashton's other full-length ballet, *Ondine* (1958), is a much more artistic and more integrated work; it is also easily the least popular of his full-length ballets. This may be partly due to the music, by the contemporary German composer Hans Werner Henze, who has not found a very big following outside Germany. It is suitable to the story, like a film background score but not particularly tuneful or memorable; it livens up in the last act with a jazzy piano concerto for the divertissement, but the combination of lively dancing and music comes too late to cheer the audience up, and seems inconsistent with the style of the rest of the ballet. The story itself is not particularly interesting, though no worse than that of many full-length classics. Two lovers, Palemon and Berta, are separated by an Ondine, or water sprite (a kind of mermaid), with whom Palemon becomes infatuated (shades of *La Sylphide*). The jealous Berta chases Palemon and Ondine onto a ship and incites the crew against the water sprite. But the god of the sea raises a storm, the ship is wrecked and Ondine returns to the depths. In the last act, Palemon and Berta are reunited, and about to be married, when Ondine reappears and explains to Palemon that if he kisses her again, he must die. He accepts this, and they end up in the water together. There is more miming, as distinct from dancing, than is usual in an Ashton ballet, especially in the scene on board ship. Ashton has devised some ingenious swaying motions to suggest the rolling of the ship, and the ship-wreck provides an excuse for an exciting bit of stagecraft.

The ballet centers on Ondine to such an extent that it has been described as a "concerto for Fonteyn." Certainly Fonteyn gave a remarkable interpretation of this part—her movements really suggested a creature more at home in water than on land. She has a charming dance with her own shadow in the first act—the first time the Ondine has seen a shadow—but unfortunately this effect was invisible from the stalls at Covent Garden. In the last act, too, Ashton invented an illusion of floating in the water—Ondine is supported by men in black who cannot be seen when the lighting effects work properly. But there is not enough brilliance or variety in the dancing to excite an audience. Perhaps because *Ondine* depends so largely on acting and theatrical effects, the film of it is at least as successful as the stage version, if not more so. This is quite contrary to the usual experience, which is that stage ballets lose a great deal in being transferred to the screen. It is also significant that *Ondine*, the least popular of Ashton's full-length works, is the one in which he is most faithful to Fokine's principles.

The other category of ballet, as distinct from the full-length story ballet, in which Ashton led the counterrevolution against those principles, is the so-called abstract ballet. The abstract ballet has become extremely popular in western Europe and the United States in the past twenty years, though many of the choreographers themselves and writers on their work dislike the label "abstract." They are plotless ballets—pure dance works. Sometimes they have a setting, mood or emotion; in that sense

Les Sylphides or *Les Patineurs* might be called abstract ballets. But when we speak of abstract ballets, we usually mean something more abstract than that, something in which there is no definite setting and the mood or emotion is only vaguely suggested. Sometimes there does not appear to be any at all, though some people argue that no performance in which human beings take part can ever be totally abstract. They say the mere presence of people, with expressions on their faces and making movements at or with each other, must suggest some form of human relationship. I think the extent to which this is true depends on the spectator; some people can watch dancers going through a quite romantic pas de deux without realizing what is being expressed, others can see emotional or psychological significance in even the most academic or gymnastic movement.

Ashton always has some idea in his own mind—some setting or theme—when he creates an abstract ballet, but he does not reveal what it is and he does not mind whether the audience divine it or not. They can read what they wish into his work. For example when he made *Sinfonietta* (1967), to music by Malcolm Williamson, he thought of the first movement as suggesting earth, the second the moon, and the third the sun. But he did not indicate these ideas in the program and was content for audiences to take the ballet as they wished. Personally I prefer not to read much into works of this kind, but just to enjoy the fusion of music and movement much as one may enjoy a totally unpretentious dance routine in a revue, or ice skating, or the abstract patterns made by a kaleidoscope. Though of course I find the combination achieved by an expert choreographer more satisfying than any of those things, I can perfectly well understand that other people may get the same satisfaction out of watching a bullfight, or athletics, or the formalities of Japanese drama. Obviously the music used in an abstract ballet plays a particularly strong part in the ballet's success; as there is no drama, or certainly no explicit drama, and as very often there is no scenery either, and only plain practice costumes, the entire appeal of the ballet depends on the choreography and the music. Inevitably, therefore, one's judgment of the choreography tends to be influenced by one's view of the music. In my case this explains why I have never been able to get as enthusiastic about abstract ballets to music by Stravinsky, whether by Ashton, Balanchine, Cranko or MacMillan, as I have about similar works by the same choreographers to music I prefer. One ought to be able to judge the choreography independently of the music; in practice, this is almost impossible.

Fortunately Ashton's most popular and successful abstract ballets are to music which I do like. The two which are generally accepted as his finest, and among the finest of all ballets, are *Symphonic Variations* to the music of César Franck and *Monotones*, to pieces by Erik Satie. Two others which were also very successful but which are more rarely performed because they are designed for special occasions are *Homage to the Queen* to music by Malcolm Arnold and *Birthday Offering*, to Glazunov.

Symphonic Variations, the first ballet made by Ashton at Covent Garden, was created in 1946. It has a very simple but effective backdrop and costumes, designed by Sophie Federovich. The dominant color of the set is green, with lines and dotted lines forming an abstract pattern over it; the male costumes and tights have similar patterns on them, the female ones are short bodices and dresses cut off at an angle above the knee. The total effect of these clothes is something more than practice dress, something less than a full-scale costume. The ballet is a pas de six for three girls and three boys: originally Margot Fonteyn, Moira Shearer, Pamela May, Michael Somes, Henry Danton and Brian Shaw. In other words, the first cast consisted of the company's three leading ballerinas at that time and two of its leading men. For many years, *Symphonic Variations* remained inseparable from Fonteyn; recently Antoinette Sibley and Merle Park have each successfully appeared in the central role. One of the difficulties of dancing this deceptively simple lyrical work is that the six dancers are a team, but they are also all soloists. The central ballerina must stand out sometimes, but not by any ostentation, and she must also be able to take her place in a perfect ensemble. And all the dancers must go through the movements with a sense of purpose. It is like a joyous rite. The audience may not have the key, but they must feel that the dancers have.

Monotones does not have such a starry cast but it also exerts this strange ritual spell. It has two parts, which were created separately, and Ashton has toyed with the idea of adding a third section but so far there is no sign of this. The section he made first was first seen in 1965; set to orchestrated versions of the Satie piano pieces called *Trois Gymnopédies,* it is a pas de trois which was danced by Vyvyan Lorrayne, Anthony Dowell and Robert Mead. Mostly the three dance together, in allover white tights and close-fitting white caps designed by Ashton himself which make the dancers appear more or less sexless. Ashton once told me that he was fascinated by people walking in space when he made this section, and tried to imagine the sort of movement they might do. The other section was made a year later, to the Satie piano pieces called *Trois Gnossiennes,* specially orchestrated by John Lanchbery. Again a pas de trois, it was performed by Antoinette Sibley, Georgina Parkinson and Brian Shaw. The new pas de trois became the beginning of the ballet, being immediately followed by the old one, and the complete ballet was at first known, confusingly, as *Monotones 1 & 2.* It is now simply called *Monotones,* though the numbering is still used when one of the pas de trois is performed on its own in a divertissement. The costumes for the *Gnossiennes,* also by Ashton, were similar to the others, but had a greenish tinge. This, together with the shape of the headdresses, suggested gnomes and I found myself seeing the first section as an earthly ritual, the second as a more sublime one. In 1969 the first section was recostumed in orange-brown, and the gnomelike look was lost. Now the dancers seem to be moving in a sun-drenched desert. But I am breaking my own rule about not reading situations into abstract ballets!

Homage to the Queen and *Birthday Offering* are quite different: they are brilliant displays of pure classical virtuosity, directly descended from the Petipa divertissements. The former was created for the Coronation of Queen Elizabeth II in 1953. It used the four ballerinas of the company—Nadia Nerina, Beryl Grey, Violetta Elvin, and Margot Fonteyn as Queens of Earth, Water, Fire and Air, each with her partner, and with a special part for Alexander Grant as the Spirit of Fire. Ashton exploited the particular skills of these dancers, and the specially written music by Malcolm Arnold was tuneful and highly danceable. I very much wish that he could be persuaded to write more ballet music. *Birthday Offering* celebrated the twenty-fifth anniversary of the company, in 1956. It assembled all seven ballerinas the company then boasted—Elaine Fifield, Rowena Jackson, Svetlana Beriosova, Nerina, Elvin, Grey and Fonteyn—with their partners, in spectacular costumes by André Levasseur. The music is from various scores by Glazunov, mostly from his ballet *The Seasons*. There were a grand processional entry, separate solo variations for all the ballerinas, a pas de deux for Fonteyn and Michael Somes, and a pas de sept for the men. When the ballet was revived in 1968, with only Fonteyn remaining of the original cast, an additional solo was introduced for Nureyev. Both of these works have always been very successful when performed but the company does not often put all its eggs in one basket by assembling casts like these, and ballets which were designed to show off particular dancers lose something when revived with other casts. Still, audiences would welcome the chance to see these works more often.

Both Ashton's principal successors in British choreography, the South African John Cranko and the Scottish Kenneth MacMillan, have also created full-length story ballets and short "abstracts."

Cranko's *The Prince of the Pagodas,* to specially written music by Benjamin Britten, was one of his comparatively early works (1957). Despite the fact that Britten's music is attractive and melodic, and has since been used by other choreographers in Germany, the ballet was never really popular at Covent

Garden. This was partly due to a complex fairy-tale plot, which incorporated elements of various other fairy tales and fables but did not seem to have any compelling life of its own. Cranko's choreography too was possibly overelaborate, demanding a lot of hard work from the dancers without sufficient returns. Nevertheless there were many admirable sections in the ballet, and it might yet be successfully revived in some simplified and shortened form. Cranko's later full-length ballets, created for his own company in Stuttgart, have been considerably more satisfying.

Cranko has also made, both in London and Stuttgart, a number of abstract ballets, in particular since he went to Germany. He has a tendency to demand a bit more from his dancers than they can easily accomplish; this may help to develop and extend a budding talent but it may also simply show up inadequate techniques. This happened most notably with his Bach abstract, *Brandenburg Nos. 2 & 4,* which worked brilliantly when danced by the Royal Ballet's best male dancers but began to look strained as soon as replacements started to take over. However, it is clear that Cranko has found an abstract style midway between the lyricism of Ashton and the cooler classicism of Balanchine.

MacMillan's only full-length work to date for the Royal Ballet, his version of Prokofiev's *Romeo and Juliet,* has been an enormous success, even more with the public than with the critics. It has also been staged by the Royal Swedish Ballet. Sir Frederick Ashton once told me that "you can't fail with *Romeo and Juliet,*" but in fact several choreographers, including Serge Lifar at the Paris Opéra, have done so. On the other hand it is amazing how many choreographers have been very successful with this work, no doubt because of the combination of one of Shakespeare's most familiar and effective plots and Prokofiev's most dramatic, tuneful and coherent score; there are no extraneous divertissements, and almost all the action—fights, the deaths of Mercutio and Tybalt, the first meeting of the hero and heroine, their balcony scene, and their final parting and reunion in death—is depicted through choreography set to highly appropriate music. Only the music for the wedding ceremony performed for Romeo and Juliet by Friar Laurence poses a difficulty, and this tends to be an old-fashioned mime scene. In general, however, *Romeo and Juliet* has proved that a full-length ballet can be a unified and coherent dramatic work, which even Fokine might have approved.

MacMillan, like Cranko, has also produced a number of abstract ballets, especially since he went to Berlin. One of his first was to Stravinsky's *Agon,* but in this there seemed to be some uncertainty whether he intended a completely abstract ballet or whether there were elements of plot. The costumes were overelaborate, and the music proved extremely difficult for the dancers. (Balanchine's setting of the same music for New York City Ballet is both simpler and more appropriate, and his dancers are more accustomed to dancing to Stravinsky's percussive, nonmelodic rhythms.)

Concerto, to Shostakovich's second Piano Concerto, one of MacMillan's recent ballets, has been mounted for several companies, including the Royal Ballet. It is a pleasantly unpretentious work, including a lyrical pas de deux for the slow movement and jolly, fast-moving sections for the first and last, and with some virtuoso dancing for the leading man. Some people objected that there was *too much* dancing—that every bar of music was paralleled by some steps—and the same criticism is often made of Balanchine's abstract ballets. Others find this style of choreography more satisfying than, say, Ashton's, which tends not to match the movements so precisely to each beat of the music, but to let the music and movement counterpoint each other. The wide variety of styles possible in even abstract choreography is one of its attractions. MacMillan's style is generally slightly drier than Cranko's, closer to Balanchine in its coolness and further from Ashton's warmth and occasional sentimentality. (It would be an amusing and possibly salutary experience for both critics and general audiences to be shown new ballets occasionally without being told the choreographers'

names. Abstract ballets would prove especially hard to identify.)

Another facet of the counterrevolution, but one which has
not been pursued by the Royal Ballet, is the development of
ballets which depend chiefly on their dramatic content. Since
the departure of Robert Helpmann it has been left to other
companies in Britain to produce works of this kind. This may
be pure chance, but it must also be said that ballet companies
and audiences tend to prefer dramatic works when they are
short of outstanding dancers. This applied to the Royal Ballet
in its early days and during the war but is far from the case
today, when the problem at Covent Garden is rather one of
finding enough opportunities for all the first-class classical
dancers. But it still tends to apply to smaller British companies
such as Ballet Rambert and the company which was called
Western Theatre Ballet until it was reborn, in 1969, as Scottish
Theatre Ballet.

During the last decade, Ballet Rambert has nurtured a new
choreographer, Norman Morrice, who became associate director
of the company when it adopted its new avant-garde image in
1966. In his very first work, *Two Brothers* (1958), he showed
the predilection which has reemerged in several of his later
ballets for the theme of jealous conflict between men. In *Two
Brothers* the setting was modern, and it seemed as if Morrice
would produce works in the style of Helpmann's *Miracle in the
Gorbals*. Later Morrice set this theme in a vaguely Biblical
context—specifically in the Garden of Eden in *Hazard* (1967)
and more abstractly with the emergence of the first men in *1-2-3*
(1968). Both these works were concerned with the corruption
of early man's innocence by woman, and with the first fight
between men, possibly between Cain and Abel. But while remaining obsessed with the same themes, Morrice has gradually
increased the amount of actual dancing in his works, which
have ceased to be mime plays and now make considerable use of
energetic classical technique, especially for the men. This trend
first became particularly noticeable in *The Tribute,* a very

interesting but overcomplex and rather obscure work which Morrice did for the touring section of the Royal Ballet in 1965. The experience of working with highly trained classical dancers no doubt stimulated him to use their technique, and it would be good if he could do more work with a classical company. The more he is tempted to rely on dramatic situations, rather than on choreography, the shorter the life of his works will be. Indeed they do not seem to remain very long in the Rambert repertoire, but are always being replaced by his own later works of a similar type.

The same applies to the ballets created for Western Theatre Ballet by Peter Darrell, who like Morrice started as resident choreographer and became his company's artistic director. Big claims have been made for Darrell and Western Theatre Ballet by the company's skillful publicity experts, and by some of the critics. At one time we were constantly being told that Darrell was pioneering a new path for ballet. It is true that he tackled subjects like mental instability and sexual perversion that are not the normal diet of ballet. It is also true that he used two established playwrights, John Mortimer and David Rudkin, to provide the scenarios for his ballets *Home* and *Sun into Darkness*. (One unkind colleague alleged that after the premiere of the full-length *Sun into Darkness* there had been despair backstage because Darrell had just thought of one perversion he had left out of the ballet!) Unfortunately the law of diminishing returns applied to these ballets even more quickly than it did to Helpmann's or Morrice's, because they were much weaker in actual choreographic invention. Darrell's dancers tend to use the same limited range of steps in nearly every situation, and one rarely feels impelled to see one of his ballets a second time. An exception is *The Prisoners* (1957), one of his earliest works, which provided such good opportunities for acting that it repaid repeated viewing. The plot—two men escape from jail, then one has an affair with the other's wife, kills the other in a jealous fight, and remains the woman's prisoner for fear of being betrayed and caught—lends itself to powerful mime in a series of short effective scenes. Dramatic action mimed and partly danced to music can make very effective and exciting theater, but for the reasons I have indicated it does not win such a firm place in the regular repertoire as either the full-length classic or imitation classic, or the modern abstract work.

CHAPTER IV

New Revolutions?

COUNTERREVOLUTION inevitably prepares the ground for the next revolution, and we have already seen that some of the developments which seemed to be taking ballet back to pre-Diaghilev and pre-Fokine days have in fact been taking it forward. The new full-length ballets pioneered by Ashton and now being made by other choreographers are a real advance on the old full-length classics in two respects. First the dancing and the action is usually much more integrated and more care is taken to have appropriate decor and costumes. In other words, Fokine's principles are being incorporated in the very full-length works which he thought belonged only to the past. Ashton's *La Fille Mal Gardée* and Ashton's, Cranko's, and MacMillan's versions of *Romeo and Juliet* are good examples. Moreover producers and choreographers are looking more carefully at the classics, sometimes revising the story or tightening production details to make them more convincing. And the new abstract ballets constitute a complete new branch of the ballet repertoire, often incorporating a new sort of music with corresponding new styles of choreography.

It is notable that most of these tendencies are international. Choreographers and audiences everywhere seem to want ballets which concentrate on dancing, rather than on story line or decor. In the Soviet Union, for example, abstract ballets were long sneered at as examples of bourgeois decadence. Socialist realist theory demanded not merely that ballets should have a story, but that it should be clear, easily intelligible and, above all, morally uplifting. Admittedly the early years of the Soviet regime saw modernist experiments in ballet, as in the other arts. It was the Soviet Union which provided a home for a time for Isadora Duncan, that notorious exponent of experimental free dance. This enabled apologists in the restricted days of Stalinism to deny that Soviet ballet had never experimented with the avant-garde. "We've tried it and didn't like it," they said. Virtually all new productions were elaborate full-length works in the old-fashioned style, with stories which frequently had a strong propaganda content. The music was often trite and inappropriate, as we in London discovered when we saw the Bolshoi Ballet in *The Fountain of Bakhchisarai,* in which tinkly palm-court music by Asafiev is used for the oriental harem scene. Even these productions were to some extent viable because of the sheer brilliance and virtuosity of the dancing.

Now Soviet ballet masters are increasingly inclined to reduce the amount of spectacle, mime and storytelling in the traditional classics, and to concentrate on the dancing. The Kirov's production of *The Sleeping Beauty* was criticized by some people in the West for not paying enough attention to the story and becoming almost a pure-dance concert. Konstantin Sergeyev's new version of *Cinderella* contained less mimed acting and comic business than Ashton's and the Kirov *Raymonda* too evidently omits a lot of the traditional mime. Grigorovitch's *Nutcracker* for the Bolshoi tells the whole story in dance rather than mime, and his *Spartacus* omits the realistic mime scenes and carries the action forward through danced "monologues."

The decor in most of these productions is comparatively simple and functional, and does not compete for attention with the dancers.

Rudolf Nureyev, who imbibed some of the same artistic ideals as his contemporaries at the Kirov when he trained there, has staged several of the Petipa classics in the West in versions which exclude the mime and most of the story line. His *Raymonda* for the touring section of the Royal Ballet and later for the Australian Ballet is a series of spectacular solos, pas de deux, group and chorus dances to the ravishing Glazunov score, with scarcely a trace of the complex and somewhat ludicrous original scenario. His *Don Quixote* for the Vienna State Opera Ballet is evidently similar; certainly the version mounted for Ballet Rambert in 1962 by the Polish ballet master Witold Borkowski also dispensed with most of the story and the mime.

One act of another Petipa classic, *La Bayadère,* is performed on its own by Soviet ballet companies and has been staged for the Royal Ballet by Nureyev, for the Dutch National Ballet by Elena Chikvaidze, and for the National Ballet of Canada by Eugene Valukin. It too is virtually an abstract ballet, starting like the second act of *Swan Lake* with a processional entry for the female corps de ballet in white, but building up to some fast-moving and exciting virtuoso solos for three female soloists, the ballerina, and her partner. This sort of choreography shows that some of our modern abstract ballets are not as modern as we like to think; on the other hand the fact that this act is now taken out of context, and performed without the rest of *La Bayadère* shows the change in taste which Diaghilev, Fokine and others spotted and hastened. We have accepted their revolt against pantomime but not their attack on dance virtuosity for its own sake.

In Stuttgart, Cranko's full-length *Eugene Onegin* is an attempt to create a new full-length ballet which tells a story mainly through dancing. Opinions differ about the success of this work; personally I find it immensely effective and enjoyable and wish it were available to other companies. Cranko's original idea was to use music from Tchaikovsky's opera of the same name, but eventually he was dissuaded from doing this and instead a score was compiled from lesser-known works by Tchaikovsky. The result is virtually a new full-length score by the greatest ballet composer of all time. Pushkin's story lends itself to dancing, especially as two of the crucial scenes in any case take place at balls. Cranko's ingenuity is displayed in his transcription of the famous letter scene; instead of Tatiana singing an aria, as she does in the opera, she dreams a romantic pas de deux with Onegin, whom she has just met. There is scarcely any conventional mime in the whole ballet, yet the story is crystal clear. Nureyev, also using the dream formula, tells the story of *The Nutcracker* in his Royal Ballet production with scarcely any mime. It looks as if there may be a considerable future for streamlined versions of the classics, concentrating on the dancing, and for new full-length ballets in which choreography will count for considerably more than story, and probably for more than music or decor as well.

The acknowledged great master of abstract choreography is George Balanchine, born a Georgian called Balanchivadze, trained in Russia, apprenticed with Diaghilev, and later the founder, artistic director and resident genius of New York City Ballet. Not all his ballets are abstract, even now. In addition to *The Nutcracker,* he has done a full-length *Don Quixote* to a specially written score by Nicolas Nabokov which unfortunately I have not seen but which evidently depends rather more on mime than on dance. His re-creation of *Harlequinade,* to the music originally written by Drigo for Petipa, and his full-length *Midsummer Night's Dream,* to an arrangement of the Mendelssohn music, are comparatively recent examples of his counter-revolutionary side, usually forgotten in Europe where none of these works have been performed. But it is the development of the abstract ballet with which he is most closely associated, and on which he now mainly concentrates. Most of his abstract works are simply concerned with adding the dimension of movement to music, without any suggestion of time, place, or emotion. Some of them, like *Serenade* to Tchaikovsky's Serenade for Strings, or even *Ballet Imperial* to the same composer's second piano concerto, have faint suggestions of human relationships, though Balanchine himself is reluctant to admit this.

Being a particularly musical choreographer, Balanchine has worked on a remarkably wide range of scores, from Mozart to Webern, from Bizet to Stravinsky, from Bach to Ives, and from Glazunov to Xenakis. And because his choreography is always closely bound to the music, one's response is inevitably equally closely bound to one's response to the music. People with highly sophisticated, highbrow musical tastes find it difficult to accept *Stars and Stripes* (Sousa), *Western Symphony* (Hershy Kay) or even possibly *Glinkiana* (Glinka). On the other hand those of us who have not yet learned to appreciate the latest trends in music find it equally difficult to enjoy *Movements for Piano and Orchestra* (Stravinsky) or *Episodes* (Webern). Music of this kind seems inherently unsuitable for dancing, and it is part of Balanchine's genius that he can not only use it, but create new movement styles which seem inevitably matched to it. Lesser choreographers grappling with the same or similar scores usually only succeed in setting insoluble problems, both for their dancers and their audiences. Obviously ballet will have to accommodate itself to the new music, and Balanchine is showing that it can be done.

Jerome Robbins, who, perhaps significantly, is also of part-Russian origin, has done it too, but in a different way. In his choreography for the hit musical *West Side Story*, and in some of his work for his own short-lived company Ballets U.S.A., he transformed the cool jazz and discothèque dancing of contemporary teenagers into formal theatrical terms. His dances, with their finger clicks, athletic jumps, and high-speed runs across the stage, have since been imitated by would-be modern choreographers everywhere. But Robbins' recent work, *Dances at a Gathering* (1969) for New York City Ballet, is an experiment of a very different kind, an essay—and a supremely successful one—in abstract classical dancing with emotional undertones to piano music by Chopin.

Robbins is also one of those who have experimented in ballet without music. His *Moves* is one of the more interesting examples of this genre, which was probably started by David Lichine with *The Creation,* a partially successful attempt to show a choreographer at work on a ballet. Choreographers sometimes feel the urge to liberate ballet from the shackles of music, so that the dancing can stand on its own, ideally perhaps without drama or decor either. But to most of us, dancing without music still seems unnatural. It involves the dancers in difficult counting under their breaths to keep their movements in time, it tends to substitute the noise of their breathing, their shoes squeaking, and their toes tapping for the more agreeable sound of music. And it seems to demand an almost unnaturally high level of concentration from the audience. I suspect too that the idea of ballet in silence appeals most to choreographers without much sense of music; this suspicion is reinforced when the ballet begins in silence, as so often happens with the more experimental companies nowadays, and the music comes in later, or when the music stops and starts, leaving the movement to go on without it. Good choreographers who have done works in silence have not been tempted to continue such experiments and the silent ballet seems likely to remain an occasional curiosity.

Certainly the two greatest choreographers of our time, Ashton and Balanchine, normally work from the music. Ashton has repeatedly told me that the idea for a new ballet usually comes from a piece of music. On the other hand Maurice Béjart, the French choreographer who directs the Ballet of the Twentieth Century in Brussels, said in a television interview that he would prefer to choreograph without music. This preference has not stopped him from using Berlioz' *Romeo and Juliet,* Beethoven's ninth symphony and excerpts from Wagner's operas as backgrounds to his ballets.

Actually what Béjart is doing is believed by some people to indicate one of the paths along which ballet may now advance. His latest works have mostly been "total-theater" spectacles, designed for the Circus building in Brussels and also staged at the Palais des Sports in Paris and other large arenas. He uses speech, song, music, spectacular costumes, classical dance steps and acrobatics, and he has captured a large, enthusiastic, young audience which is not self-consciously artistic and probably would not go near normal ballet.

The only recent one of these works that I have seen is *Baudelaire*, but I am assured it is fairly typical. It is an impressionist re-creation of the poet's dreams, visions and love affairs. It obviously appealed to Béjart, and appeals to his audiences, because Baudelaire could be called one of the first hippies. Seven male dancers, dressed and made up identically, represent seven aspects of Baudelaire with five different girls as his wife. Some of the male dancers speak (with the aid of microphones) and one of the females appears to sing. The speech includes quotations from Baudelaire, comments on the action (one female is constantly rushing on and condemning the proceedings as *"artificiel"*), and an American voice describing experiments with hallucinogenic drugs. The music ranges from Wagner to pop, and includes South-Sea island melodies. But although the music (recorded on tape) changes rapidly from classical to modern and from the sublime to trash, the movements remain obstinately similar throughout. And this is the great weakness of Béjart's work. It is not just his arbitrary use of music, which must shock ordinary musical people as well as purists, but also the monotony and uninventiveness of his actual choreography. His dancers tend to perform the same limited range of steps in all situations. Béjart's company always includes a number of good-looking and talented male dancers, but one wearies of seeing them spin in the air to no particular purpose, and often out of time with each other. There is a very striking moment in *Baudelaire* when one of the heroes leaps around the ring, then rolls down a ramp and right across the floor. On one occasion, the contrast between classical and pop music is used to highlight the contrast between the poet and the crowd. But mostly, there seems to be no particular reason for either the music or the movement.

Moreover it is not at all clear what the message or moral of *Baudelaire* is intended to be. We are not stimulated to any new thoughts about the nature of man, or given any new ideas for his salvation. Of course there is no reason why a ballet should provide either of these things, but Béjart does seem to be attempting this. One quotation from Baudelaire is spoken at both the beginning and end of the performance—a quotation in which he denies love for family, friends, country, beauty or gold, and ends by declaring love for the clouds, the marvelous clouds. Just before the end, there is an explosion and all the cast fall dead on the floor; then the girls drop their gaudy colored scarves on the men, who rise again. Perhaps all this captures the nihilism and unsatisfied questing of modern youth; and perhaps that is why it strikes them as an exciting experience. But I cannot help thinking that it can only make such an impression on comparatively unsophisticated audiences, especially those who have not seen much modern art, let alone much ballet.

However there is no doubt that a total-theater spectacle of this kind could be an exciting and important new art form. I cannot help wondering whether someone like Robbins, or possibly Helpmann, could manage it better than Béjart. With him, the idea is so much more exciting than the execution. At least, however, when Béjart mixes the media, he tries to mix them all. There is a sort of dramatic content, intended to be relevant to the problems of our time, as well as psychedelic use of lighting, amplified sound effects, and abstract movement. Many of the choreographers and producers experimenting with mixed-media ballets seem content to ignore the dramatic aspect altogether. This is especially true of choreographers on the fringe between ballet and modern dance, who frequently prefer to leave audiences to draw what conclusions they may from an enigmatic title, some abstract movement (usually including a lot of writhing on the floor), electronic music and constantly changing lighting effects.

Sometimes this mixture is theatrically effective; more often, it seems like a rite designed for the gratification of the performers rather than an entertainment for a paying audience. Time and time again I have sat through "experimental" new works in which the dancers appeared to have some sense of purpose of their own but their movements looked to the outsider too much like the sort of thing a reasonably athletic and musical child might improvise in a nursery. Admittedly this criticism can be made equally of recent developments in other branches of the arts. Many paintings now look like the random daubings of a child, just as many sculptures look like objects accidentally piled up in a scrapyard. There would be no objection to theatrical performances looking like this too, as long as they communicated something to the audience. But communication is normally best achieved by careful planning and a clear sense of purpose.

Nowadays, however, not everyone even admits that a theatrical performance need communicate anything at all. And some ballets do not merely look as if they were assembled by chance; it is proudly claimed for them that they actually *are* assembled by chance. The most notorious examples are the works presented by the Merce Cunningham company. This American modern dance group represents a collaboration between John Cage, the avant-garde composer, Robert Rauschenberg, the artist, and Cunningham himself, a dancer and choreographer. All of them believe in what are called "aleatory" effects, in other words effects depending on pure chance. The "music" leaves lots of room for improvisation, including dropped trays, banged piano lids, and chairs scraped on the floor; the "decor" may consist of bits of furniture and other objects found in the theater and its vicinity; the "dancing" is sometimes improvised by the dancers and often looks improvised when it is not.

Obviously such a chance combination *could* lead to an interesting performance. But it is unlikely to do so regularly, each time there is an audience. Moreover the element of improvisation is likely to disappear; once the artists find a satisfying combination they are likely to repeat it. In any case it is difficult to see what virtue the aleatory principle is supposed to have, apart from the explicit abdication of artists who realize they have nothing to express. When the exponents of this sort of thing are asked what a particular performance is meant to say to the audience, they reply that it is not meant to say anything in particular and that they do not care how the audience reacts, if at all. Theoretically, they do not even care whether there is an audience though presumably the facts of economic life make one desirable in practice.

Another disadvantage of this kind of performance is that attention is distracted from the dancing to the more gimmicky ingredients. This would normally be a crippling disadvantage, but as the dance content of these works is often minimal, and the actual technical standard poor, the distractions may be a blessing, enabling a company to get away with performances which would not be tolerated on their merit as dance attractions. Many avant-garde "ballets" nowadays include no dancing at all. We have seen a dancer walking around behind the backs of the audience, and then dropping eggs on the floor. We have seen dancers getting in and out of sacks. We have seen, endlessly and repeatedly, dancers entwining themselves in strips of plastic, or hiding in plastic bags. (A thesis could probably be written on the effect of plastic on modern art, and on its apparently erotic appeal to modern artists and choreographers.) And we have seen, even more frequently, dancers lying on the floor, or writhing on it, out of view of most of the audience in the stalls, and unable to use anything of their laboriously acquired dance technique.

That is the tragedy of much of this experiment. Nobody wants to restrict the freedom of creative artists in the theater to devise any kind of play, mime, ballet or happening which they want. But it does seem a sad waste of talent to use highly trained classical dancers to perform movements which could be done by

any untrained but reasonably trim, fit young person, or in some
cases not even to perform any recognizable movement at all.
And it is not really sufficient compensation to be invited to look
at changing colored lights, or to listen to a taped montage of
sound effects, or to hear the dancers trying to speak or sing
instead of dance. When the performers are not trained dancers
at all, but drama students or amateurs, and when the performance is not given in a theater but in a studio, attic, cellar or
"arts laboratory," at least there is not the same sense of wasted
talent or wasted opportunity. But this sort of performance
usually does more for the performers than for the audience and
is scarcely what one would call a theatrical event.

   In any case the use of mixed media is nothing like as new as
this fashionable label itself. All sorts of attempts to use speech
and song in ballet have been made over the years. Sometimes
song is simply an integral part of the music—the choral singing
in the snowflakes scene of *The Nutcracker,* for example, or in
the dances from *Prince Igor* or in Ravel's *Daphnis and Chloë.*
Sometimes ballets are set to songs—Mahler seems especially
popular for this purpose; Tudor used Mahler's *Kindertoten-
lieder* for his *Dark Elegies* back in 1937, MacMillan turned
to another famous Mahler song cycle for his *Song of the
Earth* (1965) and Eliot Feld set *At Midnight* (1967) to the
Four Rückert Songs. Sometimes poems are recited—verses by
Gertrude Stein are read by a narrator as an accompaniment
to the dance in Ashton's *A Wedding Bouquet* (1937), prerecorded lines from Shakespeare are played between dances in
MacMillan's *Images of Love* (1964) and the ballerina herself
speaks poetry by André Gide in Ashton's *Perséphone* (1961).
In general, the least successful way of using words in ballet is to
have the dancers speak them. For one thing, dancers do not
usually have good speaking voices, and cannot project them. At
the first performances of *Perséphone* Svetlana Beriosova danced
with a transistor microphone concealed in her bosom, but it
crackled and on one occasion burned her! Later, her voice was

prerecorded, and she mouthed the words but quite obviously was not really saying them. In any case, an audience is usually disconcerted by the sudden breaking of the convention that the message of ballet is conveyed through movement and mime. If the dancers are going to speak, why do they bother to dance?

The use of speech or song as an accompaniment to dancing can be more successful. Recent outstanding examples are Balanchine's *Liebeslieder Walzer* (1960), a charming atmospheric work to the Brahms song settings, and the Dutch choreographer Hans van Manen's *Solo for Voice 1* (1968) to music by John Cage. In this work, performed by Netherlands Dance Theatre, a soprano moves around the stage, goading a pair of lovers with a stream of nonsense song directed at them, so that the ballet becomes virtually a trio for two dancers and a singer.

But even the best works of this kind have less impact for me than pure ballet, or pure drama, opera or oratorio either for that matter. In the case of the great Mahler song cycles, for example, I have never found the effect of the Tudor and MacMillan ballets as overwhelming as good concert performances of the same works. The standard of the musical performance in the theater cannot be expected to equal that achieved by the world's greatest singers and conductors in the concert hall. And during the ballet attention is divided between the song and the dance, so that neither can make its full effect.

I realize, of course, that this reaction is highly subjective, though I know it is widely shared. There is no doubt that both Tudor and MacMillan have made remarkable ballets: many people find them tremendously moving. *Dark Elegies* has maintained its place in the repertoire for over thirty years, and *Song of the Earth* may well do the same. But I find that the sight of dancers emoting, however expressively, subtracts from rather than adds to the music, and comes between the music and direct appreciation of it. The words of these songs really require intellectual attention, though as they are usually sung in the original German most English-speaking audiences cannot provide this.

It may actually be easier to concentrate on the ballets if one does not understand the words, but that can hardly be what the choreographers, let alone the composer, intended.

Similarly when words are spoken during the performance, either on stage or through loudspeakers, our attention must be to some extent divided between our eyes and our ears. Some people are evidently better at this division than others; perhaps it is a matter of getting used to it. Personally I find that once I am tuned in to ballet, any spoken words jar on me, whether they are part of the performance or merely a comment from a neighbor in the audience. It even jars me slightly when the male poodle in Massine's *Boutique Fantasque* goes "bow wow"!

This is not to deny, however, the possibility of a successful mixed-media or total-theater spectacle, which in effect would be something other than ballet. In ballet, our attention is focused primarily on the dancing, and other ingredients—whether they are musical, verbal, or decorative—can be distracting and irritating if they assume too great an importance. In a spectacle like Béjart's *Baudelaire*, for example, the dancing is intrinsically less interesting and less important than in most ballets and we can divide our attention more easily between all the ingredients. My objection to *Baudelaire* is not the mixture of ingredients, but the fact that none of them seems to me particularly distinctive or original. And of course it must be a temptation for the director or creator of a show of this kind to think that the mere mixing of ingredients is entertaining enough in itself, and that not too much attention need be paid to their actual quality. Many experimental shows put on in small halls and studios tumble cheerfully into this error. It may be that for some comparatively unsophisticated audiences, this mixing is enough. The combination of almost any loudly amplified music with rapidly changing colored lights, some sort of poetic or quasi-poetic speech, and some more or less significant movement is bound to have a theatrical effect. But once people have seen a little of this kind of thing, they are going to demand more subtlety or more sense of purpose in the mixture.

Although the addition of speech or song to ballets in one form or another is not at all new, it has now been made much easier technically by the invention of high-fidelity and stereophonic sound reproduction, and by tape recording. The only obstacle to high quality music and realistic sound effects nowadays is the objection of the trade unions in many countries to the use of recorded music.

The musicians' unions, both in Britain and the United States, normally insist on a live orchestra to accompany a ballet performance, especially in big towns and in theaters with orchestra pits. In the United States, the union even lays down a prescribed minimum number of musicians for a particular theater. This means that an orchestra may have to be paid to remain silent while an electronic or complex score is played on tape, or that some musicians may have to be employed unnecessarily if only chamber music is to be played, or that a work may have to be abandoned entirely if the score requires a bigger or more talented orchestra than is economical. In some ways live music, even if played by an inferior orchestra, is preferable to the best taped recordings; recorded music in the theater undoubtedly diminishes that elusive quality, atmosphere. But the complex sound effects and electronic scores devised by advanced composers today cannot be played live, and it is ludicrous that performances of this kind sometimes cannot take place because of union insistence on the expensive employment of live musicians.

Recent technical advances have also made possible far more elaborate lighting effects. Psychedelic lighting (though the term was not yet invented) and film projections played important parts in the Diaghilev production of Massine's *Ode* in Paris as early as 1928. The idea of mood lighting is, of course, not at all new. In the thirties, the curtains in front of the cinema screen, the walls of the auditorium, and the electric organ console, all changed colors between films in what would nowadays be called a psychedelic manner. Most cinemas long ago gave up this sort of thing but now pop groups and experimental theater clubs have taken it up. All sorts of ingenious devices now exist for creating light patterns of a kaleidoscopic type, in endless random variations. There are devices which are intended to translate music and other sound effects automatically into appropriate lighting, just as we are promised devices which will translate human movement automatically into appropriate sound effects, so that a live composer will no longer be essential. And we have already seen experiments with automated mobiles or abstract sculptures "dancing" instead of human beings.

Pieces of scenery which move around the stage apparently of their own volition, either on conveyor belts in the stage, or pushed by unseen hands, or with small motors inside, are becoming common in ballet as they are in the rest of the theater. Drop curtains now sometimes roll upwards from the floor, instead of coming down from the flies. All these things exercise a certain fascination, and can be used to intrigue an audience and divert attention from the absence of dance invention or dramatic content. They often make modern ballets look more like art exhibitions than ballets in any normal sense. Sound and lighting effects can also be used to similar effect. Gerald Arpino's *Astarte,* perhaps the most popular work in the repertoire of the Joffrey Ballet, depends for its effect more on the skillful and technical blending of the media—film, lighting and sound effects—than on its actual dance content. Many of the works created in recent years by Glen Tetley and Anna Sokolow come into this category. The movements required of the dancers are rudimentary and in some cases there are virtually no movements at all. Instead we are given tape recordings of atomic explosions, heartbeats, newborn babies, breaking glass and erotic-sounding words in many languages, suddenly changing colored lights or blinding spotlights trained on the audience—a new device which is becoming distressingly popular with advanced lighting experts.

These developments are of course part of a general trend in all branches of experimental theater. Actors are now frequently expected to improvise without scripts, to mime instead of speak, and to appear on bare, open stages without costumes or scenery, in the quest for greater naturalism, more intimate contact with the audience and the destruction of artificial illusion. The result, all too often, is that we get a nonplay instead of a play. Ballet, in any case, is essentially an art of convention and of illusion; if these are destroyed, the resulting nonballet tends to be even more painful than a nonplay. Close proximity to breathy, sweaty dancers is fairly disagreeable, as is the sight of fellow members of the audience on the opposite side of the stage when ballet is presented in the round. Nevertheless it is quite possible that a choreographer using some at least of these new theatrical techniques will succeed in creating a truly contemporary ballet. Maybe it will be about the Bomb, or germ warfare, or the war in Vietnam, or about drugs and dropouts, or world overpopulation and starvation, the new sexual freedom or the quest for a new religion or a new morality. There is no obligation on ballet to depict or comment on these things, and there is certainly no reason why dancers or choreographers should be particularly well qualified to do so. But these are the things which many of the experimental ballets are obviously trying to do. So far, however, all their revolutionary and quasirevolutionary techniques and gimmicks have obstinately failed to achieve a revolution in the art of ballet itself.

CHAPTER V

Evolutionary Progress

MOST OF THE REVOLUTIONARY MOVEMENTS in ballet seem likely to weaken or destroy the dance element in ballet, and develop a new form of theater which may be part dance, part mime, part circus, part art display, part happening. Sometimes there is no dancing, sometimes no dramatic or emotional communication, sometimes no music; sometimes indeed scarcely anything appears to happen at all, which constitutes a very bizarre form of "happening." Some of these experiments are interesting and effective, and exert a particular fascination for young audiences —art students, hippies or their latest equivalents, and others who would not go near a conventional ballet or theater. They may in time develop into something attracting a wider audience.

All this does not mean that ballet, as it has been known and as we have understood it, is no longer being created. We have already considered two types of ballet which are proving popular both with choreographers and audiences—the neoclassical full-length ballet and the short, abstract pure-dance work. We have labeled these counterrevolutionary, because to some extent they represent a return to styles denounced by Fokine and the whole Diaghilev revolution. There is also a type of modern ballet, less popular just now perhaps than the other two, which represents a kind of extension of the work inspired by Diaghilev. This is the one-act ballet which tells a story of some kind, attempts to fuse drama, decor, music and choreography in a coherent whole, and yet retains the preeminence of dance. In these works the story is often suggested or sketched, rather than made explicit; there is little or no mime, so that the action is conveyed through the dance, and the impact of the work is made primarily by the choreography.

Most modern choreographers make works of this kind from time to time. Even Balanchine is not totally divorced from the short ballet with a story or theme. His *Prodigal Son* (1929) was created for Diaghilev but he revived it for New York City Ballet in 1950 and it is regularly in their repertoire. It is still extremely effective, with its astonishingly modern use of mobile properties, its striking tableaus, its daring orgiastic dances and its dramatic Prokofiev music. Edward Villella gives a great dancing and acting performance in the title role, which was originally created by the young Serge Lifar. Balanchine's *Apollo* (1928) which is now in the repertoire of the Royal Danish Ballet, the Dutch National Ballet, the Stuttgart Ballet, and the Royal Ballet, as well as of New York City Ballet, is mainly abstract but with the three muses occasionally miming and with Apollo unwrapped from a swaddling cloth at the beginning. It is an uneasy mixture but it can make a considerable effect when danced by someone with a strong personality and a good physique, like Jacques d'Amboise of New York City Ballet. More recently, in 1946, Balanchine made *Night Shadow* (*La Somnambule*) * for Ballet Russe de Monte Carlo. The most fervent admirers of Balanchine's modern style may find it old-fashioned but it is one of his best-known and most popular

---

* *La Somnambule* was the title for the revised version of the earlier ballet *La Sonnambula*.

works. It was performed by the Cuevas company and by Ballet Rambert, and is now in the repertoires of numerous companies.

Night Shadow is a particularly good example of the way in which a choreographer can create an atmosphere, and hint at a story entirely through dance and without resorting to explicit mime. It opens with a distinguished-looking middle-aged man receiving guests at a garden party. He is with a younger woman, who is evidently his mistress. Then a good-looking young man (the Poet) arrives and there is a slightly embarrassed meeting. Presumably the Poet is a former lover of the Coquette, and the Baron knows this. Everybody behaves correctly, there is a divertissement for the entertainment of the guests, and the Poet dances with the Coquette but the Baron takes her from him just as they are leaving the stage together. The Poet is left alone, when a light is seen coming down from window to window inside the house, and a woman in a white nightdress, carrying a candle, comes out—sleepwalking. She is the Baron's wife. She moves around in a trance, seemingly unaware of the Poet, who turns her around, pushes her this way and that, and lies on the floor where she steps over him. Finally he follows her back into the house. The Coquette has returned in time to see them together, and in a jealous fury she calls the Baron. He rushes into the house and kills the Poet, who comes staggering out and collapses on the stage. The Sleepwalker returns, still in an apparent trance, picks up the Poet's body in her arms, and takes it into the house.

We are not really told the relationships between the characters—we can infer them as we wish. Nor do we know how much the Sleepwalker is aware of the Poet. Perhaps because of these very uncertainties the ballet is moving and effective, even if not everyone interprets it in the same way. The music is taken from Bellini's operas, including *La Sonnambula,* his opera about a sleepwalker, and is both melodious and dramatically effective. Various designers have worked on different productions of the ballet—the decor plays an important part in the drama, as the audience should be able to see the light of the Sleepwalker's candle through the windows, as she walks along the corridors and up and down stairs.

But the most memorable things about *Night Shadow* are all choreographic. The first entrance of the Poet with the awkward pause and embarrassed glances exchanged between the Baron and the Coquette, the divertissement, including an unusual Harlequin suffering from lumbago, the general dance which ends with the Baron taking the Coquette off the Poet's arm, and the appearance of the Sleepwalker are the highlights. The Sleepwalker moves almost entirely on her points, so that when the Poet gives her a gentle push, she goes weightlessly off across the stage as if without any will of her own. Similarly she turns around when he turns her, and when he lies on the ground with his arms outstretched and clasped to catch her feet, she steps delicately over them. The finale consists of the Sleepwalker picking the dead Poet off the ground and carrying him horizontally in her arms, which should look effortless but is not managed by all interpreters of the role.

There have been many memorable interpreters of the principal parts: George Skibine, Serge Golovine, Henning Kronstam and John Gilpin among the Poets, Ethery Pagava, Marjorie Tallchief, Margrethe Schanne and Galina Samtsova among the Sleepwalkers. Strangely enough Margot Fonteyn, who has given a few performances of the Sleepwalker as a guest artist with Festival Ballet, did not seem very well suited to the part when she danced it in London. The secret seems to be a combination of moving lightly and effortlessly on the points and an enigmatic facial expression which suggests a trance with suspicions of awareness underneath. However it is performed, *Night Shadow* scarcely ever fails to make a moving and romantic effect. There are many other modern ballets in similar style, which are equally effective. Outstanding examples are Cranko's *The Lady and the Fool* and *Antigone,* Ashton's *Enigma Variations,* Tudor's *Shadowplay,* Robbins's *Afternoon of a Faun* and MacMillan's *The Invitation* and *Solitaire.* Two of MacMillan's most recent works—*Anastasia* and *Cain and*

Abel, both created in Berlin—probably come into the same category.

The Lady and the Fool (1954) shares with *Night Shadow* the use of operatic melodies, this time from the lesser-known works of Verdi, and there are other similarities as well. Again the setting is a party given by some sort of rich nobleman. This time the enigmatic guest is a masked lady, La Capricciosa, who picks up two clowns in the street outside and brings them with her to the party. The clowns—one tall and one short—contribute an element of pathos and entertain the guests with a touching dance in which they squabble over a rose, tear it to pieces and end by dividing the loose petals between them. La Capricciosa rejects the advances of various rich suitors, each of whom removes one of her masks only to reveal another underneath. Instead she falls in love with the tall clown, who succeeds in removing her last mask. The smart society people reject her, because she prefers a humble clown, and she leaves with him. The little clown is left alone, nose pressed against the window watching the festivities, huddled up against the cold, but La Capricciosa and the tall clown come back for him, and the three of them depart together. This sentimental little tale of a beautiful but lonely woman, surrounded by riches but afraid of life, finding sympathy and comradeship and sacrificing the social whirl, contains a wealth of comment which can be taken as applying to class, racial or any other prejudices.

Again it is Cranko's choreography, rather more than the music or the decor, which makes *The Lady and the Fool* memorable. There are contrasted solos for the various suitors, and a pas de quatre in which La Capricciosa dances with each of them in turn, a dance perhaps inspired by the Rose Adagio in *The Sleeping Beauty.* There are a number of ingenious and effective lifts in the air for the ballerina, a part which was charmingly created with the old Sadler's Wells Theatre Ballet by the South African dancer Patricia Miller and has since been danced at Covent Garden by Beryl Grey and Svetlana Beriosova, among others. David Blair had one of his best parts as the spoiled, arrogant host, and there have been a whole succession of moving clowns. The original tall clown was Kenneth Mac-Millan, who soon gave up dancing and became Cranko's principal rival as the heir to the British choreographic crown.

My preference among MacMillan's ballets in this genre is for *The Invitation* (1960), to my mind one of the very best of all his works. Once again, the setting is a party—not that a party is necessarily the ideal setting for a ballet! This time it is a gathering of parents and their children around the turn of the century. The prudish mother drapes the naked statues, while the prurient adolescent children steal naughty peeps at them. The daughter of the household is sensitive; she turns away shocked from the statues and is just beginning to feel the pangs of romantic first love for her handsome cousin. Among the guests is a seedy married couple. The wife seduces the cousin, who is educated by the experience and the more anxious to make love to the girl, but the husband rapes the girl, who is put off sex for good and looks destined to become a withered old maid. The story was suggested to MacMillan by two novels—Colette's *Ripening Seed* and Beatriz Guido's *House of the Angel*—and has struck some people as excessively perverse, or as revealing a hostile attitude to sex. It strikes me, on the contrary, as hostile only to hypocrisy and repression, and showing the crippling effect they can have on youth and innocence. Like *The Lady and the Fool,* therefore, it seems to me to make a worthwhile social comment. And like the other ballets of this type, it makes its comment primarily through the dance. Admittedly the specially written music by Matyas Seiber and the decor by Nicholas Georgiadis help very considerably in building up the atmosphere. But it is the choreography and the performance that one remembers.

The most notorious scene is the rape, very graphically portrayed with the girl shuddering against the man's body and then dropping slowly to the ground, twined around him in a circle, in a manner used earlier by Balanchine in his *Prodigal Son.* But all the choreography for the heroine is appropriate and touching; the part was created by Lynn Seymour, who inspired MacMillan in many works. She conveyed exactly the required mixture of virginal timidity and adolescent curiosity, in her gentle dances with her cousin and in the provocative way she danced with the older man, without realizing what she was provoking. Her frightened rejection of her cousin at the end, and her final shriveled walk towards the footlights always gripped the audience and earned her an ovation. Indeed all the original interpreters—Christopher Gable as the cousin and Desmond Doyle and Anne Heaton as the older couple—were highly memorable and have scarcely been equaled by the many talented subsequent casts. The formal dances for the children, supervised by a cane-tapping governess, lead naturally towards the disaster as the girl senses the older man's interest and begins to dance for him, and then with him. The mother's look of shock when she arrives to see her daughter whirling away with the man, her reproachful glance at the governess and the husband's shame after he has been carried away into committing the rape are among the details which contribute to the credibility and power of the drama.

What is more debatable is the acrobatic divertissement, including an erotic pas de trois for two cockerels and a hen, which was obviously intended to provide a contrast and indicate the sexual undertones running through the party. Most people found it distracting and an unnecessary dilution of the party atmosphere, and many people urged MacMillan to omit it. He has now integrated it further into the action, so that the dancers of the divertissement mix with the guests and help to whip up passions all around. He has also provided a chorus of old-fashioned servants to heighten the period nature of the piece and to set out chairs for the divertissement, making clear it is a formal entertainment provided for the party. This is an improvement, but *The Invitation* might be even better without this divertissement.

Ashton's *Enigma Variations* (1968) is also about a kind of house party. The ballet is a surprisingly literal interpretation of

Elgar's program for his well-known music. The Variations characterize Elgar's wife and friends, and Ashton and his designer, Julia Trevelyan Oman, had the idea of assembling them all in a realistic setting representing Elgar's country house. Some of the items are comic: Stanley Holden as Hew David Steuart-Powell smokes a pipe and rides a bicycle, Brian Shaw as Richard Baxter Townshend rides a tricycle, and Alexander Grant as William Meath Baker scurries around the stage in ceaseless and seemingly purposeless haste. There is a charming lyrical pas de deux for Vyvyan Lorrayne and Robert Mead as Isabel Fitton and Richard Arnold, the lovers on the hammock, and an incredibly difficult fast-moving solo for Anthony Dowell as the young blade Arthur Troyte Griffith. But the main achievements of the ballet are the astonishing sense of nostalgia and period atmosphere it evokes and the choreography for Derek Rencher and Svetlana Beriosova as Elgar and his wife, and for Desmond Doyle as their friend Jaeger. To the famous Nimrod Variation, Ashton created a pas de trois in which they scarcely do more than walk together, yet all their close companionship and understanding is fully expressed. Beriosova is particularly moving and effective, whether standing in the background watching Elgar's flirtation with the young Dorabella (Antoinette Sibley) or sharing his joy at the end, when he receives a telegram informing him that Richter has agreed to conduct his music. Ashton has succeeded, entirely through dance and restrained mime, in conveying Elgar's creative problems, his difficult human relationships, and the deep love he inspired in his wife and friends. Even if one knows nothing about Elgar, and has not read the printed program note, the ballet still makes its very considerable theatrical effect.

An earlier ballet of Ashton's, *Daphnis and Chloë* (1951), is even more obviously evolved from Fokine's principles and is indeed set to the Ravel music which Fokine originally used in 1912. By using some slightly modern-looking dance steps and some equally modern-looking costumes designed by John Craxton, Ashton has succeeded in giving the Greek legend a timeless quality. He has also given Fonteyn one of her very best parts. As the innocent Chloë who is abducted by pirates and then happily restored to her lover, she was able to show both the touching, gentle side of her personality and the lively vivacious one. Alexander Grant scored one of his biggest successes as the pirate chief, who is closely related to the Polovtsian warrior in Fokine's dances from *Prince Igor*.

Another of Grant's big successes is as Bottom, who is transformed into an ass, in Ashton's Mendelssohn-Shakespeare ballet *The Dream* (1964). Unlike Balanchine's full-length *Midsummer Night's Dream*, Ashton's work is in one act and is virtually all dancing. It includes neoclassical and romantic dancing for Titania, Oberon, and the attendant fairies, a mercurial part for Puck and lots of comic invention for the human lovers. The pas de quatre in which the two pairs of lovers are all chasing or running away from each other is particularly funny; there is also pathos at the end when Bottom half-remembers his temporary fate as an ass and when Puck is left alone to shrug off the proceedings. Antoinette Sibley and Merle Park have both been delightful Titanias, Anthony Dowell is outstanding as Oberon, growing in authority each time he dances the part, and Keith Martin and Wayne Sleep have both been successful Pucks. John Lanchbery's arrangement of the music is extremely skillful, so that *The Dream* seems to have a coherent Mendelssohn score; it is one of the best recent ballets in the Fokine tradition.

Tudor's *Shadowplay* (1967), the first ballet he ever made for the Royal Ballet, is an allegory using music by the little-known French composer Charles Koechlin, suggested by Kipling's *Jungle Book*. A "boy with matted hair" sits alone under a tree, and is then joined in turn by a group of monkeylike creatures ("arboreals"), birds ("aerials"), a semioriental male figure ("terrestrial") who initiates him in sex, and an enigmatic female figure ("celestial") who seems to love him but then turns on him aggressively and swoops down on him from on high. In the end, the boy is back under the tree surrounded by the monkeys, scratching himself a little as they do, yet apart from them and clearly different. At its simplest level it is an atmospheric work about man, nature and the animals but it obviously has deeper allusions to man's search for love and the meaning of life. It provides Anthony Dowell with a part which exploits his youth, enigmatic expression, and speedy, light dancing style, and it also gives good opportunities to Merle Park and Derek Rencher as the ambiguous celestial and terrestrial characters. Michael Annals's part-realistic setting, with ropes for the monkeys to climb and an unusual spreading tree on one side of the stage, contributes considerably to the total effect.

Similar works, in which men get involved with animals and in which there is some allegorical message, are Roland Petit's *Le Loup,* created for his Ballet de Paris in 1953 and now in the repertoire of the Royal Danish Ballet and the National Ballet of Canada, and John Taras's *Piège de Lumière,* created for the Cuévas Ballet in 1952 and later staged for New York City Ballet and London's Festival Ballet. The former concerns a girl who falls in love with a wolf and is hunted to death with him; it was originally notable for the performances by the young Violette Verdy and by Petit himself, and for the very attractive forest decor by Carzou. The latter is about convicts who live in the forest, hunting animals and catching exotic butterflies in a light-trap, so as to sell them. Their newest recruit becomes infatuated with a spectacular female butterfly, allows it to escape, and becomes an outcast again. Serge Golovine, at one time the most sensational virtuoso dancer in the West, had a tremendous success as a male butterfly, and Rosella Hightower used her formidably strong technique as the female one. The butterflies' costumes were designed by André Levasseur and looked very colorful and spectacular; but somehow they looked less striking when Festival revived the work in 1969.

Robbins's *Afternoon of a Faun* (1953), to the Debussy music previously used by Nijinsky, is a particularly lovely and compelling work, yet still comparatively little known. Robbins had the brilliant idea of transforming the narcissistic eroticism of the faun into the narcissistic eroticism of ballet dancers practicing in a studio. A boy and a girl catch sight of each other in the studio mirror, dance languorously while scarcely aware of each other and part. That is all, but somehow we seem to learn a lot about their personalities, their self-absorption, their loneliness. When the ballet was originally produced for New York City Ballet, and later for Robbins's own Ballets U.S.A., the male part was taken by a colored or seemingly-colored dancer, and the ballet therefore appeared to be in part a comment on race relations. But Robbins denies that this was his intention, and when the ballet was mounted for the Royal Danish Ballet both roles were taken by white dancers. Niels Kehlet and the very young Dinna Bjørn were particularly successful, and the ballet gained by being stripped of its irrelevant racial associations. It would undoubtedly be a useful acquisition to any company, large or small.

All these ballets are logical developments from the Fokine tradition, with the actual choreography playing a more dominant part than it often did in his ballets, and usually with more intricate and technically demanding dancing. They also contain an element of implicit comment so that without being in any way propagandist tracts or having any specific message and without abandoning classical ballet technique, they yet seem relevant to the world in which we live; some such element does undoubtedly strengthen a mixed program of short ballets.

In this connection it may be significant that the first work to enter the Royal Ballet's repertory by its latest choreographic hope, Geoffrey Cauley, is also of this type. *In the Beginning* (1969), to the clarinet and oboe sonatas by Francis Poulenc, is—as the title implies—about Adam and Eve: characters who seem to have exerted a peculiar fascination for choreographers in the last few years. The program for the ballet carries only one sentence of description or explanation, "One man's paradise is another man's purgatory." And the ballet, which is full of beautiful groupings and contains two touching love duets for the hero and heroine, is not easy to understand completely, certainly not at first viewing. There are four principal characters—

Adam and Eve, a girl who is evidently the temptress-serpent, and an enigmatic male character who is part tempter or devil, part the pleasure-loving, promiscuous side of Adam's nature. The ballet ends with Adam and Eve chained together, while the serpent triumphantly sits above them, and with Adam looking longingly towards the other male character who walks gaily off, throwing the apple up in the air and catching it in his hand like a ball. This is evidently some sort of comment on monogamous marriage as a kind of imprisonment. But Adam and Eve have chosen it; perhaps it is their paradise. The message is obscure, and possibly not fully worked out by the choreographer, but in performance that only makes the ballet more intriguing.

The other sort of ballet which seems to be developing successfully from the traditions of the past is the short comedy ballet. There are two types of comedy ballet—the comic story ballet, a development of Massine's comic character ballets, and the comic abstract ballet, derived from the dances which used to be performed in revues, musical shows, and music halls.

David Lichine's *Graduation Ball* was first staged in Australia in 1940 and is now performed by many leading companies including Festival and the Royal Danish, who do it with particular style and wit. It is in some ways similar to a Massine ballet, but less artificial than *La Boutique Fantasque* and more like *Mam'zelle Angot,* which Massine created for Ballet Theatre in 1943 and which has in recent years been a popular success for the Royal Ballet. *Graduation Ball* takes place in a smart girls' finishing school, probably around the turn of the century in Vienna or St. Petersburg, when the cadets from a nearby military academy are invited to the ball. There is a naughty girl with pigtails which stick out, an amusing flirtation between the headmaster and the headmistress, who is also usually played by a man, a touch of sentimentality with the partings at the end, and a jolly divertissement as part of the ball. With its lilting melodies by Johann Strauss, it always cheers up the audience and in a good performance it has just enough period atmosphere and charm to seem like a miniature work of art rather than a mere frolic. Unfortunately the humor is often broadened and all credibility lost.

The same is true of John Cranko's *Pineapple Poll* (1951), a remarkably successful Gilbert and Sullivan ballet. Originally made for the Sadler's Wells Theatre Ballet, it remained in the repertoire of the Royal Ballet for many years and was staged by David Blair for the Joffrey Ballet in 1970. The story is roughly based on one of Gilbert's *Bab Ballads* and the music is taken from several of Sullivan's comic operas. It is a tale of a handsome naval captain, his rich, well-bred fiancée, a bumboat girl who swoons at the sight of the captain and dresses up as a sailor to get on his ship, and the potboy from the inn who is pining for love of the girl. All ends happily, of course, and wittily too, with the fiancée's aunt dressed up as Britannia and the cast celebrating around her. But before that there are jolly dances, including an inevitable hornpipe for the captain, an amusing pas de trois in which the captain keeps rushing from his fiancée to her aunt, who is supposed to be chaperoning her but keeps dropping her umbrella and scarf while talking endlessly to herself.

Most mixed programs are the better for a comic work, and most choreographers attempt to produce one sooner or later. Even Antony Tudor, mostly associated with psychological dramas (though he hates the label) has often relaxed with comedy—in the early days with *Gala Performance* and *Judgement of Paris* (1938), and thirty years later with *Knight Errant* (1968). Opinions differ about the success of this bawdy tale, roughly based on an episode from Laclos' novel *Les Liaisons Dangereuses*, set to music by Richard Strauss (mostly his incidental music for *Le Bourgeois Gentilhomme*) and created specifically for David Wall of the Royal Ballet's touring section. There is no doubt that the central part, a carefree libertine who seduces three women as a kind of game and then arranges dates for them with their husbands, to the surprise and embarrassment of all concerned, gives David Wall marvelous dancing and acting opportunities, which he seizes to the full. There are also excellent parts for the three ladies, all in contrasted ways keen to be seduced, and the humor is often bawdy and farcical. Some people find that there is too much complicated activity on the stage and that the plot is too difficult to follow, criticism which can also be made of many Massine ballets. But *Knight Errant* has a sense of period style and unusual wit which should win it a permanent place in the repertoire quite apart from its fashionably risqué story.

Among the most successful recent examples of more abstract comic ballets have been Cranko's *Card Game,* Robbins's *Fanfare* and Ashton's *Jazz Calendar.* Strangely enough, the first two are much more popular in Germany and Denmark than in Britain and the States. *Card Game,* to Stravinsky's *Jeu de Cartes,* was created for Cranko's own company in Stuttgart and later mounted by Cranko for the Royal Danish Ballet and the Royal Ballet. By a coincidence, the leading role of the ambiguous and slightly sinister Joker, who spends part of the ballet parodying a ballerina, was taken in both Stuttgart and Copenhagen by brilliant Danish dancers, Egon Madsen and Niels Kehlet respectively. When the ballet was mounted for the Royal Ballet, with Christopher Gable as the Joker, its humor seemed to get lost in the wider spaces of the Royal Opera House, and it struck many people as crude and vulgar. The male dancing lacked brilliance and both Gable and his successor Anthony Dowell seemed too soft and at something of a loss. Yet most experienced critics who saw the ballet in Stuttgart or Copenhagen thought it an excellent work, and the best staging of this music we have yet seen.

Fanfare, created by Jerome Robbins originally for New York City Ballet in 1953, was performed by them in London in 1965, but without making much effect. Yet this ballet too is one of the biggest successes of the Royal Danish Ballet. Set to Benjamin Britten's *Young Person's Guide to the Orchestra,* it has the dancers impersonating and parodying the instruments of the orchestra. To be successful, the ballet requires dancers of great personality and comic acting ability—not the strong points of

New York City Ballet. When danced by the Danes, *Fanfare* combines brilliant dance display with a great deal of amusement, especially from the older, heavier dancers who impersonate double bass and tuba.

Jazz Calendar (1968) was set by Ashton to the suite by Richard Rodney Bennett, which in its turn was suggested by the nursery rhyme "Monday's child is fair of face." There is a section for each day of the week and Ashton has been most ingenious in translating the verse into dance terms. Monday's child is a girl preening herself in a mirror, Tuesday's ("full of grace") is a fast-moving, acrobatic pas de trois, Wednesday's ("full of woe") is a parody of exaggerated mourning by a ballerina, slightly reminiscent of Lady Capulet's histrionics after the death of Tybalt in Lavrovsky's version of *Romeo and Juliet*. As performed by Svetlana Beriosova, with her natural feeling for the Slav tragic manner, it is very funny. Thursday's child ("far to go") is Alexander Grant, endlessly running, spinning on the ground, and traveling by train, boat and plane, all simulated by his six girl companions. This literal interpretation of the verse is followed by an equally literal one for Friday's child ("loving and giving"). Ashton has concentrated more on loving than giving, and loving of the most sensual kind. This is an erotic pas de deux, with a boy and a girl dressed and made up alike to look like a narcissistic couple—originally performed by Antoinette Sibley and Rudolf Nureyev. Saturday's child ("works hard for his living") is the best invention of all, a boys' ballet class which is made to work harder and harder by the insatiable ballet master. This gives the younger boys of the company a chance to show their paces, to make fun of some of the standard classical steps, and to pretend to drop from exhaustion. It always brings the house down. Sunday's child ("bonny and blithe, and good and gay") is an excuse for a jaunty little dance by a girl, who then leads all the company into the final ensemble, ending with them pretending to go around on a revolving stage waving at the audience, in the manner of a television or Radio City spectacular. There are a lot of apparent quotations from other works in *Jazz Calendar* but Ashton denies that these are deliberate and disclaims any intention of parodying his own or anyone else's work.

A great part in the success of *Jazz Calendar* is played by Derek Jarman's trendy settings. They are very simple—a few cubes here, hoops there, a drop curtain showing a calendar for January 1968, when the ballet was created—but all in bright colors, all linking neatly together for the finale, and all in the right cool, abstract style for the jazzy music and witty choreography. The ballet was criticized by some people as too much of a revue sketch; comic ballets always tend to be dismissed as slight and unimportant. But they make a highly desirable contrast in the average mixed program, and are among the most difficult ballets to create. They are also very difficult to judge, because sense of humor is such a personal and subjective thing. Sophisticated audiences and professional critics usually prefer the more abstract comedies, and get a bit restless with old-fashioned comic story ballets. These generally have first to win favor with the public, which they do very easily; children and less experienced audiences have not yet grown to regard farcical plots as corny and cannot always follow the allusions of the more abstract comedies. Massine's *Mam'zelle Angot* was rather condescendingly received at first, but is now popular with nearly everyone. After all, most of us welcome an excuse to laugh at a bit of nonsense from time to time.

CHAPTER VI

What Is Ballet?

THIS SURVEY of the various kinds of ballet which have been produced over the years, and which have survived and retained their popularity to the present day, makes it apparent that ballet can be almost anything. There is ballet as entertainment and ballet as art, to say nothing of ballet with pretensions to be Art. There is ballet as silent theater, ballet as a concert, ballet as athletics, and ballet as an animated museum or exhibition. And the borderlines between ballet and its sister arts—drama, opera, painting, sculpture and music—are sometimes very indistinct.

Just as some ballets seem to have more to do with one of the other arts, so some spectacles labeled theater or art may strike us as having more to do with ballet. Experimental theater today, in the attics and cellars off Broadway, off Shaftesbury Avenue, and off the main streets of most European capitals, makes much use of mime and expressive physical movement. Young actors are now highly trained in controlled movement and near-acrobatic skill. The Living Theater, one of the leading American avant-garde theater companies, appeals at least as much by its use of movement and groupings as by anything spoken by its actors. Jean-Claude van Itallie's *The Serpent,* performed by the Open Theater of New York, was virtually choreographed by its director, Joseph Chaikin. The actors mimed exactly the sort of realistic sexual orgies and fights which feature in many modern ballets. Nobody called *The Serpent* a ballet, but it could have been performed by one of the experimental ballet or dance companies without seeming in any way out of place. Jerzy Grotowski's Laboratory Theatre also relies heavily on movement, especially when performing in the West, to audiences who do not understand Polish. Ryszard Cieslak's performances as the Simpleton-Christ in *Apocalypsis cum Figuris* and in the title role of Calderon's *The Constant Prince* would have won applause from any ballet audience for their exciting athleticism, and would have been beyond the ability of most conventional actors. In London, "Stage Two" of James Roose-Evans's Hampstead Theatre Club has started by training actors in mime and movement rather than speech; approaching the same point from the opposite direction, the Sadler's Wells Opera has replaced its ballet by a Movement Group. Similarly, art galleries now frequently feature mobile and automated sculptures and elaborate lighting displays "which seem just like ballets." When the same thing is done by a dance company in a theater, it apparently *is* a ballet.

There is not much point in a long semantic argument about what is, and what is not, a ballet. There is something to be said for the point of view that it does not matter what we call a work of art, or a performance, so long as it is interesting, or entertaining in some way. But there is also something wasteful about using highly trained classical dancers, who have devoted most of their lives to acquiring their ballet techniques, in works which could equally well be performed by actors, or gymnasts, or any group of reasonably fit young people. And it is important to remember—though it is often forgotten—that as soon as ballets are performed in art galleries, or college halls, or in the open air for that matter, they lose something of their essential theatrical appeal. Ballet is defined in most dictionaries as a theatrical art consisting mainly of dancing, and it is at least mildly curious that the word is now often applied to performances which are not theatrical, and which are not intended to be, and which in some cases contain no dancing.

It is no good restricting the use of the term ballet more than is absolutely necessary; certainly not as much as most of the theorists of ballet have done. It must be crystal clear by now that ballet is not confined to works with a dramatic theme, as Noverre thought it should be, nor need it be a perfect blend of dance, drama, music and decor, as Fokine proclaimed. The surprising thing is that so many people should have tried to lay down restrictive rules and dogmas for such a young and untheo-retical art.

Fokine's five principles, of course, were intended to liberate ballet from the conventions and shackles of the Petipa classics. He outlined them in his celebrated letter to *The Times*, published in June, 1914. Choreography must not consist of combinations of ready-made steps but should be newly created to suit the subject, the period, and the place of the ballet. Dancing must not be used as a mere divertissement or entertainment. The whole body must be used expressively, to convey emotion and drama, instead of using conventional mime gestures. Composers and artists must be given complete freedom; there need be no specific ballet music or ballet costumes. Of course it was highly desirable to liberate ballet in this way and to get away from the ideas that the ladies of the ballet must always dance on the points of their toes, or wear conventional ballet dresses— either the short tutu or the romantic ankle-length one—and that ballet music must necessarily consist simply of pretty, easily danced tunes. Unfortunately, Fokine in his turn became too dogmatic and started to insist that his kind of ballet was the only kind. But ready-made classical steps can still be selected and arranged by a choreographer of talent into a new and successful ballet, divertissements can still be entertaining and effective, and there is still plenty of scope—indeed a real need—for pretty, danceable music. More and more ballets nowadays are performed in varieties of practice dress—plain tights and bodices of different patterns and colors—which has become as much a conventional ballet costume as the classical and romantic tutus of the past. And the uniform which is rapidly developing for avant-garde ballets—various kinds of underwear or even total nudity—is just another convention and likely to become an even more boring one.

The truth is of course that all ballet is necessarily a convention, which the balletgoer must accept, just as the operagoer accepts the convention of songs or the theatergoer often accepts the conventions of a proscenium arch and the telescoping of time. If art were exactly the same as real life, it would scarcely be art. Of course peasant girls and modern teenagers do not really move on their points, any more than princes or soldiers leap or spin in the air, or balance girls on one outstretched arm. And there is no purpose in dressing Swanilda or Giselle or their friends as real-life peasant girls, complete with dirt, darns, and clashing colors, if they are still going to indulge in the highly artificial thing called classical dancing. There may be some purpose in replacing the longer and more obscure passages of classical mime by simpler dumb show in the modern "method" manner, simply because this may be a way of making the action more easily intelligible to a modern audience. But this is only replacing one artificial convention by another, not abolishing them altogether. And in many cases the traditional mime is still as short and clear as anything that could replace it.

Since Fokine, many other people have tried to lay down the law about the nature of ballet. Fortunately, most of their laws cancel each other out. In the Soviet Union, for example, socialist realist theory demanded that ballets, like all other works of art, should tell a story with a political or moral content and an uplifting, not a depressing ending, and should be immediately intelligible to the general public, including the factory worker and the collective farm delegation. *Swan Lake* was given a new, happy ending, with the Prince killing Rotbart in combat and holding hands with Odette in the dawning light, presumably to live happily ever after. Many full-length story ballets were created which were evidently more notable for their naive, propagandist themes than for their choreography. After Stalin's death a reaction set in, and many of these ballets were criticized for not being true works of art, and for not giving the dancers enough opportunities to dance. But a general presumption seems to linger that any story is better than no story, and that a happy ending is better than a sad one.

The opposite extreme has been expressed, as might seem natural, in the United States. This is not the result of a subtle ideological conflict but merely a reflection of the fact that Balanchine has developed a preference and special talent for abstract works. This has led some of his admirers to make exaggerated claims for this style, as if it were the only worthwhile style today: story ballets are old-fashioned, acting and mime only get in the way of the dancing and true ballets should simply add a visual dimension to the music.

But the story ballet has had its propagandists in the West too. When Robert Helpmann's powerful dramatic works were prominent in the repertory of the then Sadler's Wells Ballet, Audrey Williamson wrote that the future of ballet rested to a considerable extent in a broadening and strengthening of the subject material, along the lines being pioneered by Helpmann and Michael Benthall, his scenarist. She thought, on the other hand, that "because of its lack of emotional interest" Ashton's *Symphonic Variations* was not the greatest of his works nor the one which would prove to have most staying power. Time has shown that the emotional interest of Helpmann's works wanes with repetition and with the changing mood of the times but that the abstract beauties of *Symphonic Variations* survive frequent viewing and continue to delight audiences on all occasions.

All balletgoers have their own preferences among types of ballets, but the luckier or more skillful are able to enjoy almost all ballets, provided they are good of their type. There are more sophisticated dogmas than those which assert that ballet must always be abstract, or dramatic, or uplifting, but even these tend to be rationalizations of a personal preference. One of the most experienced British ballet critics, James Monahan, has repeatedly expressed the opinion that it is not really the function of ballet to tell stories, which can be done better in books or plays, nor to present a straightforward display of technical skill, which borders on the gym display. What ballet can do best and what makes it unique, he argues, is the conveying of emotion through movement to music, especially by a lyrical ballerina. The epitome of this sort of communication is Odette's role in *Swan Lake;* supreme twentieth-century examples are *Les Sylphides* and *Symphonic Variations.* The ideal ballerina for it is, or was, Margot Fonteyn, of whom Mr. Monahan has written the definitive critical study. It is significant that he is also a poet, for his argument is really for ballet as visual poetry.

There is much to be said for this. It is true that this sort of dancing and this sort of ballet are among the greatest experiences which ballet can provide. And there is obvious sense in ballet concentrating on those things in which it is unique, and not on effects which can be achieved as well, or better, by novels, plays, films, operas, music hall or the circus. But following this approach to its logical conclusion would deprive us of the ballet versions of *Romeo and Juliet,* of *The Invitation* and *Enigma Variations, Hamlet* and *Miracle in the Gorbals,* most of Balanchine's creations, and a great deal of entertaining classical virtuosity, such as the *Don Quixote* pas de deux. Mr. Monahan would certainly not wish to push his argument so far—he admits to an inconsistent penchant for *The Invitation*—but some people might. It is amazing what hostility all these works can provoke from some alleged ballet lovers, including critics.

Our most senior critics still tend to cling, consciously or unconsciously, to Fokine's principles. The late A. V. Coton, whose early death in 1969 robbed British ballet criticism of one of its most outspoken and distinctive voices, explicitly pleaded for a return to those principles in the making and judging of new ballets. Arnold Haskell, whose books introduced a whole generation to ballet, has argued that ballet is weaker today for not paying as much attention to decor as in Diaghilev's day, an assertion combining two extremely dubious propositions. Those of us who learned about ballet well after Diaghilev's day learned in very large part from the writings of critics like Haskell and Coton, to whom we all owe a very great debt. We therefore imbibed their approach to ballet in our formative years, and it was only with our own growing experience of ballet in performance that we may have come to revise our original approach. The resulting shift of critical standards helps to explain why New York City Ballet got such a poor critical reception on its first visit to London in 1950, and such a good one on its second visit in 1965. It may also explain the disappointment of many critics with Ashton's *The Two Pigeons* when it was first produced in 1961, though it is enthusiastically greeted by most of us now. The application of inappropriate Fokine principles possibly accounted for much of the bewilderment when we first became acquainted with the Bolshoi and Kirov companies.

It now seems to me self-evident that ballet can succeed in many different styles and forms, and that any attempt to dogmatize about it should be avoided. It can be dramatic like a play, or aesthetically satisfying like painting or sculpture, or physically exciting like athletics, or vaguely emotional like a poem. It can add an extra dimension to music, or use music as a mere background, or exist without music at all. It can be intellectual, or escapist, or erotic. It cannot be restricted to any one of these things; it embraces them all and may embrace many more besides. My only dogma is that ballet must involve dancing, and make good use of the highly trained, skilled being who is a ballet dancer. Maybe even that is too dogmatic. Perhaps the only safe rule about ballet is that there are no rules. In that freedom is its glory and its appeal.

Part Two

HOW IS IT DONE?

CHAPTER I

The Choreographer

THE ACTUAL STEPS danced in a ballet are selected or invented by the choreographer, a title which has only come into use in this sense during the twentieth century. Originally choreography meant writing down dance steps in some system of notation, but nowadays we speak of "dance notation" or use the new word choreology. Choreographer, which was sometimes spelled and pronounced "choregrapher" from the French *chorégraphe,* means dance writer, if one sticks to its original Greek derivation. It now means writing in the sense of composition: the choreographer is the composer of the dance.

But the choreographer usually does far more than merely arrange steps for a ballet, though that is difficult enough in itself and perhaps should not be dismissed with a "merely." In practice the whole of a ballet is normally the brainchild of the choreographer. He chooses or invents the story, if any; he selects the music or commissions a composer; he chooses a designer and indicates what sort of decor and costumes he requires. He also directs the work, guiding the dancers in their acting, in their placing on the stage, and in their understanding of the style and mood required. All these functions are not inevitably linked. Sometimes the scenario or story is specially written for a ballet by a dramatist or poet, and then a choreographer is found. Diaghilev sometimes decided to use a certain piece of music, and then engaged a choreographer. There have been experiments in commissioning writers for ballet; Western Theatre Ballet twice employed dramatists for this purpose—John Mortimer for *Home* and David Rudkin for *Sun into Darkness*. For the latter work they also employed an experienced operatic producer, Colin Graham, to supervise the production in co-operation with the choreographer, Peter Darrell. The results were not particularly auspicious, but this does not invalidate the idea of using outside writers or directors. The great classic ballets were often suggested by existing books or poems and so are many modern ones. There is no reason why a specially commissioned story should not serve equally well, provided the author understands the requirements of a ballet and is in close sympathy with the choreographer.

All the ballets of the past must obviously be produced by someone other than the original choreographer. There are now many rival productions of the standard classics like *Swan Lake* and *Giselle,* quite apart from variations in the choreography and "improved" choreographic versions. And indeed these works, with their elaborate scenic effects and the need to integrate dancing into the action, cry out for skillful production. Audiences nowadays expect the story to make some sort of sense; for example, they like to be given a reason for characters to go on or off the stage, and even for them to start dancing. Although it is not possible to make the classics completely logical and coherent, a great deal can be done in that direction. Peter Wright, for example, did wonders with the touring section of the Royal Ballet's *Giselle,* without altering much of the traditional choreography. He opens the ballet with a scene showing Hilarion being very friendly with Giselle's mother, presenting her with a bird he has just shot for Giselle. This helps to explain why the mother is hostile to Albrecht later. Hilarion is depicted as an intelligent burly villager, suspicious from the start of the mysterious visitor who is disguised as a peasant. He spies on Albrecht, spots him with an aristocratic cloak, and breaks into his hut, finding a sword and matching it up with the royal party's hunting horn. Albrecht starts the flirtation with Giselle as a lighthearted escapade but is genuinely involved with her by the time of her death, and has to be dragged from the scene at the end of the first act by his esquire, in the face of mounting village hostility. The second act is less logical: a few Wilis are first seen flitting about the glade, then they all rise up from under the stage on a lift—an effective stage picture but causing confusion about whether they live in the air or under the ground. At the end Giselle, instead of sinking into her grave, disappears gradually behind some gauzes; perhaps we are to think she melts into thin air. At least all this represents an intelligent attempt to rethink the ballet, even if it only confirms that these classics can never be completely logical and consistent. David Blair's production for Ballet Theatre is also extremely intelligent, with some effective new touches, but occasionally it veers so far towards realism that the sense of poetry is lost—for example, when the Wilis kick the dead body of Hilarion off the stage.

Peter Wright's new production of *The Sleeping Beauty* for the Royal Ballet was much more controversial. Many people felt that this is such an essentially classical work, depending on its bravura display of pure dancing, that the effect was muted by too much emphasis on the story, while others thought Wright had reduced the story element too much. Most of his changes struck me as improvements: the tedious game of blind man's buff in the hunting scene was omitted, Aurora was given the near-fatal spindle accidentally by an old woman, instead of by a disguised Carabosse, and the Prince had to climb up an ivy-clad wall to reach Aurora's bedroom. I liked too the crumbling away of the palace after Aurora's awakening, leaving the stage clear for a romantic pas de deux for the newly met lovers.

It would be fascinating to see what one of the great operatic or drama producers, like Franco Zeffirelli or Peter Hall, might make of one of these romantic or classic ballets. It is difficult nowadays to recapture their period atmosphere; one reason for this, as Fonteyn once pointed out to me, is that the Wilis of *Giselle* and the Sylphs of *La Sylphide* were originally lit by gaslight and dressed in old-fashioned tarlatans and cottons. With electric lighting and synthetic fabrics, the effect is often much too modern, and is not necessarily remedied by gauzes and artificial steam, two modern conventions for this sort of ballet. (It really is not very satisfactory to watch dancers through a gauze, and the clouds of steam which are now beloved of every *Swan Lake* and *Giselle* producer often get out of hand, obliterating the dancers from view and swirling into the audience as well.) Perhaps a producer of genius may even be able to give the classics a convincing new look, as Wieland Wagner did for his grandfather's operas.

Equally there is no reason why a producer should not work in collaboration with the choreographer on a new ballet. Some modern ballets in any case seem to be more produced than choreographed. By the time the dancers have wrapped or un-wrapped themselves in transparent plastic, lain down on the stage while bits of scenery move around them, or climbed on and off symbolic abstract sculptures, there is not always any time left for actual dancing. But a choreographer who is creating new and exciting dances, admirably fitted to the music, may have comparatively little sense of stagecraft. Especially if his work is a dramatic one, he might benefit from an experienced producer. In practice, however, the general rule is for the choreographer to do everything himself. Ashton, for example, combines his supreme gift for choreography with a superb sense of theater. In *The Two Pigeons,* the choreography is inextricably mixed with the production: the use of the doves to symbolize the human lovers and of the chair on which humans and birds are all finally reunited are two examples.

What sort of person is a choreographer? Most of them started their professional lives as dancers. It seems to be virtually impossible to create dances without first going through rigorous training and learning exactly what a dancer can do and how. It is sometimes said that choreographers are failed dancers and there is an element of truth in this gibe. It stands to reason that dancers who are not doing as well as they had hoped, or who have to stop dancing for some reason, may decide to use their knowledge by trying choreography. On the other hand, dancers who are successful and devoting themselves to their careers may never attempt choreography simply because they have not got the time or the energy left over from their dancing. Margot Fonteyn told me, when I asked her if she had ever been tempted to try choreography, that being a ballerina was a full-time job. Neither of the two greatest living choreographers, Ashton and Balanchine, made great reputations as dancers, though Ashton was an extremely accomplished mime. Cranko and MacMillan both started their careers as dancers but neither looked likely to achieve greatness in that direction.

On the other hand, by no means every comparatively unsuccessful dancer can become a choreographer, as has been proved in countless experimental workshops and Sunday-night tryouts at which various dancers have attempted to make ballets. Most of these efforts look imitative and are quickly forgotten. In any case many of the great choreographers of the recent past were also outstanding dancers. By all accounts Fokine was an extremely distinguished soloist at the Maryinsky Theatre at the beginning of this century; Massine was at least as famous for his performances, especially in his own ballets, as for his choreography; Nijinsky, the most famous male dancer of all time, seemed likely to become a great choreographer as well.

A talent for choreography generally becomes apparent early in a dancer's career. There are few if any examples of dancers successfully switching to choreography in middle age. A dancer with a certain sort of personality, with wider or more intellectual interest than average and with an innate creative flair, is unlikely to rest content with constant repetition of someone else's steps, and will possibly insist on trying to create something of his own.

Choreographers are scarcely ever trained; they just happen. Massine was one of the few exceptions. He was consciously trained by Diaghilev, introduced to leading composers and artists, taught about literature and the arts, taken to art galleries and concerts. It is often said that all choreographers must have such a catholic education in the arts, but few of them do. Their knowledge, such as it is, is acquired over the years as they work. It is scarcely to be wondered at, therefore, that when they attempt ambitious psychological or metaphysical dance dramas, the results are often trivial compared with what one might expect in literature or the legitimate theater. What is surprising is the number of times a choreographer, with no pretensions to intellectual or academic stature, can create a work which seems to illuminate our knowledge of our fellowmen, or our understanding of the world in which we live.

In creating new dances, the choreographer may be doing one of two things: he may be arranging existing steps in a new way, or he may actually be inventing new movements. Many people assume that it is all one or the other, that all possible steps must already have been invented and performed by now or that choreography is not worthy of the name unless it consists of totally new movements. In fact, neither of these assumptions is correct. Some choreographers are very inventive, in the sense of constantly devising new and unusual movements, so that the spectator is constantly impressed by the invention. John Cranko was once congratulated by a distinguished ballet critic on his skill in inventing new movements; he confessed to me that he was a bit surprised to be congratulated as he had always assumed that the invention of new movements was the essence of choreography. Certainly all choreographers must invent new steps from time to time, though equally certainly most of their work must involve the use of existing steps. "New steps" does not mean steps in the literal sense; most possible foot movements have probably been invented by now, though one is still sometimes surprised by a new foot movement during a jump. A familiar step becomes unfamiliar if performed out of its usual context. And choreographers seem to be very good at finding new positions in which girls can be carried by their partners, new ways of dragging dancers along the floor (very popular in the most self-consciously modern works), new acrobatic stunts and new combinations of foot, arm, and body movements.

When one sees a particularly inventive new abstract ballet by Balanchine, Cranko or MacMillan, one is inclined to think that the invention of new movements and combinations of movements is indeed the crux of choreography. This is less true of a new work by Ashton, which tends to impress more by the apparent inevitability of the movements set to the music, and by the lyrical flowing quality of the whole. Ashton *is* inventive, especially in pas de deux; but his skill lies equally in his selection and arrangement of existing steps to suit the music and to suit the dancers concerned. One reason why so many dancers enjoy working with Ashton is that he has a knack of showing them at their best, not only by letting them do the steps they already know they do well but also by helping them to discover talents they had not previously suspected.

How does the choreographer go about his work? There are almost as many methods as there are choreographers. Ashton generally starts by falling in love with a piece of music, listening to it over and over again until it becomes a part of him, and then developing a theme to suit it, and some ideas about dances and dancers. In rehearsal, he creates with the dancers, who may suggest steps or experiment with different ways of doing what Ashton suggests. The choreography is developed through trial and error on the dancers. Balanchine's technique is evidently very similar. Sometimes, on the other hand, Ashton starts with a theme and searches for the music, as happened with *Marguerite and Armand*. Dumas' story of the Lady of the Camellias seemed a good subject for Fonteyn and Nureyev, but there was considerable debate about suitable music before Humphrey Searle was finally commissioned to orchestrate Liszt's Piano Sonata in

B minor. Or again, in the case of *Enigma Variations,* it was the designer, Julia Trevelyan Oman, who suggested the original scenario about Elgar and his friends, though this was simplified and adapted by Ashton.

Sometimes choreographers carry subjects for possible ballets around in their heads, waiting to find suitable music and an opportunity to stage the works; sometimes they may carry around both subjects and pieces of music, without being able to fit them together. Antony Tudor told me he had wanted to use the Richard Strauss incidental music for *Le Bourgeois Gentilhomme* for a long time before he actually used it for *Knight Errant.* Then various things fortuitously combined: an invitation to do a new ballet for the touring section of the Royal Ballet, the desire to exploit the particular talents of David Wall, and the thought that an episode from *Les Liaisons Dangereuses* would suit the purpose and could be well matched with the Strauss music.

Choreographers cannot always wait for inspiration; if they are resident choreographers with a ballet company they are probably expected to produce a certain number of new works each season. In Germany, where the subscription ticket system operates, subscribers demand two or three totally new programs a season. This places a great strain on the choreographer, who may also, like Cranko in Stuttgart, be the director of the company; he must be adept at producing acceptable works at regular intervals, even if not all of them are highly original or remarkable. Or of course he can try to find suitable guest choreographers.

Some choreographers arrive at rehearsal with a much more fixed plan than Ashton or Balanchine. They may have elaborate notes on paper, or an exact idea in their head of where the dancers are to be and what they are to do. Massine's ballets were apparently worked out in this way, and MacMillan's tend to be now. Even so, of course, the original ideas will probably get altered and adapted in rehearsal. Theoretically a ballet could nowadays be completely written out in notation and then rehearsed without the choreographer being present at all. The day for this may come, but at present no leading choreographer works in this way. Most of them would prefer to see their ideas executed by dancers, and then tailor them to suit the cast, rather than to impose a written script. At the moment, it is inaccurate to speak of a ballet being "written" by a choreographer; it is made or evolved on the dancers. His work is more like that of a sculptor, but with living material, than that of a writer or composer.

Where the various systems of writing or notating choreography are most useful is in preserving a ballet once it has been made. There have been systems of notation for centuries: the Stepanov system was used in Imperial Russia and the full-length classics were notated in it. Some of these scripts were brought to England by Nicolai Sergueyev, who was a producer at the Maryinsky Theatre until he left Russia in 1918. He mounted the five principal classics for the Sadler's Wells Ballet in the thirties from this notation, and it is thanks to him that the Royal Ballet has had such authentic versions of *Swan Lake, The Sleeping Beauty, Coppélia* and *Giselle*. Many of his other scripts are still available, and could be used if any company wanted to revive some of the forgotten nineteenth-century works.

The Stepanov system has also been adapted by Massine into a system of his own, which he has been teaching at the Royal Ballet School recently as part of his course in choreography. Unlike most choreographers, he believes that a practical system of notation is an invaluable aid to choreography.

The best-known systems of notation today are Labanotation, based on a method suggested by Rudolf von Laban, a pioneer of central European modern dance in the early years of this century, and Benesh Notation, developed in London in the last twenty years by Joan Benesh, a former dancer with the Sadler's Wells Ballet, and her husband Rudolf Benesh. Large claims are made on behalf of both systems, between which there is great and sometimes bitter rivalry. Labanotation is more widely used

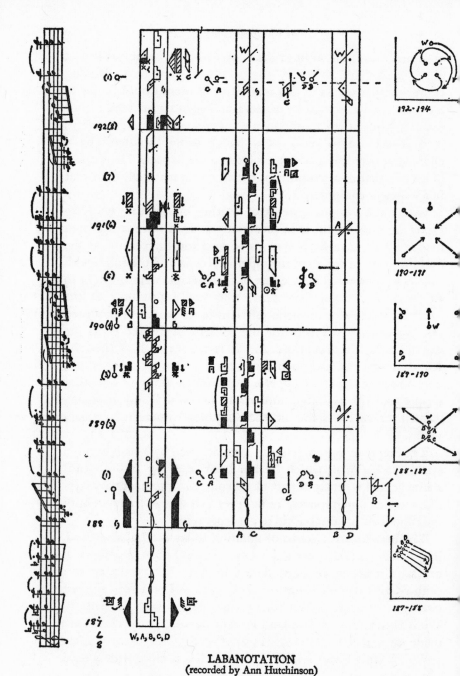

LABANOTATION
(recorded by Ann Hutchinson)

Excerpt from 1st movement of *Serenade* (Choreography Copyright © 1964, by George Balanchine) to Tchaikowsky's *Serenade for Strings.*

BENESH MOVEMENT NOTATION

(Copyright © 1955, Rudolf Benesh   Notator: Monica Parker)

Excerpt from 2nd movement of *Anastasia* (Choreography Copyright © 1967, by Kenneth MacMillan) to Bohuslav Martinu's *Fantaisies Symphoniques* (Copyright © 1957, by Boosey & Hawkes Inc.).

in the United States, where it has been developed and where there is an office administering it. The Benesh system uses the term choreology, and choreologists trained at the Benesh's Institute of Choreology in London are now attached to the Royal Ballet and to many of the European companies with directors or choreographers trained in London. Several ballets have been successfully reproduced from it; for example Kenneth MacMillan's *Concerto* and *Olympiad,* created in Berlin, were staged at Covent Garden from Benesh notation.

The advocates of Labanotation claim that their system is more thorough and can record more detail than Benesh. In return, the supporters of Benesh claim that it is simpler and quicker to learn. Perhaps both are right, though neither side will admit this, and it is virtually impossible for an outsider to judge, without spending a great deal of time studying both systems. One thing they certainly have in common is that they take a lot of time and work to master, and also to use. It takes so long to record a ballet in one of these systems that nothing like the complete existing repertoire is yet notated. New works created for the Royal Ballet are now notated during rehearsal, however. Maybe notation will become quicker and simpler as the systems develop, or as more dancers and choreographers become familiar with them.

The advantages of notation are obvious. By its means, ballets can be preserved and reproduced in their original form. They can either be staged simultaneously in various countries in the lifetime of the choreographer but without his participation, or they can be preserved and revived long after the original choreographer and cast are dead. Until recently, ballets were mostly handed down by direct inheritance from dancer to dancer, from ballet master to ballet master. Little alterations crept in as memories faltered, or as dancers decided to insert "improvements" for themselves. Choreographers wishing to mount ballets for companies other than their own either had to find time to travel or had to send trusted emissaries to stage their ballets for them. Balanchine, for example, has regularly used various colleagues to remount his ballets for other companies. Notation can save the time of creative artists, leaving the work of staging and reproduction to experienced stage directors and readers of notation, and can ensure authentic re-creation of the choreographer's intentions.

Ballets can also be preserved to some extent on film. Most of the Royal Ballet's repertory has now been filmed for reference and filing purposes; Massine has an extensive collection of private films of his old ballets which he uses as aids in his revivals. In addition there are of course the commercial ballet films made for the cinema and television, which usually alter the original stage versions of the ballets in some respects. In any case it is not possible to stage a ballet entirely from a film record.

The potential disadvantages of all these methods of recording ballets may not be as obvious as the advantages. Nevertheless they exist. For one thing, natural selection has always operated to a large extent in the life of ballets; good ones survive because they are remembered, and because dancers and ballet masters want to go to the trouble of maintaining them. Bad ones die because they are forgotten. If all new ballets are to be preserved on paper, there is a danger of some of them living unnaturally prolonged lives. On the other hand it could well be argued that a ballet which is not appreciated today may be ahead of its time, and that future generations would be glad to have the opportunity of reviving it. How valuable it would be now, for example, if we had exact notations of Nijinsky's ballets.

A more subtle and probably more real danger is that ballets may become ossified by being notated. The very changes which have crept into ballets over the years in the past may have helped to keep them alive. In the classics, each generation of dancers has introduced new steps in accordance with developments in technique and taste. Choreographers themselves alter their own ballets to suit new casts and changing times. Fokine did innumerable versions of many of his ballets, especially *Les Sylphides*. New dancers taking over a ballet may be able to make the same effect as their predecessors only by changing a step or a gesture here and there to suit their own techniques and personalities. An attempt merely to reproduce the exact movements of the original cast may lead to a feeling of deadness, so that the ballet becomes a museum piece.

It is true that the original cast of a ballet usually comes nearest to the choreographer's intention, having worked with him and the steps having been created on and for them. Sometimes, however, even the original cast improves on the ballet at subsequent performances. Fonteyn regularly deepens and develops her interpretations well after the first night, possibly introducing new gestures and new subtleties of timing and accent in her dancing. Robert Helpmann, when he took over the title role in de Valois' *The Rake's Progress* from Walter Gore, was widely considered to have improved on the original.

Admittedly changes could still be made in a ballet that has been notated. Ballet masters and dancers would then have to make the changes consciously, instead of unconsciously. They could no longer kid themselves that they were still doing the original ballet. It will therefore require more courage and self-confidence to alter ballets in future. Perhaps this is as well, but it would be a pity if the scripts came to be regarded as sacrosanct.

This may seem paradoxical. Surely the choreography of a ballet should no more be tampered with than the score of a symphony or opera, or the text of a play? But such a parallel is not exact. The fact that living interpreters are involved, and that they will change, means that exact repetition of the same movements cannot be preserved. The original cast will get more mature, which will affect their emotional interpretations and gestures, and their physical technique. Unless the ballet is to die, they must be replaced by younger dancers, who should not be expected to attempt to be carbon copies. Equally, of course, they should not be allowed to substitute all their own favorite movements and mannerisms for those originally prescribed.

Sometimes, in practice, dancers introduce their own personal touches even while the ballet is still new and the choreographer is still present. The most striking recent example of this was MacMillan's *Romeo and Juliet,* which was created on and for Lynn Seymour and Christopher Gable. The first performance was actually danced by Fonteyn and Nureyev, who in several places departed from the choreography set by MacMillan and have departed further from it in later performances. Indeed, in 1969 MacMillan once went so far as to ask to have his name removed from the program when these stars were dancing! In one particular scene, when Juliet is left alone in her bedroom after the ultimatum from her parents that she must marry Paris, almost every interpreter has her own version. Seymour sat still on the bed, gazing straight out at the audience, and succeeded in conveying the turmoil of thoughts going through her head. This was what MacMillan intended, and this was also done later by Annette Page and Georgina Parkinson. Fonteyn obviously felt uneasy about this idea, and experimented at different performances with various bits of expressive mime, until she succeeded in achieving a similar effect by different means, turning sideways to the audience and gripping the bed post in anguish. Antoinette Sibley and Merle Park have performed other mime sequences at this point. It may be that MacMillan deliberately left this passage, like a cadenza for a soloist in a concerto, to be improvised by the ballerina, but I believe that in fact he simply was unable to impose his will on all the various ballerinas.

If so, this would be in line with what happened to the Russian classics in the lifetimes of Petipa and Ivanov. Different ballerinas inserted their own favorite steps and variations, and this was accepted as normal. It was the Italian ballerina Pierina Legnani, for example, who introduced the thirty-two fouettés in the third act of *Swan Lake* because they were her particular virtuoso speciality. So there is not necessarily any one absolutely authentic version of the classics, which must all have been further altered in the years since their creation. Nevertheless there are certain versions, such as those brought to London by

Sergueyev, which are the product of the continuous tradition handed down in St. Petersburg-Leningrad at the Maryinsky-Kirov Theatre. A second generation export of Russian classics to the West has now taken place through the agency of Rudolf Nureyev. His versions of *Raymonda* and an act of *La Bayadère,* based mainly on his remarkable choreographic memory but with a few of his own inventions and innovations, are essentially the same as those performed at the Kirov, as can be seen when Soviet companies or producers stage them in the West. On the other hand Nureyev's versions of *Swan Lake, Don Quixote* and *The Nutcracker* are more original, though even these probably incorporate remembered passages from various Russian versions. Many of us have now come to accept new versions of *The Nutcracker,* such as Balanchine's, Cranko's, Grigorovitch's and Nureyev's, as superior to the original Ivanov.

There are choreographic passages in the classics, however, and in outstanding modern ballets, which are so celebrated and so closely identified with the ballets that producers or choreographers alter them at their peril. Most of Odette's dancing in the second act of *Swan Lake* is in this category—the gentle nestling of her head on Siegfried's shoulder, the small birdlike beats of the feet, the way she climbs up on to her points from the kneeling position and the swooning fall at the end of the pas de deux. Ivanov's choreography and groupings for the swans is, or ought to be, equally sacrosanct. Gorsky's version of this act, performed by the Bolshoi, is markedly inferior. The dance of the four cygnets in the same act, on the other hand, which was originally intended for young girls from the ballet school, is now frequently performed by larger and more mature ladies of the corps de ballet and looks more like a cancan than a dance of little swans. The ladies link their arms and bounce their knees jauntily up and down and the effect is always a hit with the audience, often getting more applause than all the lyricism of Odette and the other swans. Many true lovers of *Swan Lake* would like to see this dance omitted, as out of keeping with the mood of the rest of the act, but audiences insist on it. If performed as originally intended, however, by small girls, it can still seem charming and appropriate, as it did when cast in this way by the Royal Danish Ballet.

All the classics are full of these choreographic trademarks and signatures. In *The Sleeping Beauty,* the most famous are Aurora's Rose Adagio, with its balances on one foot and the hand raised delicately in the air between the support of the four suitors, and the male Blue Bird's flying jumps across the stage. In *Giselle,* there are Giselle's dance across the stage on the point of one foot, her dance with Albrecht at opposite ends of a long line of peasant girls, so that they are constantly running around to try to catch each other, and their later pas de deux in which she throws him flowers. (The Bolshoi's Giselles and Albrechts did not run after each other at Covent Garden in 1969, which made this dance duller. Giselle always used to throw her flowers while jumping, and Albrecht was supposed to catch them, which made a nice romantic effect. Now she frequently throws them on the floor *after* she has jumped, and he simply picks them up, which is much less attractive.)

These trademarks or signatures are passages which could be quoted out of context, even to quite different music, and yet still be immediately recognized by balletgoers as quotations. The movements designed by Fokine for Pavlova in her most famous solo, *The Swan*—usually called *The Dying Swan*—especially the final section when the ballerina lies on the ground with her arms and then her hands making their final flutters, are in the same category. To turn to more recent works, much of Ashton's choreography is similarly identifiable. In *La Fille Mal Gardée,* for example, there is a lift for Lise which ends with her hands fluttering down, reflecting movements of the ribbons around her, which could not be seen elsewhere without immediately recalling that ballet. All balletgoers could add their own countless examples to this short selection.

It is tempting to say that these signature passages of choreography should never be altered, however much a ballet is revised or restaged. Indeed it is tempting to say that the works of the greatest masters—Petipa, Ivanov, Fokine, Massine, Ashton, Balanchine—should not be tampered with or altered at all. If those rules had been followed, we should still be seeing the nineteenth-century classics as they were created, or as near to that pristine state as memory and research could manage. We should have been spared some of the lamentably inferior choreographic travesties, particularly of *Swan Lake,* which have spread like a rash in recent years. But we should also have been deprived of versions of *Swan Lake,* like those by Bourmeister and Cranko, which have found favor in their own right. It would obviously be impossible to enforce a rule that only good choreographers should revise the classics. All one can do is apportion praise or blame to any particular attempt.

Many of the short dances which feature as divertissements in the classics, for example, can undoubtedly be improved. Some of the pseudo-Spanish and Neapolitan dances which may originally have been Petipa's work and which became traditional look ludicrous or boring today, with our greater knowledge of national dance styles. Ashton's version of the Neapolitan Dance in *Swan Lake* is generally regarded as superior to other versions; it is always one of the most popular and successful items in the Royal Ballet's production. On the other hand his more recent pas de quatre for the first act, which has replaced the traditional pas de trois, is widely felt to be too brilliant and exciting in style for the mood of that act and would probably fit in better as part of the third act divertissement, for which the music was originally intended. Many productions now follow the Bolshoi example in having a jester in the first act who mocks the Prince's tutor, dances with the peasant girls, and introduces a bit of virtuoso male dancing. But this too seems out of keeping with the mood of the ballet. The introduction of a melancholy solo for the Prince is a much more appropriate way of increasing the amount of male dancing which in itself is one of the commoner and most sensible reasons for revising the classics.

The last act of *Swan Lake* traditionally had some black

swan maidens interweaving among the white ones, providing a nice visual contrast. There was also a touching pas de deux for Odette and the Prince, to music not originally intended for *Swan Lake* but incorporated in Tchaikovsky's lifetime, presumably with his consent, and sounding suitably poignant. In the Helpmann-Ashton production for the Royal Ballet, the black swans are omitted in favor of an endless procession by the white ones, who form quite interesting patterns if seen from above but look boring from the stalls. Instead of the previous pas de deux, we have a new one to a slowed-down piece of music written for one of the would-be fiancées in the previous act. This scarcely seems more authentic than the traditional version and, after several years of familiarization, still sounds less effective.

The least satisfactory act of *The Sleeping Beauty* is generally agreed to be the hunting scene, in which the Prince first sees a vision of Aurora. The original version, with little or no dancing for the Prince and some rather staid courtly dances for his entourage, now seems boring. It is becoming customary to insert a solo for the Prince and to reduce the antics of the court party. In particular the game of blind man's buff played with the Prince's elderly tutor is now often omitted, an omission for which one can be grateful as elderly tutors and blind man's buff have both become familiar ballet clichés—like jesters. Nijinska rechoreographed this scene for Diaghilev and also for the late Marquis de Cuevas, introducing far more varied dancing. It seems a pity that her version has not been retained by any existing company. A very successful innovation in the 1968 production by the Royal Ballet was an entirely new pas de deux by Ashton, inserted after Aurora's awakening by the Prince. So there are times when both additions and alterations to the received choreography of the classics can be justified and successful.

The case of *Giselle* and *Coppélia* is even trickier than the Tchaikovsky-Petipa classics, because it is doubtful if much of the original French choreography survives anyway. The versions we see and regard as authentic today are mainly based on revisions done in Russia. The "peasant" pas de deux is not part of Adam's original score for *Giselle* but is by Burgmüller, an even more obscure composer. Ashton added a new solo in Bournonville style for the peasant girl in 1960, and in 1968 Peter Wright rearranged the pas de deux as a pas de six, with two of the boys dancing one of the "solos" together, three girls doing another, and all six dancers starting and finishing together, and joining the rest of the villagers in the carnival crowning of Giselle. These innovations have proved popular and there seems no reason why alterations of this kind should not be attempted from time to time. Peter Wright also arranged a different solo for Elizabeth Anderton, one of the ballerinas who danced Giselle, omitting the famous balancing variation on the point of one foot, which led me unfairly to criticize the dancer for simplifying the choreography. Nureyev has been adversely criticized for introducing extra vertical jumps (entrechats) in the second act and some people also condemned Vasiliev, with the Bolshoi, for introducing extra jumps and spins at the beginning of the first act. Enrique Martinez, in his staging of *Coppélia* for Ballet Theatre in 1969, introduced extra dancing for Franz and made some of Swanilda's dances more demanding and exciting. The whole ballet is more enjoyable as a result. Each case must be judged on its merits. Personally I have no objection to great dancers like Nureyev or Vasiliev making their roles more difficult for themselves, especially as in both cases their extra dancing strikes me as appropriate to the dramatic situation. But I do normally object to choreography being simplified for dancers who cannot quite manage the original, though even this is sometimes forgivable in the case of veteran ballerinas. In fairness to all concerned, any alterations in the original choreography should be clearly indicated in the printed programs; too often new choreography is still credited to dead choreographers, or described as "after Petipa," when the original has been drastically altered or totally replaced.

It is evident that there are times when choreographic revision of the classics can be beneficial, and also that a great choreographer can sometimes successfully rechoreograph a complete work. Each choreographer of real distinction has his own personal style, which will be recognized throughout the ballet by the experienced and perceptive spectator, just as a concertgoer can identify the composer of a piece of music or at least make a fair guess at his period and nationality, or a filmgoer can recognize a Fellini, a Godard, or a Hitchcock. Cranko's *Nutcracker*, or Ashton's *Fille Mal Gardée* are works of art in their own right, quite independent of earlier versions and possibly as good or better. Choreographers have preferences for particular steps, particular ways of linking steps together, particular ways of using music, and particular sorts of dancers. Balanchine likes working with cool, long-legged girls who can move in the extremely rapid and accurate musical way he demands and who do not intrude their personalities. Sometimes he is accused of using his dancers like machines, and certainly he seems less concerned than most choreographers with facial expressions. Soul is a word he abhors when applied to a dancer. And he is noticeably less interested in doing choreography for male dancers and for mature ballerinas than for young girls, though in recent years the exceptional technical gifts of Edward Villella have inspired him to create some interesting and difficult male solos.

Ashton has always been inspired by the particular technical and emotional gifts of certain dancers, notably Fonteyn, but also Svetlana Beriosova, Antoinette Sibley, Merle Park, Vyvyan Lorrayne, Rudolf Nureyev, Stanley Holden and, especially, Alexander Grant. He is usually as interested in their personalities and interpretative powers as in their technical strength or physical appearance. MacMillan too has been particularly inspired by dancers like Lynn Seymour and Christopher Gable whose personalities and dramatic powers were even more remarkable than their actual dancing. Cranko often created roles for Beriosova who has rather lacked a choreographer to develop her full potential since he left London for Stuttgart; in Stuttgart he has created a number of remarkable ballerina roles for Marcia Haydée and he has shown exceptional skill in exploiting the varied talents of his other dancers. Both Cranko and MacMillan have recently done very demanding and intricate choreography for male dancers, though MacMillan retains his reluctance to use the entrechat, which I have always found one of the most exciting and effective male classical steps. And both of them have found difficulty in getting the boys of the Royal Ballet to perform their choreography with the ease of the male dancers in Germany.

One choreographer specializes in speed and athleticism (Balanchine), another in lyricism (Ashton), others in intricate movements with lots of original twists, lifts and bends (Cranko and MacMillan). Cranko and MacMillan have many similarities, but Cranko's work is more sentimental, more romantic while MacMillan's tends to be drier and more classical. We recognize Petipa by the correct display of a comparatively small range of formal steps, ideally fitted to the music. We recognize Bournonville by the softer, bouncier style and by certain trademarks—sudden quick sideways movements and equally sudden freezing in the middle of a quick dance—which are very difficult for dancers unaccustomed to his style to master. We recognize much recent Russian choreography by the spectacular one-handed lifts and the near-acrobatic way in which the girls throw themselves through the air to be caught horizontally by their partners. We recognize certain other choreographers, too numerous to name, by the arbitrary way they mix all these styles together, usually to totally unsuitable music. And we recognize, or hope to, an important new choreographer by the sudden realization that we are seeing steps which are either new or are being used in a new way, with a strong new personal trademark.

Exactly the same steps can make very different effects, depending on how they are linked together, how they are set to the music, and how they are performed. A girl dancing on her points can be romantic and ethereal, as in *Les Sylphides* or *Giselle*, or cold and hard as in *Checkmate* or William Dollar's *Le Combat* (*The Duel*), or deliberately ludicrous as in Balanchine's *Bourrée Fantasque* and Tudor's *Gala Performance*. It is partly a question of the way the feet are used; they can be touched lightly and softly on the ground, giving an impression of weightlessness, or loudly stabbed down like a tap dancer's feet so as to seem aggressive. All the classical movements can be slightly exaggerated, or the positions held too long in relation to the music, so as to make the effect look ridiculous and comic. The dancer's arms, facial expression and whole style of movement all contribute to the final impression the steps make.

Choreographers vary greatly in the way they set dances to music. Some, like Lifar and Béjart, seem to use music mainly for its dramatic or emotional effect, or simply because they like the sound of it; their choreography often looks as if it could equally well be danced to any other music. Petipa, Balanchine and MacMillan all tend to set dancers moving in exact synchronization with the music; this is one thing they have in common and partly explains why Balanchine and MacMillan can so conveniently be labeled neoclassical. On the other hand, Fokine, Ashton and Cranko generally have their dancers moving *through* the music, not matching a movement to every beat of music but feeling the sense of the musical phrase. That is part of the explanation of the label romantic. Fanatical admirers of Ashton often find Balanchine's and MacMillan's works too fussy—"too many steps." The devotees of Balanchine and MacMillan often find Ashton and Cranko "less musical."

It is this endless variety of possible choreographic styles that causes dancers and critics to be always looking hopefully for new choreographers. It might be thought that there are quite enough good ballets in existence to provide a satisfying repertoire, even if no more new ones were created at all. And so there are. The demand for new ballets can certainly be exaggerated. It is unreasonable to expect the constant creation of works which can compete with the established masterpieces, any more than we expect the constant creation of new classic novels, paintings, symphonies, or operas. The example of opera is particularly apt. The operagoing public still mainly wants to hear works by Mozart and Wagner, Rossini, Bellini, Donizetti and Verdi, Gounod and Bizet, Tchaikovsky and Moussorgsky. The most recent operas to be generally accepted as part of the standard repertoire, those by Strauss and Puccini, are about the same age as Fokine's ballets. The number of operas composed in the last fifty years which are box-office attractions is extremely small and the staging of a new opera is a much rarer event than the staging of a new ballet. The greatest singers still prefer to display themselves in the older works, and very few of them appear in contemporary ones.

Ballet is far more up-to-date. A substantial part of the repertoire of every major company was created in the lifetime of the dancers, at any rate of the older dancers. New works are added every year. Obviously not all of them survive, but a surprisingly large proportion do. This is probably the most creative period in the history of ballet, because of the extraordinary way in which ballet has proliferated all over the world, and gained immensely in popular appeal. There are more and more companies and dancers looking for choreographic talent. As a result, dancers, critics and the paying public are inevitably subjected to a large number of new works which should never have got further than the rehearsal studio. But these do no great harm, except to the companies' budgets, and are soon forgotten. There does not seem to be any satisfactory way of sifting the choreographic grain from the chaff before production; even Diaghilev could not always do so and artistic directors with his strength of conviction and courage are much rarer than choreographers. Most artistic directors are rightly nervous of stifling original new talent at birth, though some of the more absurd and predictable flops of recent years could well have been spotted in advance and prevented.

It is sometimes said, mainly by unsuccessful choreographers, that there are not enough opportunities for new creative talent.

In fact every company is only too anxious to give an opportunity to anyone showing the slightest spark of originality. The sad aspect of most choreographic workshop and tryout performances is how little new talent there is and how imitative and uninventive most of the would-be choreographers are. Although both audiences and dancers, and especially dancers, need the stimulus and challenge of new works, I see nothing to be ashamed of in the fact that a large proportion of the present ballet repertoire except that of the New York City Ballet dates from the last century and the first half of this one. It is fashionable in some quarters to sneer at the silly "irrelevant" plots of the old works; perhaps the same people sneer at Mozart's operas. But just as singers and their audiences need to be constantly tested and exposed to the great music of the past, so dancers and their audiences need the great choreography of the past. Dancers need the technical discipline and challenge; audiences need to sharpen their standards and increase their knowledge by comparing different interpretations of the standard works. Indeed one of the greatest pleasures for the regular balletgoer is comparing all the different Odettes, Auroras and Giselles, Siegfrieds and Albrechts.

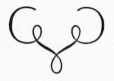

CHAPTER II

The Dancer

PRESUMABLY MOST CHILDREN who start ballet classes dream of being a Pavlova or a Fonteyn, a Nijinsky or a Nureyev. Not all do so, though: Fonteyn herself says she did not start with any hope of becoming a ballerina; she only thought she might get into a corps de ballet. ("Ballerina" strictly speaking is the title of a dancer who takes the leading female roles in the full-length classics or in their modern equivalents. It should not be used, as it commonly is, to denote just any female soloist.) Some dancers were passionately determined to dance from a very early age, others drifted into it because of parental ambition or because they were sent to ballet classes for health reasons. Male dancers in particular need great determination when they are young, as the combined prejudices of family, friends, school and society are usually against ballet dancing as an occupation for a boy. Both David Blair and Graham Usher have told me of their boyhood determination to dance; Blair used to play truant from his Yorkshire school around the age of nine to attend dancing lessons. Christopher Gable and Anthony Dowell were both stagestruck and thought of themselves as potential actors or dancers. It was chance that Gable got a scholarship to the Royal Ballet School, and he did eventually leave ballet to take up acting.

On the other hand, girls are often encouraged by their parents to go to ballet classes, even against their will. Antoinette Sibley says she does not remember ever wanting to be a dancer, it just happened. Her father was an avid balletgoer and thought she should audition for the Royal Ballet School. She did, at the age of nine, and got in. By the time she was fourteen, she knew she could never give it up. Alicia Markova took her first classes as treatment for flat feet. Far from wanting to be a dancer, her ambition was to be a doctor. Only when she was taken up by Diaghilev, and became involved with Russian ballet and acquired a Russian name, did she get caught up in ballet.

Not quite so many adoring parents would send their daughters to ballet classes if they fully realized the tough life, and the comparatively poor rewards, which face the girl who makes ballet her career. On the other hand many parents welcome the discipline and strict routine involved in ballet training. More parents of boys might well forget their prejudices and realize that a ballet training is as tough and virile as any athlete's. Although ballet is now so well established in Britain and the United States, the stigma on male dancing remains. In Russia and in Denmark, parents are apparently as proud and happy for their boys to be accepted by the state ballet schools as they are for their girls. The Russian and Danish male dancer is not thought of as necessarily effeminate or odd. There is unfortunately something of a vicious circle in Britain and the United States: as long as ballet is regarded as an unsuitable occupation for a boy, it will not attract many fit, tough normal boys who might find it extremely rewarding. It must be admitted though that the rewards, for both boys and girls, are likely to be intangible rather than material, for all except the most famous and successful dancers. And the amount of time and energy which must be given to training, combined with the frightening insecurity and uncertainty of the profession and the arduous life it involves, do not make it the most tempting of careers.

Although children may take simple dancing lessons, which soon show whether they have any sense of movement to music, from a very early age, say four or five, proper ballet training usually begins between nine and eleven. The Royal Ballet School now starts both girls and boys at eleven, and does not particularly want them to have had any previous ballet training. They look for lively, likable personalities, with the right physical attributes. The girls must be well proportioned, slim, with a well-shaped neck and not too large a head, with loose leg extensions and good feet. There are height-prediction tests: girls should not grow to much less than 5 feet 3 inches or much more than 5 feet 6 inches, though there are exceptionally small ballerinas, like Maryon Lane and Lucette Aldous, and exceptionally tall ones like Beryl Grey and Jane Landon. Tall girls tend to look awkward in classical lifts, and they have difficulty in finding partners. Boys must have a good athletic frame and physique, a good jump, plenty of vitality, and of course musicality. They should grow to about 5 feet 8 inches.

Full-time ballet schools combine ballet training with general education, and the importance of this is now widely recognized, though the general education given is not always as thorough as it should be. The ballet training itself should not be purely technical; it should also include the history of ballet and some training in the appreciation of music, art—and ballet. It is amazing and disquieting, how often dancers seem to know little or nothing even about their own immediate predecessors, let alone the dancers and ballets of fifty years ago. General school subjects are essential for them to become reasonably educated men and women, and as an insurance against their careers in ballet not materializing, or coming to a premature end.

Some children never complete the course at ballet school, because of illness or injury, or because it gradually becomes apparent to them or to their teachers that they have not sufficient talent. And even when the course is completed, finding a place in a ballet company is not at all easy. The junior section of the Royal Ballet School, for example, takes in about thirty children a year, only about twenty of whom stay till they are fourteen. The senior school takes about sixty students a year but only fifteen can expect to get into the Royal Ballet. Some of the rest find places in other British companies which have not got their own schools and many more join companies abroad, especially in the Commonwealth and in Germany and Scandinavia where they do not mind employing foreigners. Others dance in opera, musical comedy, revue and on television. Girls may take up teaching; there is an ever-growing demand for teachers, to produce even more unemployable dancers. Others drift into office jobs, or get married. Boys find it easier to get into ballet companies, because of the shortage of male dancers.

The world's principal companies have their own schools, and usually prefer to take dancers from them. The Royal Ballet School, of course, trains dancers for companies all over the non-Communist world; similarly the Bolshoi and Kirov schools train dancers for other companies in the Soviet Union, and all over eastern Europe. A few western students have succeeded in training there too. The Royal Danish Ballet recruits virtually all its dancers from its own school, though it does now audition outsiders, including foreigners. John Cranko has started a school in association with his company in Stuttgart, and the main American companies all have their own schools, as does the National Ballet of Canada. The Russian and Danish schools seem the most successful in providing a good general education, and the Russian and Danish companies also provide the greatest security for dancers, with plenty of roles for the older ones and with full pension schemes.

Once accepted as a professional dancer, a girl or boy always faces the risk of disabling injury, of putting on too much weight, or of simply getting stuck on the ladder of promotion and being doomed to years of soul-destroying routine in the corps de ballet. If all these risks are avoided, professional life is still absurdly short. Great ballerinas like Ulanova, Markova and Fonteyn dance till around fifty, but they are exceptional. Many ballerinas retire much younger, and most girls give up around forty. Physically and technically they are likely to be at their peak at about the age of thirty; later, artistic skill and interpretative ability must increasingly make up for lost glamor and virtuosity. In some cases they easily do so. The three ballerinas mentioned gave some of their most deeply felt and moving performances in their forties. The famous Italian teacher and ballet master Enrico Cecchetti once told Ninette de Valois that there could not be a true ballerina under twenty-eight, though he added the rider that it could be marvelous to watch a potential ballerina of twenty-one. It is one of the ironies of ballet that when a dancer is still the age of the teenage Giselle, she usually lacks the experience and emotional depth to project the role fully; when she has these things, she may have difficulty in looking the part. The great Giselles shed their years and look eighteen again as they dance. The problem is exactly the same as that facing the actor or actress playing Hamlet or Juliet.

The life of a male dancer tends to be even shorter than that of the female. He may well be at his fittest and most presentable in his early twenties; around thirty he will probably already start to lose speed and elevation, and he can rarely continue virtuoso dancing beyond the late thirties. Partnering, mime and national dances can be performed till much later; Massine danced till he was sixty. But audiences nowadays are unwilling to accept heavy, middle-aged princes in the classics, however well they may lift their ballerinas. The Bolshoi ballet produced principal dancers of this kind on its first visit to London, but no longer does so. On the other hand, companies like the Bolshoi, and the Royal Danish Ballet, provide plenty of scope for older dancers in mime and character parts; crowd scenes in productions by those companies look more realistic because of the proportion of heavy, mature people on the stage. The Royal Ballet should ideally do likewise, but has never yet been able to afford to keep on sufficient dancers for this purpose. Instead they engage actors ad hoc for particular productions, which does not solve the problem of employment for the older dancer and does not look as convincing on the stage. New York City Ballet, with its repertoire almost entirely devoted to abstract dancing, could not accommodate older dancers in any case. The plight of the male dancer who gives up dancing in middle age is generally worse than that of the girl; unless he is going to teach, produce ballets or become a choreographer, he may find himself unemployed with no particular training for other work. Some male dancers who gave up while still fairly young have succeeded in making quite new careers in business and commerce.

Quite apart from all these risks, even the most successful dancer's life consists of unremitting hard work for comparatively small financial rewards. People are still often surprised to hear of famous dancers attending class; in fact all dancers must attend class every morning of the working week to maintain and improve their techniques and to keep their muscles supple. The class, which starts with exercises balancing with one hand on a fixed horizontal bar by the wall and builds up to fast jumps and other technically demanding steps in the center of the stage or studio, keeps dancers fit and also gives the ballet master or teacher a chance to point out any faults which are developing. It also gives dancers the opportunity of working at any particular steps which they find difficult, or want to improve. Dancers who are conscious of a particular weakness often go to a special teacher who specializes in that step. Professional dancers may well have rehearsals with their companies, or matinees, in the afternoons, and performances in the evenings, and must regularly face a long and tiring day. The performances themselves can be unbelievably exhausting. Fonteyn has spoken of the sheer fatigue she feels during and after a difficult role, and has said that if people knew how much the dancers suffer, they would be unable to bear to watch. Graham Usher has told me that roles like the Blue Bird in *The Sleeping Beauty* and the Blue Skater in *Les Patineurs* "practically kill you"; he says, "I often felt I must have split a gut." And Annette Page gave as one of the reasons for her premature retirement that she just did not want to have to work as hard as Fonteyn does.

Only the greatest devotion to dancing can see a boy or a girl through the arduous training and the equally arduous professional career which may follow. The basic techniques of classical dance must of course be taught to children from an early age; unlike modern dance, ballet is not something which can be picked up in one's late teens. Turnout of the leg from the thigh, in which the foot is turned out sideways at an angle of 90 degrees, must be practiced from the earliest stage while the muscles are still flexible. Good turnout is regarded by most experts as the essential basis of classical dancing; only when the thighbone can rotate freely in its socket has the dancer got sufficient freedom of movement to perform the range of leg and foot movements required. It is also held by some people that dancers with good turnout look more pleasing on the stage, though there are times when one cannot help wishing that dancers would not walk or stand about with their feet artificially in this position. Turnout is one of the many aspects of classical technique that modern dance has revolted against, and turned-in feet (called parallel position) are almost a hallmark of the modern school.

Girls also start from a fairly early stage to dance on their points, though it is now realized that too early a start is both painful and harmful. They should never start before they are twelve and at the Royal Ballet School they sometimes start as late as fifteen. Nowadays girls can wear heavily blocked shoes to help them with point work, but these are noisy and unromantic. Men do not normally dance on their points, though Anton Dolin did so in his youth and more recently Alexander Grant has done so most effectively as Bottom transformed into an ass in Ashton's *The Dream*. Flemming Flindt also dances on his points in Petit's *Carmen*. All sorts of exercises to strengthen the arches of the feet, and the use of the thigh, knees and ankles, are of course essential to every ballet class. But it is a mistake to think, as many people outside ballet do, that dancing is all a matter of legs and feet.

It is true that footwork is one of the basic aspects of ballet technique. The famous five positions learned by every ballet student begin and end every classical movement—the legs in one of the positions, with the feet always turned out. Similarly there are appropriate positions of the arms, to match the positions of the feet. But the dancer has to be trained in the disciplined use of the whole body. A dancer may be notable for an expressive face, lyrical, soft arm movements, a supple back, good posture, balance, speed, elevation, precision in turns on the ground and in the air, or quick, neat footwork. The ideal dancer would be remarkable in all these qualities. And the effort to acquire them demands constant and determined self-discipline; that is why ballet schools still cherish the old-fashioned virtue of discipline and it is said that ballet students never become delinquents! Certainly many people who have been to ballet school, but not remained in ballet, say the self-discipline was the most valuable thing they learned, and something for which they are always grateful.

In addition to all the physical attributes and skills, there are also a number of less tangible qualities which affect the popularity and success of a dancer. Two of the most important of these are "line" and musicality. They are both easy to write about in a general sort of way but very difficult to define at all precisely, and even more difficult to locate in particular dancers. Line is the ability of a dancer to move and stand in such a way that the whole body—head, torso, arms, and legs—always forms a harmonious and attractive pattern. It is partly a matter of good physical proportions, partly a matter of instinct, and partly a matter of training. Fonteyn is always held up as a superb example of good line, which can be seen in almost any of her photographs. A dancer with short arms or legs, out of proportion to the rest of the body, can hardly acquire good line. A very tall dancer may have beautiful line or the legs may be always getting in the way, looking ungainly in jumps and classical lifts. A short, thick neck, or an unusually large or small head, will also affect the line. Most people do not notice line when it is good, but become aware of it, even if only unconsciously, when it is bad and the dancer looks ugly or ungainly. Line is also important when a man and a woman are dancing together. Very often the man must mirror the woman's line, holding his arm or leg in parallel with hers; or else he must provide a contrast, say by holding his arm at right angles to the angle of her body or keeping his raised leg on a lower but parallel plane, making an effective overall pattern or shape for the two of them.

Musicality in dancers does not necessarily mean a deep interest in music or great knowledge of it. Fonteyn, as famous for her musicality as for her line, says she rarely goes to concerts or listens to music, outside the ballet. But she has an instinctive feeling for movement to music, which she developed in the early days of her career in collaboration with Constant Lambert, then musical director of the Sadler's Wells Ballet. Lambert has been quoted as saying that when conducting he would sometimes ask himself how Fonteyn could possibly get right across the stage in the prescribed phrase of music. Yet she would always arrive on time, without any sign of haste or doubt. Some dancers often seem to be out of time with the music, others can only keep in time by constant counting to themselves, which usually conveys a sense of strain to the audience. Some modern scores, without any melodic line or clear rhythm, make counting essential, unless the dancer has developed an instinctive rapport with this kind of music. The Royal Ballet had enormous difficulties, for example, in dancing Kenneth MacMillan's *Agon*, to Stravinsky's music, because they were not used to the percussive, nonmelodic idiom and to constant counting. New York City Ballet, on the other hand, takes to this music, and even more difficult pieces by Webern and Xenakis, like ducks to water. Modern dance companies nowadays think nothing of dancing to electronic tapes, to recorded sound effects, to speech or in silence. But a truly musical dancer will always prefer to feel the music, rather than to count beats, and that is why Fonteyn is happier with more conventional scores, as Pavlova was too.

Of course, dancers moving out of time with the music may be the fault of the conductor adopting speeds faster or slower than the dancer can physically manage, or thinks appropriate. Good dancers can adapt themselves to various speeds; Fonteyn has danced *Swan Lake* or *Les Sylphides* at many different speeds on different occasions. She says that it is not so much the speed, as the sense of rhythm, that is important to her. Even so, there are limits to what a dancer can do. A tall dancer usually cannot move as fast as a short one, nor an older one as fast as a young one. Few dancers anywhere can move as fast as the highly trained young athletes of New York City Ballet. So conductors must to some extent follow the dancers, and adapt their speeds to them.

A third quality, even more intangible than the others, which affects the success of a dancer, is sex appeal. This is usually ignored by writers on ballet, perhaps because it is thought to lower the status of ballet as a serious art form, perhaps because in the past it was not thought quite nice to refer in print to sex, and perhaps because some serious balletgoers are genuinely unaware of its importance, or manage to be so abstract in their attention to the dance that they immunize themselves to the sex appeal, or lack of it, of the dancers. Yet in the past, ballet was widely regarded as a display of pretty girls for tired businessmen and rich aristocrats; those days are gone, but there are still many people who go to ballet primarily for similar motives. It is obvious that physically fit young people wearing brief costumes or close-fitting body tights must have a strong erotic appeal; this is often emphasized today by the deliberately suggestive and sensual movements devised by many modern choreographers. Every sort of sexual activity is simulated. In 1970 Netherlands Dance Theatre produced the first classical-style ballet with totally nude dancers—*Mutations* by Hans van Manen and Glen Tetley.

Sex appeal is a main reason for widely different opinions about the same dancer. It is very difficult to resist a dancer who appeals in this way, even if the actual quality of the dancing leaves something to be desired. Equally if a dancer's sex appeal is blatant, but not of the kind that attracts a particular member of the audience, the effect may be merely irritating and may arouse more violent criticism than is objectively justified. It hardly needs making explicit in this permissive post-Freudian age that sex appeal is not simply a matter of attractive girls appealing to men, and vice versa. We all have some elements of both sexes in us, and are capable of responding to some extent to the glamor and sex appeal of our own sex. At least one in twenty of the population is reckoned to be homosexual, and that proportion is likely to be higher in big cities and particularly in the artistic circles that frequent cultural events. Tall, strong-looking muscular female dancers are quite as likely to be appealing to certain ladies in the audience as to men; indeed, men may dislike their "unfeminine" strength. Some people find petite lady dancers attractive, others complain that they are dwarflike. Virile, tough male dancers will appeal to some men and women, but will strike others as too much like sportsmen, too inartistic. A pretty, willowy young male dancer will excite some spectators and revolt others. In one way or another sexual preference is bound to influence our reaction to dancers. People who believe that all their judgments and preferences are completely objective are fooling themselves.

It is this sexual element in dancing which accounts for much of the prejudice against male dancers. While ballerinas, at any rate until recently, had a demure, remote image and were always conservatively dressed, male dancers have for years exploited their faces and their physiques. Nijinsky was no glamor boy, but evidently had a remarkable magnetic personality. Later stars of the Diaghilev ballet, like Massine and Lifar, were sensationally good-looking and appeared in scanty costumes which exploited the fact. In our own day the screams of the teenage girls for dancers like David Blair, John Gilpin, Chris-

Photo Frederika Davis

The greatest present-day ballerina in her greatest role: a study of Fonteyn as Odette in Swan Lake.

Merle Park and Rudolf Nureyev in the "fish-dive" ending of the last-act pas de deux of The Sleeping Beauty.

Photo Zoe Dominic

Photo Houston Rogers

Giselle: *Galina Ulanova in Act I.*

Photo Houston Rogers

Giselle: *The Bolshoi corps de ballet in Act II.*

Photo Houston Rogers

Alla Sizova and Yuri Soloviev in Blue Bird pas de deux from the Kirov State Ballet production of The Sleeping Beauty.

Photo Frederika Davis

Ekaterina Maximova in Grigorovitch's version of The Nut-cracker, *with Alla Shcherbinina as the doll and Vladimir Levashov as the conjuror.*

Erik Bruhn and Carla Fracci in the second act of La Sylphide, *which they dance regularly with American Ballet Theatre.*

Photo Fred Fehl

Photo Houston Rogers

Stanley Holden as the Widow Simone in Ashton's La Fille Mal Gardée.

Photo Houston Rogers

Fonteyn and Nureyev with the Australian Ballet in Nureyev's production of Raymonda.

Ashton's Marguerite and Armand with Fonteyn and Michael Somes (as Armand's father).

Photo John Blomfield

Photo Houston Rogers

Fonteyn in the "shadow" dance in Ashton's Ondine.

Photo Zoe Dominic

Ashton's Enigma Variations *with Desmond Doyle, Derek Rencher, and Svetlana Beriosova as Jaeger, Elgar, and Lady Elgar.*

Kenneth MacMillan's The Invitation *with Lynn Seymour, Christopher Gable, Desmond Doyle, and Anne Heaton.*

Photo Zoe Dominic

George Balanchine's abstract ballet Agon, as performed by the New York City Ballet.

Photo Fred Fehl

topher Gable, Flemming Flindt, Attilio Labis, Henning Kronstam, Jacques d'Amboise, and David Wall have had as much to
do with their physical appearance as with their admittedly first-
class dancing. The critic Richard Buckle once suggested that
Rudolf Nureyev's fans might well be chanting "We want Rudi,
preferably in the Nudi"! Part of Nureyev's sensational success is
due to his animal magnetism and sensuality. He appeals to the
mothering instinct in middle-aged women, the mating instinct
in younger ones, and the desire of many male homosexuals.
Equally he arouses strong dislike in people who are repulsed by
his particular brand of sensuality.

Although sex is now openly discussed and portrayed in the
theater, cinema and literature, there still lingers a relic of the
idea that it is in some way improper for a man to flaunt his
sexuality. A woman making herself as glamorous and appealing
as possible is regarded as normal; a man doing the same thing is
not. Just as some people still object to men using perfume, or
wearing jewelry, so they find it difficult to accept the idea of
men in tights, displaying their figures for the admiration of an
audience. This prejudice is reinforced by the suspicion that
many male dancers are themselves homosexual—and by the
effeminate costumes sometimes designed for them. The suspicion is hotly denied by most ballet propagandists, who protest
rather too much for credibility that because male dancers must
be strong and athletic, they therefore must be "normal." On the
other hand, the homosexual propagandists can also be heard
claiming, with more plausibility but no more truth, that only
homosexuals make great male dancers. Many great male dancers
have been bisexual or entirely heterosexual, married and the
fathers of families. Massine's son and daughter both have careers
in ballet; so has André Eglevsky's daughter. George Skibine and
David Blair are both fathers of twins. Danish and Russian male
dancers generally give a more normal, virile impression than
their counterparts in Britain, France and the United States. It is
significant that we tend to speak of our male dancers as boys;
the Russians and Danes seem more aptly described as men. But

it is equally true that many Russian male dancers, including
Nijinsky, have been bisexual or homosexual. Nor can audiences
always tell which are which. There are soft, effeminate-looking
dancers who live heterosexual lives and there are strong, virile-
looking ones who are homosexual.

The prejudice against male dancers would not matter much
if it did not prevent many suitable boys from training for ballet.
Kenneth MacMillan caused a stir in 1969 by saying, in a radio
interview with me, that British male dancers are too small and
lightweight, and that he intended to import foreign dancers of
greater strength and muscularity when he took over codirection
of the Royal Ballet in 1970. Partly this is simply a statement of
MacMillan's preference for a burlier kind of male dancer, and
partly it is a criticism of the selection policy adopted by the
Royal Ballet School. But there is such a shortage of male talent
that the school probably accepts any male talent that offers; the
fact is that the more athletic, burlier kind of boy is assumed, by
his friends, his teachers, and his family to be unsuitable for such
a sissy occupation as ballet. It is this assumption which must be
destroyed if western male dancing is to compete with what we
have learned to expect from the Slav countries and from Denmark. Television programs showing the tough training of
dancers are now helping to create a better image.

Ballerinas have not on the whole been regarded as sex sym-
bols. Pavlova and Ulanova, Markova and Fonteyn were thought
of as remote, slightly unworldly figures, an image which may or
may not have tallied with their private lives. The female
dancers who have been most famous for their glamor—Tcherni-
cheva, Baronova, Moira Shearer, Colette Marchand, Renée
(Zizi) Jeanmaire—have not on the whole been the greatest
ballerinas. But in the second and third ranks—the minor soloists
and members of the corps de ballet—good looks certainly help.
Naturally audiences prefer, other things being equal, an attractive dancer to an unattractive one. And a dancer must be
exceptionally talented to succeed despite an ugly face. People
sometimes say that one should not blame a dancer for her face;

but it is not a question of blame. A pleasant, expressive face is as much part of a dancer's necessary equipment as well-trained feet and arms.

What the great stars have got, which may or may not include some form of sex appeal, is sheer strength of personality, or what it is at the moment fashionable to call charisma. They need personality to fight their way to the top and they need it to hold the audience's attention when they are on the stage.

Strength of personality is particularly well illustrated by the most famous ballet partnership of our day: Fonteyn and Nureyev. Fonteyn was not gifted with a naturally strong technique, and she always had to work extremely hard to conquer weak feet and to acquire the necessary virtuosity for the great classical showpieces. But she was determined that anything she did should not be done worse than by other people. She was always prepared to make a fresh effort. In later years she has astonished everyone by the quiet skill with which she coped with the problems of her private life, as well as with her demanding professional career. In addition to her dancing, as President of the Royal Academy of Dancing she attends committees, personally supervises the revision of the teaching syllabus, and organizes fund-raising galas. She is never at a loss for the right word, either in committee, in a public speech or at a press conference. The same gift showed when she got involved in Panamanian politics through her husband, Roberto Arias. The skill with which she parried questions after she was arrested for a short time in Panama was later equaled by the calm poise with which she tended her husband after the attempt on his life which left him in a wheelchair, partially paralyzed. For a long period she commuted between Covent Garden and the out-of-town hospital where Dr. Arias was being treated, but the physical and nervous strain was never allowed to show. Several people who have worked with Fonteyn have remarked on her remarkable control of herself and her life, and her capacity to deal with and accept life's problems as they arise.

Nureyev, as he recounts in his own book, already showed the

strength of his personality in Russia, first by his determination
to be a dancer, leaving his home in Central Asia to start training in Leningrad at an unusually late age. Later he resisted
powerful pressures to send him back to dance in Asia, and
managed to stay in the Kirov company. He continued to rebel
against the rules imposed by the authorities in all sorts of ways
and when the company visited Paris, and he suddenly found
himself being recalled to Russia, he made his celebrated and
successful dash for freedom at the airport. It is not surprising
that his colleagues in the West have found him hard to work
with; but his personality and his temperament are essential keys
to his fantastic success. What makes Nureyev a great star is not
his technique, which is sometimes untidy and can be equaled
by several other leading male dancers. It is the fact that he rivets
attention as soon as he comes on the stage, without dancing a
step. Of course this would not be enough in itself. But allied
with a technique which is certainly in the top class, with a
distinctive dancing style and with considerable acting ability, it
is more than enough. The charisma produced when he and
Fonteyn are dancing together, in the second act of *Giselle* or the
balcony scene of *Romeo and Juliet,* is even greater. Invisible
rays seem to make contact between them, and the audience is
conscious of a rapport, a togetherness, which is exceptionally
moving and exciting. The same thing evidently happens when
Carla Fracci and Erik Bruhn dance together; in London we got
a glimpse of this in their excerpt from *La Sylphide* at the 1969
Covent Garden Gala, and in New York their partnership in the
classics with American Ballet Theatre has become almost as
famous as that of Fonteyn and Nureyev with the Royal Ballet.

The question of a dancer's individual style of movement is
often mentioned but is hard to explain. It was once suggested to
me by Clive Barnes, now the theater and ballet critic of the
New York *Times,* that the difference between a good dancer
and a great one is that the latter has a distinctive style of
movement which one comes to recognize, just as one recognizes the style of a composer or choreographer. How else can

one explain the fact that no two ballerinas dancing a standard classic role will look exactly the same? Partly of course it is simply the difference between their faces, and the shapes of their bodies. But there will also be different nuances in the actual movements, and there are certain ways of moving which we do come to associate with particular dancers. Partly these are actual steps which particular dancers specialize in. I remember Nureyev's complicated spins in the air, Gilpin's pirouettes, Bruhn's high entrechats, Fonteyn's rapid neat footbeats, Nerina's jumps, Ulanova's fast runs across the stage and Seymour's rounded bending movements. But I also remember Nureyev's walk, Fonteyn's eyes, Plisetskaya's arms, the brash bounce of Kehlet and Villella, and the gentle charm of Sibley, Maximova and Makarova, Egon Madsen and Christopher Gable. Many people must share these and other images. These dancers who create memorable images and whom we want to watch all the time they are on the stage are the true stars.

Star is regarded as an ugly four-letter word by many choreographers, directors of ballet companies, critics—and dancers who find stardom elusive. Dancers who know they have strong techniques may wonder why they are not necessarily accepted as stars; they sometimes forget that one of the arts of a star is to make the most difficult technical feats look natural and easy, but not so easy that the audience fails to admire. In *The Sleeping Beauty,* for example, strong soloists make the fairies' variations at the christening look like efficient displays of speed and balance; dancers with potential star quality make them look like spontaneous and natural ways of moving to the music. Similarly a great ballerina will make Aurora's Rose Adagio look easy, yet at the same time miraculous. If her face shows radiant happiness, perhaps with slight surprise at her own accomplishment, but her actual balances are not held very long, the effect will still be more satisfying than impeccable balances accompanied by a strained smile or a tense or blank face.

Companies without stars understandably make a virtue of necessity and sing the praises of the ensemble; these praises can be worth singing—a starless ensemble can be marvelous to watch. But we should not be hoodwinked by such ensembles into thinking that stars are unnecessary, or even undesirable. For one thing they are essential to the classics which demand outstanding personalities in the leading roles. For another they are essential to most choreographers, who need the stimulus of working with such personalities and with dancers who give their own individual accents to the choreography. The converse, that star dancers need choreographers to develop and guide their talents, is also true, but not to the same extent. Pavlova, Ulanova, Fonteyn, Nijinsky and Nureyev would still have been stars even if not a single new role had ever been created for them; they could have shone entirely in the classics, though at the cost of their own boredom and ultimate staleness. Very little *was* created for Pavlova, after Fokine's early little numbers for her, and some people say she declined artistically for this reason. But she certainly remained a star. Some ballerinas, like Nerina and Beriosova, might have extended more aspects of their talents if a great choreographer had continued working with them regularly.

Stars are also essential at the box office. Audiences like to follow a star and soon create their own, even without any official encouragement from the ballet companies. For many years now New York City Ballet has abandoned star billing and listed its dancers alphabetically. (There is a celebrated remark attributed to Maria Tallchief when she resigned: "I don't mind being listed alphabetically, but I'm not going to be treated alphabetically.") But it is only necessary to attend a few performances to realize that the company in fact boasts several stars. When it was at Covent Garden in 1965, Suzanne Farrell was very obviously presented as the star ballerina, though London audiences raised equal, or even greater, enthusiasm for Mimi Paul. There could be no dispute about the star status of both Jacques d'Amboise, with his exciting physical presence, and Edward Villella, with his sensational technique. Before the season was over, many people were going specifically to see these dancers, rather than the company, and fewer people would have gone if these dancers had not been there.

Personally I regret the New York City Ballet's policy of not advertising casts in advance, and of changing both casts and programs at very short notice without apology or explanation. Audiences are evidently supposed to believe that they should go to see the company rather than any particular dancers, or even any particular ballets. The Royal Ballet, in its early days, had a similar philosophy. But this attitude really betrays a kind of contempt for the paying customer, who is surely entitled to prefer one dancer to another. (This contempt is also shown by New York City Ballet in the strange practice of suddenly omitting important sections of a ballet; when I saw *Raymonda Variations* in 1969, neither Violette Verdy nor Conrad Ludlow performed their principal solo variations, despite the fact that Miss Verdy was in stunning form and would obviously have been marvelous in the exciting Hungarian-style solo which is one of the main features of the work.) Moreover, many people would go to the ballet more often if they could be sure of the chance to compare different casts.

Nowadays the Royal Ballet does normally advertise its casts well in advance, but the company is officially headed by a large group of principals which includes ballerinas, character dancers, mimes and highly experienced soloists, all listed together in alphabetical order. Fonteyn and Nureyev get asterisks against their names because they are guest artists and not resident members of the company, but that is their only distinction in the printed programs. Of course this is all nonsense. Nobody seriously believes that all the people listed as principals are equal in importance, merit or popularity. And the management of the Royal Opera House recognizes the special status of Fonteyn and Nureyev in a controversial way—by charging considerably higher prices of admission when they appear.

Once or twice the touring section of the company has permitted itself posters giving individual dancers star billing, but these were only occasional departures from the company's normal democratic policy. Yet ballet is part of theater and part of show business, and I see no reason why the appeal of star dancers should not be exploited. Names like Svetlana Beriosova, Merle Park, Antoinette Sibley, Doreen Wells, Anthony Dowell, Donald MacLeary and David Wall should be in big type on the posters, and in lights outside the theaters. Why not?

Admittedly the Bolshoi and the Kirov also pursue an antistar policy. Their casts are never advertised in advance and we are supposed to book for *Giselle* or *Swan Lake* without knowing which ballerina is to dance. The folly of this was fully exposed during the Bolshoi's 1969 London season, when audiences at Timofeyeva's performances of these ballets felt cheated, while audiences at the performances by Maximova and Bessmertnova were highly satisfied. All ballerinas are not equal, not even Russian ones, and it is no good pretending they are. Nor is it any good, in the long run, conning the public into paying for performances it does not really want to see.

Some critics and directors of ballet companies appear to think that an egalitarian ensemble in which dancers take leading parts one night and are lost in the corps de ballet the next is in some way better than a clear hierarchy; it *may* be morally better, but I doubt if it is better artistically. Modern abstract ballets by Balanchine, Cranko or MacMillan may be deliberately designed for an ensemble without any outstanding solo parts. Many of the smaller companies make an impression by the sheer strength of their ensembles; Netherlands Dance Theatre is a good example. One admires it as a company without remembering any individual personalities, though audiences eventually get bored with anonymity. Even in such companies, stars tend to emerge and must be allowed to shine, or else they leave. Maria Tallchief left New York City Ballet more than once, and Mimi Paul and Suzanne Farrell did so later, for similar reasons.

There is not really much point in trying to submerge a star personality in a corps de ballet, even if the star can be persuaded to try. Modern story ballets, as well as the classics, gain immensely from stars in the leading roles. Even a semiabstract ballet like *Les Sylphides,* though in no sense a star vehicle, can gain immensely from ballerinas like Markova, Fonteyn or Fracci, who create a special aura and feeling which help to restore the ballet to life, while lesser soloists may simply go through the steps without conveying any feeling or atmosphere.

Great artists can often soften their personalities when they wish to take part in an ensemble. In Ashton's *Symphonic Variations,* for example, Fonteyn was in a sense only one of three equal ballerinas, yet she was in the center and always subtly but clearly led the team. Some people thought that Nureyev would be too strong a personality for the work and would upset its balance, but in practice he fitted into the ensemble admirably.

Classical ballerinas and their male opposite numbers are not the only stars of the ballet. Dancers with sufficient personality to justify star billing may specialize in acting or character dancing rather than in pure classicism. The label "dramatic ballerina" describes the female dancer who owes her fame more to her powerful miming than to pure dancing. The America ballerina Nora Kaye was perhaps the most famous recent dancer of this genre; she had a very strong technique but is remembered mainly for her acting in *Giselle* and such modern works as Jerome Robbins's *The Cage,* Agnes de Mille's *Fall River Legend,* and Tudor's *Pillar of Fire.* The French ballerina Janine Charrat had a similar reputation, based on such performances as in her own *Les Algues,* set in a lunatic asylum. In England, the most recent dancers of this type have been Anne Heaton and Paula Hinton who had a considerable following among the cognoscenti but never achieved the wider reputations they deserved.

An even rarer type of star female dancer is the character dancer specializing entirely in mime. The outstanding interpreters of roles like Carabosse the wicked fairy in *The Sleeping Beauty* and Madge the Witch in *La Sylphide* are usually male, and of course the male repertory contains numerous other good mime parts, from Dr. Coppelius to Widow Simone. The most celebrated female mime in recent years was the Danish Gerda

Karstens, who showed how much can be made of female mime roles given a sufficiently powerful interpreter. The Bolshoi Ballet also needs such talents, for example for the emotional and almost hammy role of Lady Capulet in *Romeo and Juliet*. Attempts to find a strong female mime in Britain have not so far been very successful; the female Carabosse in the Royal Ballet's latest version of *The Sleeping Beauty* has generally been voted a flop.

The Royal Ballet *is* strong, however, in male mimes, as it has been since the days of Walter Gore (the original Rake) and Robert Helpmann. Some star mimes, most notably Alexander Grant, give star performances as character dancers as well. Character dancing comes between pure classicism and pure mime: it includes folk dances, comic dances and, as the name implies, dances where character is shown through the dance. Grant's ludicrously comic yet touching Alain in *La Fille Mal Gardée*, his mincing hooded charlatan who is suddenly transformed into the impressive god Eros in *Sylvia*, and his Bryaxis the pirate chief in *Daphnis and Chloë* are among his large gallery of remarkable dancing portraits created in collaboration with Ashton. In some ways Grant has for many years been the greatest male star in the Royal Ballet, but because neither his physique nor his personality are suited to the princes and poets of classical and romantic ballet, his position has not always been sufficiently appreciated.

A similar stigma attaches to the ballerina who specializes in light, soubrette roles. The outstanding Swanilda in *Coppélia* or Cancan Dancer in *La Boutique Fantasque* is somehow not thought of, at least in England, as equal in importance to the outstanding Odette or Giselle. This is partly because the greatest British ballerinas, Markova and Fonteyn, have been primarily exponents of the more serious classic roles; it may also be because of the ingrained British puritanism which thinks something tragic more significant than something comic. Dancers like Moira Shearer and Nadia Nerina, whose best performances were in soubrette roles, were always slightly undervalued, and

Merle Park was in similar danger in the early stages of her career when she too specialized in soubrette roles. As a result, star soubrettes are often tempted to take on tragic roles for which they are not really suited, in an effort to consolidate their status as true ballerinas. This scale of values is not universal. When Ulanova was at her peak in Russia, she was one of three equal-ranking ballerinas of the same generation. One of the others, Marina Semyonova, was also an Odette and a Giselle, but the third, Olga Lepeshinskaya, was primarily a Swanilda and a Kitry in *Don Quixote*. She was not thought any the less of for that. (Her interpretation of the *Don Quixote* pas de deux, which I was lucky enough to see in Brussels, remains in my memory as the liveliest and most exciting performance ever.) Alexandra Danilova, the Russian ballerina whose career was mainly in western Europe and the United States, was also most famous for her soubrette roles; nobody who saw her in any of the Massine ballets, for example, can ever forget how much they gained from her sparkle, charm and sense of style.

In Denmark, too, dancers of many different types are properly appreciated. The Danes have difficulty in producing a pure classical ballerina; even Margrethe Schanne, the last one they had, specialized in just two romantic roles, the Sylphide and Giselle, rather than in the Petipa classics. But Inge Sand, a great Swanilda, was just as respected as Schanne. One of the greatest Danish male dancers of recent years, Fredbjørn Bjørnsson, is, like Grant, primarily a character dancer. Perhaps he is not as famous as male classical dancers like Erik Bruhn, Flemming Flindt and Henning Kronstam, but he too is accepted in Denmark as a star. So is Niels Bjørn Larsen, who succeeded Gerda Karstens as Madge the Witch as well as doing all the principal male mime roles. Character dancing and mime are among the principal natural talents of Danish dancers, so maybe it is natural that these skills are more fully admired there.

Part of the undermining of the stars of the ballet is financial. Like everyone else in ballet, they are badly paid despite the lengthy and intensive training, the insecurity, and the shortness of a dancer's life. Corps de ballet dancers in Britain may earn as little as £12 ($28.80) per week, though most companies pay at least £16 ($38.40). The minimum pay for a dancer in a good touring musical show is £17 ($40.80). The Royal Ballet starts its corps de ballet at £18-10-0 ($44.40), but a dancer in a West End show is likely to get at least £30 ($72.00), while much more is frequently paid in films and television. Dancers in commercial shows do not have the security of an annual contract, as members of the Royal Ballet do, but neither on the other hand are they likely to have to attend so many classes and rehearsals. Principal dancers of the Royal Ballet get upward of £44 ($105.60) per week, and some may get £3000-£4000 ($8,400.00-$11,200.00) a year.

The biggest stars negotiate their own fees—Fonteyn and Nureyev are now paid by the performance and obviously make considerable money from guest and television appearances all over the world. Even so, ballet stars as a whole are not nearly as well paid as the stars of opera, to say nothing of musical comedy or the cinema, pop music, athletics or sport.

The discrepancy between the pay of ballet dancers and dancers in musicals is not as great in New York as it is in London, though ballet dancers still come off worse. Minimum rates for ballet dancers are now about $140 a week, while for dancers in musicals they are about $160. (In Britain all dancers are members of Actors Equity; in the United States, dancers in musicals belong to Equity while ballet dancers belong to the Guild of Musical Artists.) And the Rockefeller panel which made a comprehensive study of the problems facing American dance in 1965 reported that the maximum earned by a ballerina in a year was $10,000, while an opera singer might get $6,000 for a single performance.

Nor do dancers often become household names. One can number on the fingers of one hand the ballet stars who at any one time are well-known to the world at large, and not just to those people who follow the world of ballet. If they do become well-known, their achievement is all the more remarkable for being made without benefit of the enormous publicity machine which boosts stars of cinema, television and show business. In the Soviet Union and Denmark, balletic events and ballet stars do make news of general interest, as opera does in Italy and sport in Britain. Perhaps ballet stars would not like to have all their private activities—motoring offenses, marriages, divorces and children—reported as if they were pop singers. And some ballet companies give the impression that they are reluctant to have their dancers publicized at all for fear they will get swollen-headed, become difficult about money or casting, and break up the happy ensemble. But ballet would attract an even wider audience, and become more viable financially, if it abandoned this reticence and refinement and faced up to its role as part of the world of theater and entertainment. There is really nothing to be ashamed of in that role; it is only an inferiority complex that prevents ballet from taking pride in its glamor and publicity value. I suspect that, in their secret hearts, most dancers would welcome more publicity. They are, after all, human and most people enjoy being celebrities, being recognized by taxi-drivers and headwaiters, and having their autographs sought at every corner.

At the moment the rewards of being a dancer, except for that handful of top stars, are comparatively intangible. There is the mixed pleasure of extensive travel; many companies make tours all over the world so that dancers see more countries than do most theater artists. But they are usually working and rehearsing too hard to see much of the places they visit. Most dancers also have to do constant touring in their own country, staying in lodgings which they must find and pay for, and often sacrificing their free time to long and boring journeys. Home life is almost impossible, except for those who are more or less permanently based in a capital city or who are married to fellow dancers in the same company.

Still, there are obvious compensations for the dancer visiting Paris, Brussels, Moscow, London, Baalbek or Tokyo, as many of them do sooner or later. And there are equally obvious attractions in the summer festivals which are now frequently held in Italy, France, Monaco, Spain and Yugoslavia. Perhaps partly because of their very aloofness from the commercial entertainment world, ballet dancers have a desirable social status, and are frequently invited to receptions, dinner parties, and nightclubs by local celebrities and ballet lovers. But the whole world of entertainment has recently become much more socially respectable and desirable than it used to be, with the Beatles being honored by the Queen, Grace Kelly marrying Prince Rainier of Monaco, and members of the Sinatra clan hobnobbing with the Kennedy set, so ballet dancers would not lose caste by gaining greater commercial publicity.

All these things—travel, meeting people, fame—are among the attractions of a dancer's career, and some compensation for the hard work and poor financial rewards. More important is the sheer love of dancing, and the feeling of achievement in mastering and constantly improving the complex techniques and the difficulties of interpretation. There is no doubt that most dancers enjoy their work; if they did not they could not go on. Fonteyn has said that the strict discipline of a dancer's routine is actually an advantage. She never had to stop to think what she should do on any particular day, because she always knew she was due at class or rehearsal. This permanently demanding schedule meant that she was all the more appreciative of any free time she had. Young people nowadays, she remarked, are discontented partly because they have no discipline in their lives, and do not know what to do with themselves. And the discipline learned in youth has helped her to cope with the problems of later life. It may well be that for a certain type of person the discipline of ballet is an attraction in itself.

But these attractions are not going to be enough, in this modern world, to provide the expanding world of ballet with all the talent it will need. There is no doubt that greater rewards, both in fame and fortune, will have to be found.

CHAPTER III

Music and Decor

MUSIC, AS WE HAVE SEEN, plays a crucial part in the success of many ballets and an important part in most of them. The Tchaikovsky classics owe their fame and long life as much to the composer as to Petipa and Ivanov, and it seems more than probable that many Stravinsky and Prokofiev works will survive for the same reason. However, ballet can also survive with music which would not be accounted distinguished by concert standards, but which is preeminently suited to dancing and to the particular story and atmosphere of the ballet concerned. It has long been fashionable and commonplace to deride "hack" composers like Adam, Hérold, Løvenskjold, Minkus and Drigo, but the fact remains that dancers still like dancing to their music, choreographers still like working with it, and most important of all, audiences still like hearing it.

Some of the ballet teachers attending a seminar at the Royal Academy of Dancing told me that children respond instinctively to this kind of music, and immediately start inventing their own dances to it, while more difficult and possibly more distinguished music leaves them cold. Fonteyn, too, has often stressed how much she prefers dancing to music with definite rhythm rather than the purely percussive scores provided by many modern composers.

There is no disgrace in the fact that a high proportion of established ballet music is, by concert standards, second-rate—or even third-rate. Fokine and his circle thought we must get away from the idea of "ballet music," which suggested the second-rate, but actually there is nothing wrong with special ballet music for dancing, any more than with film music for the cinema. Much ballet music is merely intended as an appropriate and atmospheric background, and there is nothing to be ashamed of in that. If ballet is primarily a matter of dancing there is no reason—not even a theoretical one—why the music should be particularly distinguished in its own right. Experience has shown that good ballets need to have good dancing music, which is quite a different thing. This is true of *Giselle, La Sylphide* (with its two rival scores), *La Fille Mal Gardée* (with its many musical versions, incorporating quotations from many composers), and of most of the Danish classics. The Danish "Tivoli" composers, like Lumbye, wrote marvelously jaunty and catchy tunes which serve the delightful Bournonville repertoire as well as Minkus and Drigo serve Petipa. And the same thing applies to many more recent works. Gavin Gordon was scarcely a well-known composer, and his score for *The Rake's Progress* is not a concert work, but that has not in any way detracted from the success and popularity of de Valois' ballet. This catalogue could be continued indefinitely. What all these scores have in common, apart from their suitability for dancing, is their appropriateness to the styles of the ballets. One can almost visualize the ballets from listening to recordings of the works. And some forgotten composers may even be brought back into popularity by the ballet boom; the conductor Richard Bonynge, for example, has not only recorded forgotten nineteenth-century operas but also forgotten ballets of the same period including Adam's *Le Diable à Quatre* and Burgmüller's *La Péri*. Festival Ballet's revival of Adam's *La Jolie Fille de Gand (Beatrix)*, and Benjamin Harkarvy's version of a pas de deux from *Le Diable à Quatre* for the Netherlands Dance Theatre and for the Harkness Ballet, though not very memorable choreographically, at least served to reintroduce these very balletic and delightful scores; an Ashton or a Cranko may yet bring these pieces back to life.

This is not to deny, however, the need for good ballet scores. Obviously ballet would benefit enormously if a new Tchaikovsky or Prokofiev could be found. Two leading composers of our day, Benjamin Britten and Hans Werner Henze, have composed full-length ballet scores (*The Prince of the Pagodas* and *Ondine*) with reasonable success, but unfortunately neither of them has followed these up, though other pieces by Britten have been successfully used for ballet, especially by Ashton and Robbins. Various concert pieces by Shostakovich have also been used for ballet, but his specifically written ballet scores have not established themselves. Khatchaturian's score for *Spartacus* is more like film background music than a concert work, and has had to be dramatically cut for the Grigorovitch production, but it is undeniably effective in the theater. Stravinsky is regarded by many people as the greatest ballet composer of this century, and certainly his work has provided Balanchine with a substantial proportion of his repertoire and his inspiration. Personally, I do not find Stravinsky's music very suitable for ballet, and I think it works better in the concert hall, though Balanchine's work can sometimes persuade me otherwise. Good ballet scores have been written in Britain by Malcolm Arnold, Roberto Gerhard and Matyas Seiber, but none of them ever worked regularly for ballet. And these modern composers would not dream of taking detailed bar by bar instructions from their choreographers, as Tchaikovsky did from Petipa.

Not all ballet music has to be dance music. Music in ballet can be matched exactly to steps, or used as atmospheric or dramatic background, or as a source of emotional inspiration.

And all these uses of music can be equally effective, and are equally valid.

One of the advantages of distinguished composers writing for ballet—apart from the pleasure given to the more musically sensitive of the ballet audience—is that distinguished conductors can then be enticed to appear on the podium and the standard of orchestral playing can be transformed. Ernest Ansermet conducted regularly for the Diaghilev ballet, and it was notable what a galvanic effect he had at Covent Garden during his few postwar guest appearances with the Royal Ballet. Antal Dorati was also a regular ballet conductor in his early career, and of course Constant Lambert played an enormous part in establishing musical standards in the early days of British ballet. (I am slightly reassured, in these days of Stravinsky idolatry, to know that Lambert was firmly against him as a ballet composer.) Yuri Faier and Gennadi Rozhdestvensky showed us, on their visits with the Bolshoi Ballet, the full beauty of the familiar Tchaikovsky scores. But ballet companies everywhere now complain about the difficulty of getting good conductors. Promising young conductors prefer to learn the ropes by working as repetiteurs with opera companies, or as junior conductors with provincial symphony orchestras, rather than as ballet pianists or conductors. The lack of intrinsic musical interest in much of the ballet repertoire must undoubtedly be blamed for this, as well as the necessity for constant soul-destroying repetition of a small handful of standard works. The attitudes of managements and dancers do not help. At Covent Garden, conductors have frequently been expected to conduct a ballet performance without any previous stage rehearsal with the dancers, and sometimes without even an orchestral rehearsal. And one experienced conductor has pointed out to me that whereas singers at the end of an opera wait to hear what the conductor thinks of them, dancers wait to tell the conductor what they think of him.

The result of all this is that even at the Royal Opera House, Covent Garden, there is often a standard of orchestral playing which would disgrace a small touring ensemble. Yet those of us who also attend opera at Covent Garden know how magnificently the very same orchestra can play under a great conductor like Kempe, Giulini or Solti.

This is not just a matter of musical interpretation. Orchestras only give of their best for conductors they respect; the wrong notes and fluffed entries which have become frequent occurrences on ballet nights at Covent Garden can partly be explained by the orchestra's lack of respect for both conductor and score and partly by inadequate rehearsal. There have even been occasions when the music stopped altogether, or when two sections of the orchestra played different sections of the score at the same time. Some musicians say that the ballet conductor is faced with insuperable problems; the music cannot sound as it should if speeds have to be adjusted to suit the physiques and whims of individual dancers and the requirements of unmusical choreographers. Strong-minded conductors can sometimes persuade dancers to alter their speeds, and the dancers are sometimes surprised to find how easily this can be done. On the other hand, tempos in the classics must be adapted to different dancers' requirements; even parts of *Les Sylphides* must be danced at speeds which are quite different from Chopin's original intentions. David Ellenberg, for many years musical director of Ballet Rambert, has pointed out to me that if tempos are distorted too much, the music sounds wrong and the conductor is blamed. Technically each group of musical instruments has a comfortable natural tempo for a piece of music and too great a departure from it produces a distorted effect. All these problems, which mean there is a permanent need for compromise between stage and orchestra pit, make it all the more important that ballet companies should have experienced and strong-minded musical directors.

It might be thought that modern methods of stereophonic high-fidelity recording and reproduction would enable ballet to dispense with live orchestras altogether. But apart from the objections of the Musicians Union, in Britain at any rate, this would clearly be impossible for works in which tempos must be adjusted from night to night to suit different dancers. In works like Stravinsky's, on the other hand, the composer's wishes generally take precedence over those of the dancers. Such scores might receive better performances in a good recording than they normally do from a live orchestra under the resident conductor, especially on tour when it is possible to have only a small orchestra which must be inadequate in size, quite apart from the difficulty of persuading the best musicians to travel with a company.

Some continental ballet companies *do* use taped music. But there is something very dispiriting and unsatisfactory about canned music in the theater; atmosphere is lost and, however good the recording and reproduction system, the performance never seems quite as exciting. For this reason too it seems probable that the live orchestra, expensive and difficult though it is, will remain an indispensable part of a normal ballet performance.

Decor is less indispenable. Indeed, when ballet companies are short of money, as they almost always are, decor and costumes are one of the first and most obvious areas for economy. For years New York City Ballet performed most of their works in various forms of practice dress and tights, against plain backcloths or a cyclorama, partly to save money and partly because Balanchine's abstract ballets are well suited by this treatment. His *Apollo,* for example, is generally thought to look better in this abstract style, as it is generally presented nowadays, than in its original decor. New York City Ballet has also made a practice of compensating for the absence of decor by the particularly skillful and varied use of lighting; the late Jean Rosenthal pioneered this technique and worked out special lighting plots for most of the ballets in their repertoire. More and more ballet companies are now employing specialist lighting experts, who are also becoming more familiar in the legitimate theater.

Soviet ballet, on the other hand, where expense is no object and public taste remains conventionally Victorian, tends to go in for realistic and opulent decor in the old style. Unfortunately

the full Bolshoi and Kirov stagings cannot generally be reproduced when the companies appear on smaller stages in the
West, but even so we can get a fair idea, aided by photographs
and films, of their methods. Costumes, by our standards, are
often overelaborate, though things have improved since the
Bolshoi's first visit to London, when the men's long tunics,
elaborate wigs and artificial facial makeup made them look like
characters from the silent films, Victorian melodrama, or at least
nineteenth-century ballet prints. Western styles have been increasingly adopted since then, but costumes for the national
dances and for the crowd scenes still tend to look gaudy and
overfussy. Scenery is usually straightforwardly realistic and unoriginal; there are spectacular and exciting effects, like the
burning of a house in *Fountain of Bakhchisarai,* but these are
not usually fully reproduced in the West. The Kirov style in
decor, as in dancing, tends to be more restrained than the
Bolshoi, and some people complain that their ballets virtually
lack decor. This is not true, but certainly the decor is never
allowed to intrude on, or distract from, the dancing. People
who want the decor to be an important part of the ballet are
disappointed.

The places where most attention is paid to decor are Paris
and, more surprisingly, London. And the tastes of these two
Western capitals scarcely ever coincide. Perhaps the most celebrated and elaborately decorated of all Parisian ballet productions was the late Marquis de Cuevas' version of *The Sleeping
Beauty* designed by Raimundo de Larrain. This was a production in which the decor and costumes came first, leaving the
dancers to manage as best they could afterwards. Some of the
costumes were so large, heavy and elaborate that dancing was
virtually impossible. The ballerinas had heavy, artificial makeup,
so that facial expression was nonexistent. Nevertheless, it was a
spectacular fantasy and was extremely popular in Paris. The
entry of the fairies in the prologue, carried aloft with endless
trains behind them, and the appearance of Carabosse, with an
extraordinary high wig, were particularly striking.

More recently there has been a production of *Coppélia* at the Paris Opéra, with decor by Pierre Clayette, which looked more like an elaborate musical comedy spectacular or even a Folies Bergère revue than what we generally expect at the ballet. The musical score and the story were revised, under the supervision of Michel Descombey, to make room for more dancing and more elaborate scenic effects. The villagers were transformed into dolls and back again, the Prince and Dr. Coppelius were likewise transformed into each other, and there was an elaborate divertissement with balloons descending from on high and disgorging troupes of various national dancers. It was not exactly *Coppélia*, but it certainly was a stunning theatrical spectacle.

The French have a strong urge for this kind of thing. They always want something new; the idea of simply reproducing a classic in fairly conventional decor is anathema to them. Some of the new ballets produced in Paris by the smaller groups have been more like works about decor than about dancing. The advantages of this are that the public is kept constantly stimulated and intrigued, and that top designers from the worlds of fashion and art are brought into ballet. André Levasseur, originally of the house of Dior, was one of the most successful of these importations; he designed many ravishingly beautiful costumes for Fonteyn and the decor for the Royal Ballet's *Birthday Offering*. From the days of Diaghilev, top French artists have been accustomed to work for the ballet and this tradition has continued. Some French stage designers, like Georges Wakhévitch and Jacques Dupont, have also made magnificent contributions to design abroad. Wakhévitch has designed for opera in Italy and Britain, as well as doing many ballet decors at the Paris Opéra. Dupont's settings and costumes for Ashton's *The Two Pigeons* are an important ingredient in its success, and his mobile lacelike tent for Roland Petit's *Pelléas et Mélisande* (1969) was virtually the only good thing about that dismal gala creation for Fonteyn and Nureyev. Petit's ballets are often dominated by their decor; his previous creation for Fonteyn and Nureyev, *Paradise Lost* (1967), was also memorable chiefly for the enormous red lips, designed by Martial Raysse, through which Nureyev plunged.

In general, however, French visual taste is much further from English than the narrowness of the Channel would suggest. Neither the Larrain *Sleeping Beauty* nor the Clayette *Coppélia* would have found favor in London; they were roundly condemned by most English visitors to Paris. Equally the French on the whole disliked the decor and costumes brought to Paris on its various visits by the Royal Ballet. The Oliver Messel *Sleeping Beauty* was dismissed in Paris as ugly and vulgar. And in general French balletgoers take it for granted that the English may have good dancers, "but of course they have no taste."

Taste in the visual arts is of course a changing and relative thing. Not only does it vary from country to country at the same period of time but it also changes quite quickly in the same country over the years. Those of us who are now in our forties were brought up to regard Victorian taste as ugly and ridiculous, but Victoriana is now well and truly back in fashion with younger people. Messel's vaguely eighteenth-century *Sleeping Beauty*, regarded in the immediate postwar years of austerity and drabness as a thing of beauty, did come to look overelaborate and vulgar, even in London, by the time it was discarded twenty years later. And taste was split over its successor, the 1968 *Sleeping Beauty* with scenery designed by Henry Bardon and costumes by Lila de Nobili and Rostislav Doboujinsky.

The overall conception was Victorian neo-Gothic, a complete change from our conventional view of this ballet, with knights in armor and a beautiful mock-medieval setting reminiscent perhaps of the musical *Camelot*. The colors were mostly gentle pastels, and much criticism centered on de Nobili for costumes which blended with the decor, rather than standing out against it. Some of us found this a welcome relief from the profusion of clashing colors in the previous production, even if it did take a little time to get accustomed to a final wedding scene taking place entirely in orange. (All the dancers except the Blue Birds were in orange costumes, in an orange marquee.) Others found it difficult to spot the dancers against the decor, and the ballerinas dancing Aurora apparently shared the view that their costumes worked against them by making them invisible.

Similar complaints were heard when the last act of *Raymonda* was first staged at Covent Garden, because the costumes were said to merge with the decor and in particular with the gold floorcloth which made the dancers hard to see from seats in the higher tiers. The floorcloth was subsequently discarded.

The other serious criticism of de Nobili's costumes for *The Sleeping Beauty* was that the girls' dresses were all too long. Instead of the now-customary short tutus, revealing almost all the length of thigh, there were romantic knee-length ones, actually more in keeping with the taste and style of Tchaikovsky's and Petipa's day. Dancers found some of the movements difficult in the longer dresses and some spectators complained that they could not see enough of the girls. (The short tutu on a well-proportioned and attractive dancer is of course very becoming. But many of the taller and more muscular girls look ungainly in it, especially when the tutu is made in such a way as to reveal a lot of underwear as well. The jockstraps now often clearly visible through men's increasingly popular transparent tights are equally unaesthetic.)

Despite all these criticisms of *The Sleeping Beauty*, which led to some modification of the costumes and scenery after the first performances, most people liked the elaborate transformation scene, with the prince's journey in a remarkably realistic boat which wound its way around the stage to Aurora's palace, and his climb up the ivy-covered walls to her bedroom. There was nothing but praise for the enchanting animal masks designed by Doboujinsky for the final divertissement. One virtue of all the argument was that it reminded doubting Thomases like me how important decor and costumes can be in making or marring the success of a ballet.

People obviously vary greatly in the extent to which they are influenced or distracted by decor. Some people find elaborate scenic or lighting effects as distracting as I find speech or song. When Ashton's *Sinfonietta* (1967) had its first performance, many complaints were heard that the constantly changing light patterns made it difficult or impossible to watch the dancers. Ashton was showing his awareness of current trends by using an optical device which cast unplanned patterns of colored lights on the backcloth throughout the ballet. Later the activity of this device was reduced. Personally, I could see the dancers perfectly clearly in all these productions, but this may have something to do with my practice of watching them through opera glasses. I confess that I am one of those people who scarcely notice the decor, at least until all the other aspects of a ballet have been assimilated. But there are certainly times when the decor is so striking, for good or ill, that it is bound to affect everyone's reaction to the ballet.

CHAPTER IV

The Critic

NOBODY LOVES A CRITIC. Critic as a term of abuse in Beckett's *Waiting for Godot* was always good for a round of applause or appreciative laughter. The very word suggests someone who is always objecting, caviling, sour. Actually the reverse is usually the case, and certainly should be. A critic should be someone in love with whatever he is criticizing; only a fanatical enthusiast for ballet could survive the endless repetitions of the same ballets with slightly different casts, the constant sorties to out-of-the-way halls and theaters to see hopeful new dance groups and the hours of boredom in the hope of minutes of illumination which are every ballet critic's lot. The same is true of every other sort of critic. Only the most determined film fan could survive all those early morning press shows, all those indistinguishable westerns, bedroom comedies, and slices of ersatz science fiction which must be sat through between occasional masterpieces. But ballet critics particularly need a great love of their subject, as they cannot be doing their work for money.

Most newspapers employ full-time theater, film and music

critics who at least earn an acceptable salary, even if they supplement it with other work. There is not enough ballet, nor enough general interest in ballet, to justify the employment of a full-time ballet critic; there are sometimes periods of weeks or even months without any ballet to be reviewed. In Britain, only the *Daily Telegraph* has ever engaged a full-time ballet critic. Clive Barnes is now theater *and* ballet critic of the New York *Times*, but he has two deputies for ballet and the total amount of ballet criticism published would certainly keep at least one critic fully employed. In Germany, where there is now ballet in virtually every city with an opera house, the principal ballet critics, Horst Koegler and Klaus Geitel, still also write about opera and music.

There is quite a tradition in many countries, including England, of ballet being reviewed by music critics. For years the music critic of the London *Times* was also the paper's ballet critic though ballet experts were engaged on an ad hoc basis when ballet performances clashed, as they often did, with a concert or an opera. My own engagement as ballet critic of the *Daily Mail* started on the basis that I was simply to deputize for the paper's music critic when other engagements prevented him going to the ballet. In practice, he disliked ballet and always found some more pressing engagement whenever there was ballet to be covered.

There is of course no logical reason whatever for ballet to be reviewed by music critics. It might be more reasonable for it to be reviewed by theater critics, as it is so essentially a theatrical art. (I often think the same applies to opera.) It could also be reviewed by art critics. Any of these people may make good ballet critics if they are genuinely interested in ballet as a whole, and not just as an example of their own speciality. Music critics frequently reviewed ballet mainly or even entirely in terms of the value of the music; this is still common practice in Italy, where I have seen reviews of the Tchaikovsky classics which discussed the alleged poverty of the music at great length and listed the dancers only briefly at the end, sometimes without mentioning the choreographer at all.

Many people assume that all ballet critics must be ex-dancers or must at least have studied dancing and thus acquired a full understanding of the technique. This is by no means the case. There are only a few critics, mostly women, who are ex-dancers and I do not think there is any evidence that this experience makes them any better or any worse as critics than the rest of us. Dancers themselves usually make the worst critics; they are so obsessed with the correct solution of technical problems that they tend to ignore the impact of a performance in the theater. For this reason, they may prefer some minor soloist with a remarkable technique to a great ballerina whose technique is getting blurred; they may favor a dancer because they know what he or she is capable of in class; they may be unresponsive to the emotional and dramatic aspects of a work. But once they have given up dancing and taken their place in the audience, they can adopt a more general approach to ballet, using their knowledge of technique as a valuable aid.

In general the type of personality who becomes a dancer is unlikely to want to become a critic. Most of the best ballet critics have only acquired such rudiments of technical knowledge as they possess through experience of watching, discussing, and reading about ballet performances and classes. Arnold Haskell, who pioneered ballet criticism in England, traveled with the Ballets Russes and thus doubtless acquired much knowledge of technique, as well of the personalities involved. Many of the new generation of ballet critics in Britain, including myself, learned our jobs by watching ballet as often as we could from a very early age, reading the books and articles about it, attending classes as spectators, and talking to dancers, teachers and choreographers. This method has produced the large group of British ballet critics of my generation, including Clive Barnes and John Percival. It is a curious coincidence that about six of us were all students at Oxford University together; Barnes and Percival were already writing about ballet and running the University ballet club then. After Oxford, and before he left London for New York, Barnes had a full-time job with the London County Council and reviewed theater and music, as well as ballet, on a part-time basis. Percival, his successor as ballet critic of the London *Times* and as European ballet correspondent of the New York *Times,* still works all day at the Greater London Council, the successor of the L.C.C. I worked for years as a BBC staff journalist and I now do a wide range of journalism, especially broadcasting as a freelance.

Quite apart from the need for money, there is a danger that too exclusive a preoccupation with ballet may narrow the critic's horizons to the point where his writing becomes finicky and sterile. Every critic should be aware of developments in the other arts; he must have time and opportunity to go to the theater, cinema, concert hall and art gallery. Moreover, too many *Giselles* and *Swan Lakes* can blunt the appetite and make one lose sight of the wood for the trees. Saturation point is different for different individuals; most of us can probably assimilate more performances than the average member of the general public and we have trained ourselves to watch two or three rival ballerinas dance Giselle in one week. On some occasions we must even watch two on the same day, matinee and evening, but that is dangerously near the limit, for me at any rate. When we feel we are seeing too much, and getting stale, there is nothing for it but to get a deputy and miss a few performances, or to take a holiday.

The critic must inevitably watch ballet through slightly different eyes from the average member of the general public, and from the average reader, if only because he has seen much more of it. In some ways this tends to make him more critical. An average person seeing a competent performance of *Swan Lake* or *Giselle* is not going to make unflattering comparisons with previous performances and is not going to notice detailed points of production which could be more logical or more attractive. The critic's function is to draw on his experience to do just this, to recall details of choreography or production which have been lost or spoiled and to compare the performance with others he has seen, and with the ideal he is always hoping to see. Moreover, the critic inevitably becomes a little blasé because he has seen so much. But in other ways the critic may be less critical than the average spectator. Precisely because of his familiarity with the classics, the standard repertoire and the regular styles of dancers and choreographers, he is likely to jump with exaggerated enthusiasm at anything that seems new and original. A new style of choreography, a new production idea, or a dancer with a "different" image are liable to be overpraised by the critics, while the ordinary members of the audience may wonder what all the fuss is about. This happens particularly with new ballet companies, which we critics are always tempted to overencourage and overpraise, for the best of motives but sometimes not in the best interests of either the companies or their audiences.

We also face the temptation to overpraise or overdamn arising from the basic fact that we are all journalists. It is obvious that a review hailing a new Fonteyn or a new Nureyev, a new Ashton or a new Balanchine, or one proclaiming that a dancer or choreographer is so incompetent that he should be banned from the stage, makes more exciting reading than one which says that the new dancer or choreographer is virtually indistinguishable from dozens of existing ones. Yet the latter is far more likely to be true. The trouble, particularly for those of us who work for mass-circulation newspapers, is that our editors are likely to think us better critics if we write in the first style, and there may just happen not to be space for our review in the paper if we write in the second.

Personally I believe it is justifiable, in a short review for a popular newspaper, to look for the bright side of a performance. By this I mean that if there is one particularly good ballet in a mixed program, one particularly good dancer in a large cast, or one aspect of the production which is striking, it is legitimate to concentrate on that, just mentioning perhaps that other things were less good. I do not feel obliged to name dancers who strike me as either averagely competent or miscast, unless their performances are so patently inadequate that they must be exposed. Equally in this book, I have not devoted much space to dancers or choreographers whose work I find uninteresting or positively offensive. (In my first years as a critic, I imagined I was being kind by not naming dancers I disliked or thought poor; now I am told, however, that the worst thing of all for a dancer is to be ignored and that most of them would prefer a bad notice to no notice at all. I certainly think it is true that all publicity is good publicity; I can think of dancers who became well-known simply by being frequently reviewed, even though most of the reviews were unfavorable.)

Logically, I suppose, it is equally justifiable to pick on the worst side of a performance, but personally I try not to do this. I suppose there is a missionary streak in all of us; if we are writing about ballet it is mainly to try to convey our enthusiasm and to try to make new converts. If I can attract someone to ballet who would not otherwise have gone, I feel I have accomplished something useful. On the other hand, of course, it is no good attracting people under false pretenses; if they do not enjoy the performance, they will never trust the critic again and, what is more serious, they may not try ballet again. One advantage of writing for a daily paper is that the notice has to be done at such speed that it is almost bound to be a genuine reflection of spur-of-the-moment reactions; there just is not enough time for a more considered, and possibly a more artificial, reaction.

Equally, of course, there is no time to do more than record a snap judgment. When writing for a mass-circulation paper, the critic tries to give some idea of the kind of work being reviewed, says "boo" or "hurrah" and perhaps find space for a brief reason for his enthusiasm or the reverse. In the papers which give more space to the arts, the critic can develop his report and his thoughts at greater length and can probably achieve a more balanced notice. In a popular paper, for example, it is usually impossible to give both the pros and cons of a performance, and critics are not popular with their editors if they sit on the fence and say they will need to see the work again before they can make a real judgment. In papers which devote more space, and attach more importance, to the arts, this sort of honesty is possible and desirable. In the Sunday newspapers and even more in the weekly or monthly magazines, the critic can sit back from the performance and discuss it in the light of his reflections at leisure and in the light of other critics' reactions. This may mean that the critic has modified his original reactions; he may even have seen the work two or three times before reviewing it. Some critics writing for Sunday papers and for magazines say they never read other reviews which appear before they write, so as not to be influenced. I understand this point of view, but personally I feel there is not much point in publishing an article a week or two after an event in ignorance of what has been said about it by my colleagues. Whether agreeing with the majority opinion or not, it strikes me as more reasonable to indicate the fact and give the reasons. Moreover there is not much point in simply writing again what has already been written in many other places, though of course many readers will not have read earlier reviews.

The need for speed in writing for the daily newspapers points to what is possibly the most essential qualification of the critic: the ability to write accurately, legally, and interestingly in a very short time.

When it is remembered that most ballet performances end between 10:30 and 11 P.M., it is clear what a rush the critic must be in. Some have to get back to their offices; others can phone their copy from the theater or from a nearby call box. Luckily one can more or less judge *Swan Lake* without seeing the last act, and therefore one can phone a review through in the last interval if necessary, or write it during the last act. *The Sleeping Beauty*, however, ends later and one cannot really review it without seeing the Blue Bird and Aurora pas de deux, and the rest of the last-act divertissement. So there is always a risk of reviews of *The Sleeping Beauty* missing early editions of the newspapers, and possibly not getting in at all. A short new ballet is often presented in the middle of a mixed program and the critic can report before the last work. Sometimes, on the other hand, a gala performance goes on so late that the notice has to be written without seeing some of the main items. Occasionally I have written one notice in the interval, for the early editions, and then a more complete one afterwards for the late London editions. But it is not always technically possible for the newspaper to change the page on which the arts reviews appear between editions.

Speed comes with practice. My own technique is to dash into a phone box immediately after the performance with the shape of my review in my head. I like to have worked out a first sentence and possibly a last one, but I leave what comes in between to inspiration as I dictate. I then ask the typist at the other end to read back what I have dictated, make sure it sounds like sense and try to check that I have not repeated myself within the space of a few sentences—something which it is surprisingly easy to do. When the notice has to be longer than usual, or when it deals with a new production which requires a lot to be said in a short space, I scribble a rough draft, which I probably alter as I dictate. When I am reviewing for a quality paper, at greater length and with rather more time, I rush home and type out a notice there, which I still probably alter a bit as I dictate. An article for a weekly magazine like the *Listener* or the *New Statesman,* or a script for broadcasting, is of course typed at much greater leisure, and probably revised several times in the process of cutting it to the exact length required.

The curious thing is that with practice the critic develops such an automatic technique for doing a snap review that extra time sometimes makes the task harder instead of easier. When I review a Saturday performance for Monday's *Daily Mail,* I have nearly a complete extra day in which to consider my notice. There is then a temptation to think about one's review too much, to try and be too clever, and by Sunday afternoon to have lost sight of what is really the most important point to be made. Notices written after this extra time are no better than the overnight snap ones, and I now try to dash off weekend notices at the same speed as if they were required at once.

The dangers of writing at speed are considerable: not only the obvious ones, that judgment may be ill-considered and hasty, that some vital point of explanation may be left out or that the writing may be sloppy and ungrammatical and include factual mistakes. All these things happen very easily. I once wrote a review of *Swan Lake* in which I forgot to name the ballet. It is tempting to critize detailed points of a performance without describing what they are. And it is hard to avoid careless slips of the tongue, or of the typewriter, like naming the wrong dancer, or using the wrong Christian name. There are also purely technical hazards, like not being able to find a free telephone that is working, getting cut off in the middle of dictation, or having a bad line so that the typist cannot hear what one is saying. And of course in the middle of dictating and revising a review, one must remember to spell all the difficult words and names.

There is also the law of libel to be remembered, though newspaper subeditors will normally cut out any potentially libelous comment, or at least refer it to the paper's lawyer. In Britain if a critic emerges from a particularly dreadful performance spluttering with rage, and keen to translate his feeling into print, he must remember that he can condemn a particular performance but he cannot cast doubts on the general competence of a professional performer, designer or musician. In other words he can say they were bad on this occasion, but he must not say that a dancer "can't dance." I once described the decor for a ballet as "incompetent" but this was cut out of my notice in case it was taken as a libelous reflection on the designer's professional ability.

The critic must also develop the journalist's thick skin. Writing for a popular paper, he not only has to compress his thoughts into four or five inches of type, but to be prepared to find them cut still further. When he reads the paper next morning he may find that what he regards as his main point has been omitted, or that his notice is not in the paper at all because of shortage of space and what were regarded by the night staff as more important items. He may also have to face the shock of seeing the headline put on his review; many people do not realize that journalists rarely write their own headlines. Personally I quite like to see a sensational or jazzy headline, without any apparent connection with ballet, on one of my reviews as I think it may tempt someone to read it who would not read a piece simply headed "Ballet" or "New cast in *Swan Lake.*" One of my reviews of Tudor's *Knight Errant* appeared on a news page of the *Daily Mail,* not on the usual arts page, under the heading *"Seduction, Tudor Style."* This broadened the appeal of the ballet and was also an apt punning description of it. Sometimes however the headlines bear little relationship to the ballets or to what the critic has written about them.

Even critics for the quality newspapers, who get more space to elaborate their views, can never be sure how their articles will actually appear. These papers are normally very good about printing their critics' reviews as written, though even in them last-minute cuts may have to be made so that the clinching final paragraph is omitted.

All these things explain why the critic, at any rate for a daily paper, has to be first and foremost an experienced and skilled journalist. My own technique of dictating items quickly from rough notes, or straight out of my head, was developed when I worked as a diplomatic correspondent for the BBC, and had to rush reports from press conferences to the newsroom in time to catch bulletins going out round the clock all over the world. All the knowledge of ballet in the world will not make a critic if he lacks an efficient journalistic technique.

Equally, of course, without knowledge of ballet, even the most efficient journalist is going to be at a loss what to say. I confess that even now there are occasions, particularly with unusual new ballets or with companies I am seeing for the first time, when I come out of the theater still uncertain what I think, let alone what I am going to write. Luckily however my view usually forms of its own accord, subconsciously, during the performance, and the only remaining problem is to drag it out into consciousness and decide how best to express it in the space available.

Critics vary considerably in their attitudes towards a performance. My own method is to forget I am a critic while watching, and to try to be as much as possible an ordinary member of the paying audience. When the performance is over, I ask myself whether or not I enjoyed it and why. I try to avoid asking myself these questions while the performance is in progress and I loathe being asked by other people as soon as the curtain falls, as I find conscious criticism—watching a performance to judge it rather than to enjoy it—blunts and may kill unconscious appreciation. But unfortunately this "noncritical" method is not always possible. If the performance is ending late, I must start planning my review before it ends. If it is a complicated new work, some notes may have to be made while it is in progress. I myself do not normally make notes about dancing and performances, but I do have to note details of scenery and costumes, including colors, for which I have no memory. If someone asks me after a ballet who was the dancer in the green dress, I generally have no idea; if they ask me which dancer played a particular part or did a particular step, I usually know. With a new work, I take a quick look at the scenery as soon as the curtain goes up, and make a quick note; I may make a similar note about any strikingly beautiful or ugly costume when it first appears.

One way of solving these problems is to attend dress rehearsals; many critics in London do this, when permitted by the management. But many other critics are working during the daytime and are not free to attend rehearsals, which are usually in the morning. Having got used to reviewing first performances without such preparation, I am now reluctant to attend rehearsals even when free to do so. I find it difficult to judge a work when it may still be in process of creation, and without a normal audience reaction, and I also find that familiarity with a work from a dress rehearsal blunts the strength of my reaction to the first performance. (Actually the same thing tends to happen the second time I see any new work. After the first performance, I usually feel strong enthusiasm or dislike. After the second, the reaction is weaker and I find myself thinking the work is not quite as good, or as bad, as I first thought. The full-strength reaction usually returns, I am glad to say, for the third and subsequent performances.)

Some critics seem able to adopt a much more detached and overtly critical attitude to performances. They make detailed notes in their programs, and at the end refrain from joining in the applause or any other public reaction. I am told that this last custom, observed by the older generation of music and theater critics as well, was based on the idea that the critic's views should be reserved for his paper and his readers, and should not be indicated in advance even by applause. Like most of my contemporaries, I regard this as both absurd and impractical. As a member of an audience, I would find it almost impossible to withhold applause without isolating myself from the general reaction to the performance in an artificial and undesirable way. I cannot believe that many people are watching to see how enthusiastically I am applauding, so as to save themselves buying the paper.

The critic is inhibited, on the other hand, from booing or any other hostile demonstration, by the fact that he is sitting in seats provided free by the management. I am not a believer in booing anyway, but there have been a few occasions when a work has struck me as so amateurish, tasteless or ludicrous that I have been sorely tempted, and only restrained by recollection of my guest status. It is often thought that critics buy their tickets, or have them bought by their newspapers. In some ways it might be better if this were the case, as then there would be no sense of obligation at all to the theater managements and critics might feel even freer to be completely frank. But most newspapers would not think it worth while buying tickets very often, and the quantity of criticism appearing would be sharply reduced. Some newspapers make it a point of principle never to buy tickets in any circumstances and not to allow their critics to review performances unless invited to do so by the management. They think this makes them safer from the legal point of view. The legal position is obscure but the general view is that professional critics are equally subject to the law of libel and equally protected against allegations of malice whether invited by the management or not. Most of us are willing to buy tickets occasionally, to review particularly interesting performances to which for one reason or another we are not invited. If a theater is not sold out, the management will usually give a critic tickets on request; but several critics have in recent years bought tickets for Fonteyn-Nureyev, the Bolshoi and the Kirov, at Covent Garden, as these performances are usually sold out and the press is only invited to a few of them. In any case critics do not feel inhibited about saying what they think because they receive free tickets from the management. Occasionally press officers or other officials of ballet companies do threaten critics that they will not find it so easy to get tickets if they write "unhelpfully," and there have been one or two incidents when a management has threatened to ban a particular critic altogether, or has actually refused to issue press tickets for a short time.

It is obviously wrong for managements to threaten a critic, or try to ban him, simply because they do not like his views. Private managements are at liberty to stop issuing invitations to a particular critic, if they really think that will serve their best interests. In such cases, they usually allege that the critic has been viciously unfair or is prejudiced against the company in some way. A determined critic who is barred in this way may well buy his own tickets; although managements reserve the right to refuse admission, they rarely go to the length of forcibly preventing a critic from entering the theater. Unfortunately there is little solidarity among critics; a few drama critics boycotted London's Royal Court Theatre when one of their colleagues was struck off the press list, but I doubt if many British or American ballet critics would show similar loyalty. If managements try to ban every critic who writes an unfavorable notice, however, they will soon find themselves with scarcely any reviews. When ballet companies receive public grants or subsidies, they are under a moral obligation to submit to public criticism, and then there can be no justification at all for differentiation between critics or attempts to discriminate against any one of them.

What are likely to be more embarrassing for critics than the threats of managements are the reactions of dancers and choreographers. Ideally perhaps, critics would never meet dancers or choreographers, and would write their notices in blissful ignorance of the effects caused. In practice the ballet world is a small world, and the critic is bound to know personally many of its leading personalities. He meets them socially, he sometimes has to interview them and in fact he needs to talk to them to amplify his understanding and extend his knowledge. Obviously it is more difficult to write a critical review of the work of someone whom one knows and likes. But it can, and sometimes must, be done. I try to avoid meeting dancers and choreographers whose work I definitely do not respect; and the ones whose work is worthy of respect are usually, but not always, sensible enough to accept honest criticism without being offended or allowing it to spoil their personal relationships. Naturally a critic can temper a hostile notice of the work of someone he generally respects by indicating that the artist is only guilty of a temporary lapse.

Many dancers and choreographers are quick to protest, on the one hand, that they take no notice of the critics but are equally quick, on the other, to resent any criticism made of them. Many of them, and also many people connected with the managements of ballet companies, seem to imagine that the critic is there to help them: to give the dancers and choreographers publicity, encouragement and advice, and to persuade people to buy tickets for the company's performances. It is true that sometimes we critics do all these things. But that is not, of course, our main function. We are employed by our newspapers to guide readers, and our first duty must always be to give as fair and honest an appraisal as we can of what we have seen.

This is the answer to the often-asked question whether critics really serve any useful purpose. Some people are sufficiently keen to go and see every new ballet and every new dancer, and to decide for themselves what they think about them. These people do not need critics, though they often enjoy reading reviews if only to have something to disagree with. But there are many more people who go to ballet only occasionally, who want some guidance about which performances to spend their time and money on. And there are others who do not normally go to ballet at all but may occasionally be tempted to attend some particularly intriguing or unusual performance. It is for these two groups of people that the critic is primarily writing. And each critic gradually acquires a small but devoted group of regular readers who put some faith in his judgment.

The balletgoer who reads the reviews regularly will soon discover which critic is best attuned to his wavelength. Some critics are very highbrow and avant-garde, others frankly enjoy more middlebrow and commercial productions. Most critics have their special favorites among ballets and dancers, and their pet hates. I do not mean that these are based on personal relationships, though this regrettably may sometimes happen. I mean that familiarity with particular dancers' and choreographers' work will inevitably condition a critic to expect pleasure or pain from them. This too can affect critical judgment. If a choreographer whose work is normally imitative or boring suddenly does something more original or interesting, he will get exaggeratedly favorable notices out of sheer critical surprise. Some critics can enjoy simple childish jokes, others laugh only at sophisticated wit, and others seem to have no sense of humor at all. Some have a preference for large, established companies; others only enjoy praising small struggling groups and hate anything that already has the smell of success. Some are so anxious not to miss out on any new trend that they praise anything which is "different," however obscure or boring it may seem to most of us: they prefer to risk praising the Emperor's new clothes than to risk being blind to an original creative genius. Others are so conservative that they scarcely ever enjoy anything new. These differences of approach do not matter; they show that the critics, on the whole, are both human and honest. If all the critics thought the same and agreed in all their judgments, it would not only be boring; it would mean the dictatorship of one particular set of standards and rules of taste. There is a danger of this in cities like New York, where one critic, Clive Barnes, dominates the field, as his paper, the New York *Times,* now dominates the field of serious journalism. He has two experienced deputies, Anna Kisselgoff and Don Mc-Donagh, who may not always share his opinions though they must presumably share his general approach. In any case, they are writing in place of him when he is reviewing a play or is otherwise engaged, not offering alternative opinions to him on the same work. Walter Terry, who used to write in the New York *Herald Tribune,* can now be read in the *Saturday Review.* Ballet is also reviewed in other papers and on various local radio and television stations, and there are three specialist ballet magazines (*Dance Magazine, Dance News* and *Ballet Review*) with their own distinctive writers. But London, with a larger number of ballet critics than any other city, is better off for variety of informed criticism, if not for variety of actual ballet. And the London critics have widely different personal approaches to their work, and widely different standards of taste.

This should destroy a widely held myth that the critics all get together and agree on a line. There are of course small groups of critics who are friendly, who in general see eye to eye, and who exchange impressions and information in the intervals. But most critics dislike talking to their colleagues during a performance, or before they have written their notices. Some critics are scarcely on speaking terms with each other anyway. Usually we are all fairly well separated from each other in the theater, and most of us do not like the rare occasions when we have to sit in a solid critical phalanx. Then we are tempted to show off to each other by making supposedly clever comments during the performance. And some of us miss the warmth and stimulation of immediate contact with the normal paying audience.

Admittedly there are certain standards which critics tend to have in common. In general what we like best is good classical dancing and interesting experiment; what gets a bad press is the company whose standards are frankly commercial and which aims for the box office by doing popular classics, usually doing them less well than the major state-supported companies. This is sometimes unfair; companies like the old Cuevas, Festival Ballet, the Dutch National Ballet and the three Canadian companies contain good dancers and give much pleasure to many people. Moreover new companies can only improve their classical style and technique by experience in performing the classics; I am sure that the classics as presented by the Vic-Wells Ballet in the first decade or so of its existence would not seem acceptable to us today but they were invaluable in developing both the company and its audience.

In any case there is nearly always at least one critic to take a different line from the majority. Critics try to train themselves to like all kinds of ballets, even the kinds that do not appeal to them naturally, but they are bound to retain individual tastes and prejudices; anybody who knows a particular critic well can usually predict his reactions. When I go to a first night, I can guess fairly accurately what each of my colleagues will say. Luckily, human unpredictability and caprice do enter as well, so that I probably get a surprise from at least one of them. He may have felt ill or irritable, or unusually happy for personal reasons, and therefore have been more easily elated or depressed. Some of my colleagues claim that they are so detached and professional that they are not affected by such subjective factors as their mood or state of health. Certainly we all try to forget our personal problems as the curtain goes up and we usually succeed in facing each new performance with an open and receptive mind. But we are only human and I do not believe we can be totally unaffected by our moods and private emotions. I find that my reactions are sufficiently consistent for me always to enjoy and admire the same works and dancers, and also to be bored and irritated by the same ones. But the *degree* of enthusiasm or hostility may vary from occasion to occasion, depending on me as well as on the quality of the performance. Of course it is this consistency of view which makes criticism possible, and enables a reader to select a critic who is likely to share his tastes and attitudes, and who is generally to be trusted. And it is surely easier to trust a critic who admits his personal tastes and prejudices than one who tries to fool his readers as well as himself into thinking that he is an inhuman machine. When I admitted in the *Daily Mail* that I dislike Stravinsky's music, I was thought by some people to be foolishly exposing myself to ridicule and by others to be injecting an unnecessary personal note into what should have been an objective review. What I was trying to do was to warn readers that any lack of enthusiasm for the ballet might be due to my subjective dislike of the music, while if I liked the ballet despite the music it must indeed have been an outstanding work or performance. Only by scrupulous honesty and by establishing such a relation of trust with readers can the critic hope to influence them. And each time someone buys a ticket as a result of reading a review, the critic may feel he has given some small service to the world of ballet. If his writing also helps people to a more discriminating appreciation of ballet, rewards dancers or choreographers for their labors, or spurs some of them on to greater efforts, perhaps the service is not too absurdly small.

CHAPTER V

How It Is Done—Britain

BALLET IN BRITAIN TODAY owes its existence indirectly to Diaghilev and directly to two remarkable women, one Irish and one Polish. It was Diaghilev who first showed that a big and artistically ambitious ballet company could be run by a private individual, divorced from the financial support and artistic stranglehold of a state opera house. It was Diaghilev who gave the British public its taste for Russian ballet. And it was with Diaghilev that Ninette de Valois and Marie Rambert served their early apprenticeships. De Valois, born in Ireland as Edris Stannus, and Rambert, born in Poland as Myriam Ramberg, created by their single-minded determination and obstinacy in the face of seemingly insoluble difficulties the two ballet companies which dominated the first decade of British ballet.

De Valois started by providing dancers from her school for plays and operas at the Old Vic, then persuading the equally redoubtable Lilian Baylis to let her stage ballets there. When Sadler's Wells Theatre was reopened by Baylis in 1931, the Vic-Wells Ballet was born. De Valois guided it and watched it grow,

first into the Sadler's Wells Ballet and then into the Royal
Ballet. For the first few years, the company had Alicia Markova
and Anton Dolin, English dancers from Diaghilev's company, as
ballerina and guest premier danseur. When they left in 1935, de
Valois launched the sixteen-year-old Margot Fonteyn (born
Peggy Hookham) on the career which was to lead to her being
acknowledged as the world's greatest ballerina. The Australian
Robert Helpmann became her partner and the company's premier danseur. With the 1939–45 war, the Vic-Wells had to leave
its home theater, performing all over the country and at the
New Theatre in the West End of London as the Sadler's Wells
Ballet. After the war it was invited to become the resident ballet
company at the Royal Opera House, Covent Garden, where it
remains. It is now called The Royal Ballet, following the
granting of a royal charter in 1956. A second company was
formed in 1946, under the name Sadler's Wells Theatre Ballet,
to perform at the ballet's original home theater, to nurture new
dancers and choreographers, and to present ballet to audiences
which could not afford the higher Covent Garden prices. Gradually this company became more and more of a touring organization, with shorter and shorter seasons at Sadler's Wells,
until it severed its connection with that theater altogether and
became the touring section of the Royal Ballet. For a few years
from 1953 there was also the Sadler's Wells Choreographic
Group, which gave Sunday performances at Sadler's Wells Theatre, and provided would-be choreographers, including Kenneth MacMillan, with their first opportunities, using dancers
from the two companies. In recent years a similar scheme, the
Royal Ballet Choreographic Group, has been started by Leslie
Edwards, giving performances in various small theaters, mostly
outside London. It has already launched at least one choreographer of outstanding promise, Geoffrey Cauley. In 1964 yet
another branch of the Royal Ballet, Ballet for All, was started
by Peter Brinson to tour small theaters, colleges and schools
giving introductory lecture-demonstrations on ballet, with dancers from the touring section of the Royal Ballet. This group

does not limit itself to items from the Royal's repertoire, though it is naturally inclined to be dominated by them. It has grown from its original six members into a miniature touring company in its own right, complete with two actors, a pianist and a stage staff. Last, but very far from least, the Royal Ballet organization also includes the flourishing Royal Ballet School, with junior and senior sections, which not only provides the annual intake for the Royal Ballet but also provides dancers for most other British companies and many foreign ones as well. The School's annual matinee at Covent Garden often reaches a higher standard than many professional performances. In addition to all this, there is also an occasional unofficial group of dancers from the Royal Ballet, organized by Petrus Bosman and affectionately known as "Bosman's Follies," which gives concert divertissement performances in small theaters in Britain and abroad.

Thus from small and fairly unpromising beginnings, Ninette de Valois has seen her little ballet company grow into an enormous and powerful branch of the British cultural establishment and become acknowledged as one of the world's half dozen leading ballet companies. British dancers, teachers and choreographers can be found at work all over the world. In the early days, the British public and the British critics thought it could not be done, and de Valois had to contend with enormously discouraging skepticism and prejudice. This may account for the lingering defensiveness of all those connected with the early days of British ballet; they retain a kind of chauvinism, a suspicion of the press, and a resentment of any criticism which sometimes suggests that they themselves have not fully accepted their own success at home and abroad.

Dame Marie Rambert's achievement has been less obvious, but not much less important. Ballet Rambert started a year before the Vic-Wells, and from the beginning its foundress took a particular interest in discovering and fostering new choreographers. She gave Frederick Ashton his first encouragement and opportunities as a choreographer and he worked with her regularly for several years, producing a number of works including

Façade, before he joined de Valois. Rambert's Ballet Club gave regular Sunday performances at the tiny Mercury Theatre, where she also had her school, and it was there too that Antony Tudor made his *Jardin aux Lilas*. Other choreographers discovered and encouraged by Rambert were Andrée Howard and Frank Staff. She also produced a number of notable dancers, especially Harold Turner, who later joined the Vic-Wells and was the original Blue Skater in *Les Patineurs*. Rambert ballerinas have included Maude Lloyd, Sally Gilmour, who did leading classical and dramatic roles during the war years, and Belinda Wright, a delicious soubrette who went on to become a leading ballerina with Festival Ballet.

Ballet Rambert was always short of money and was always losing its artists to larger companies which could afford to pay more, which could provide bigger opportunities and a more secure life, and which were not run so personally by quite such a demanding and sometimes exasperating lady. After touring the country, like Sadler's Wells, during the war, Ballet Rambert somewhat lost its sense of direction in the years immediately after the war. Then in 1955 Rambert's son-in-law, David Ellis, became associate director and the company seemed once again to be taking on a new lease of life. A new ballerina was soon found in the diminutive but dynamic Lucette Aldous, a product of the Royal Ballet School who was not at first accepted by the Royal Ballet. The repertoire was widened to include some full-length nineteenth-century classics which had not then been performed by any British company: Bournonville's *La Sylphide* and Petipa's *Don Quixote*. *Giselle*, always a Rambert specialty because of the care lavished on production details, was retained, as were the early Tudor works, and new works were produced by Rambert's latest choreographic discovery, Norman Morrice. However, audiences up and down the country came to regard Rambert as a scaled-down version of the Royal, the dancers got bored with endless repetitions of a small repertoire, for poor financial rewards, and the company could not afford to expand either the repertoire or its membership. In 1966, Ellis resigned and the company was re-formed, as a much smaller group concentrating entirely on short works, with Morrice as associate director. *Giselle, Coppélia, La Sylphide* and *Don Quixote* were jettisoned and the company soon developed into a very avant-garde and experimental group, on the fringe between ballet and modern dance, so that even the Antony Tudor works began to seem out of place.

While the Vic-Wells expanded into the Royal Ballet and Rambert took its various forms and sizes, other companies came and went. Before the war there was a Markova-Dolin company and Tudor's own London Ballet. During the war there were the Anglo-Polish Ballet and Mona Inglesby's International Ballet. These two companies provided many people, including me, with their first introduction to ballet, but both disintegrated in the postwar period. Since the war there have been Metropolitan Ballet, which first showed us the young Svetlana Beriosova, London Dance Theatre, mainly notable for introducing designers like Norman McDowell and Peter Farmer, and—still with us—Festival Ballet and Western (now Scottish) Theatre Ballet.

Festival Ballet started in 1950 as a supporting company for Markova and Dolin, managed by Dr. Julian Braunsweg. From the beginning the repertoire included both standard classics and contemporary works, and the company developed its own stars and engaged guest artists from abroad. John Gilpin joined the company from Rambert on its foundation, and eventually became not only its leading male dancer and at one period its artistic director but also the outstanding virtuoso male dancer in Britain and one of the leading male dancers in the world. Later, Festival Ballet also gave his first opportunities as a soloist to the outstanding Danish dancer Flemming Flindt, and to the Franco-Russian André Prokovsky, who later joined the Cuevas Ballet and then New York City Ballet but is now back with Festival. Unlike most British companies, Festival has always tended to be strongest on the male side, though at one time the Danish ballerina Toni Lander was a star of the company, excelling particularly in *Etudes,* created by her former husband Harald Lander. Numerous guest ballerinas have appeared with the company including Tamara Toumanova, Yvette Chauviré and Alexandra Danilova; at a time when few foreign companies visited London, British audiences were indebted to Festival Ballet for bringing them some of the greatest names from abroad.

Under Braunsweg's management, Festival Ballet specialized in long continental tours, paying repeated visits to France, Italy and Spain, and also touring eastern Europe and Latin America. In London, they appeared every Christmas and summer at the Royal Festival Hall (a happy coincidence of nomenclature, since the company had its name before any question of a season at the Hall had arisen) with seasons which attracted many tourists and people anxious to see the Festival Hall, as well as regular balletgoers.

After surviving various financial crises, Dr. Braunsweg was finally forced to resign from the company in 1965 when an enormous loss had been incurred on a spectacular new production of *Swan Lake.* A new board was formed, with Arts Council encouragement, and Donald Albery, an experienced theatrical impresario who had managed the Sadler's Wells Ballet's seasons at the New Theatre during the war, took over direction of the company. Then in 1968 Albery in his turn resigned, to be succeeded by Wilfred Stiff as administrator and the former Sadler's Wells ballerina Beryl Grey as artistic director. They had some enterprising ideas, such as inviting the young American choreographers Eliot Feld and Gerald Arpino to mount works for the company, and they revived John Taras's *Piège de Lumière,* formerly in the Cuevas repertoire. But they also allowed Jack Carter to add *Coppélia* to his list of revised classics and were forced to drop Feld's *Meadowlark* from the provincial tours because of local theater managements insisting on the well-known classics. Arpino proved unable to accept his invitation. Despite good intentions about varying the repertoire, the mixture remained very much as before though the company was less contented and the principal dancers were involved in some well-publicized arguments with Miss Grey. There has also been a return to Dr. Braunsweg's policy of engaging guest artists: in the summer of 1969, Mimi Paul of American Ballet Theatre, Lynn Seymour of MacMillan's Berlin company, and Peter Martins of New York City Ballet all appeared with the company while other guests were also booked for a very Braunsweg-style gala.

There could hardly be a greater contrast with Festival than Western Theatre Ballet, which has now become Scottish Theatre Ballet. The company was called *Western* both because it was started in the west of England, with a base in Bristol, and because its founder was a dynamic lady called Elizabeth West. It was called *Theatre* Ballet because it was intended to concentrate on ballets with dramatic and theatrical content rather than on abstract dancing. After Elizabeth West's tragic death in an accident in Switzerland, the company was run by Peter Darrell, a choreographer who had been associated with her in directing the company from the beginning. His penchant is for heavy dramatic works, often about perverted sex, though perhaps his most popular and successful ballet has been *Mods and Rockers,* which contrasts two teenage gangs dancing in a discothèque, to Beatles music. Western Theatre Ballet's occasional attempts at classical pas de deux, or at Fokine's *Carnaval,* have never been particularly successful, as the company has always been more concerned with production techniques and dramatic ability than with pure dancing skill. In 1968, Western Theatre Ballet arranged to move to Glasgow, in association with Scottish Opera, changing its name to Scottish Theatre Ballet. In 1969 Festival Ballet was invited to give its summer seasons at the Coliseum, which had already become the home of the Sadler's Wells Opera, instead of the Festival Hall.

The pattern of British ballet at the end of the 1960's thus consisted of the Royal Ballet resident at Covent Garden, with occasional foreign tours; the touring section of the Royal Ballet, with occasional seasons at Covent Garden; Festival Ballet which was finding a new London home at the Coliseum, a large and admirable theater for the dance; Ballet Rambert which gave short twice-yearly London seasons at the tiny Jeannetta Cochrane Theatre and also toured the provinces; and Scottish Theatre Ballet, based in Glasgow but still intending to tour the whole of Britain and to give London seasons at Sadler's Wells. A new ballet company, Northern Dance Theatre, was formed in 1969 by Laverne Meyer (formerly of Western Theatre Ballet) in Manchester and there were one or two other small companies, of no artistic importance, which toured the smaller provincial theaters. There was also the Ballet for All group, which filled a valuable educative and introductory function.

Everyone agreed that this pattern was far from ideal, but there was little agreement about how it could be improved, or about what an ideal pattern would be. The two outstanding problems were: how to get more and better ballet to people living far away from London, and how to provide opportunities for new choreographers. In the field of straight drama, new theaters doing interesting experimental work and achieving a high standard of performance in the classics have arisen in recent years in many provincial centers. Politicians and sociologists have been telling us for some time that too much of our cultural life, as well as too much of our economic and political life, is concentrated in London. Devolution has become a watchword and even the word "provinces" has been virtually outlawed, as too patronizing. We are now supposed to speak euphemistically of "the regions."

Unfortunately this change of nomenclature cannot, or should not, disguise the fact that taste in ballet outside London remains obstinately provincial. All companies have found that the only sure way to fill theaters on tour is to give the well-known classics. Not even lesser-known classics like *La Sylphide* or *Don Quixote*, or new versions of the classics like *Beatrix* or *The Two Pigeons* can be relied on to find an audience. The Royal Ballet had a long and hard struggle to win provincial audiences for *La Fille Mal Gardée;* although they have now partially succeeded it is still less of an attraction than the long-established works. The way to empty a theater in the provinces is to announce a mixed program of modern ballets; when Rambert and Western Theatre Ballet gave "world premieres" of their latest offerings in Bournemouth or Bury St. Edmunds, audiences remained indifferent and the theaters stayed dismally empty. In Glasgow and Manchester, two of Britain's largest cities, even the Royal Ballet has difficulty in filling the theater for anything except *Swan Lake, Sleeping Beauty, Giselle,* and *Coppélia.*

These facts make it difficult to have much faith in the various schemes which are now so fashionable for setting up ballet companies to be based in provincial cities. If audiences in Glasgow or Manchester are insufficient to support a fortnight's visit by the Royal Ballet, it seems unlikely that they would support several months by a local group. The prospects are made worse by the inevitability of the local group being less famous, and probably less talented, than a visiting company from London. They are worst of all if the local group is to be small and experimental, and unable or unwilling to attempt the classics at all. Even if curiosity does attract some people once, they are unlikely to be hooked by the more experimental and avant-garde ballets in which these regional companies specialize. A very sophisticated balletgoer or critic may be interested to see every new experiment in ballet, even if it is not particularly enjoyable or does not contain anything very remarkable in the way of dancing. There *is* a small public for this sort of thing in London. But outside London the public for it is so small that it is unlikely to provide even the nucleus of an audience.

It is usually argued, in answer to these obvious facts, that the very existence of a resident ballet company in a city will ultimately build up a sophisticated and discriminating audience. This may be true. The present large public for opera and ballet in London was to some extent created by the existence and pioneering work of the resident ballet and opera companies at Sadler's Wells and Covent Garden. Even so, London at present supports only one resident ballet company. How long would it take a smaller city to build up an audience to do so? There is a chance that a section of the Royal Ballet, or Festival Ballet, might succeed in making a home for itself in one of the larger provincial cities. There seems to me to be very much less chance for companies like Rambert or Scottish Theatre Ballet, which have not got the resources (or the inclination) to provide the sort of ballets or the sort of dancing which provincial audiences most want to see. Yet this is the type of company which people generally think of setting up in the provinces.

It follows from all this that setting up ballet companies outside London is unlikely to solve the second problem, that of providing opportunities for new choreographers. The public outside London is not going to rush to see new works, whether by known or unknown choreographers. And nothing could be more dispiriting and unhelpful for choreographers and dancers than to try out their wares in empty houses. Quite apart from the financial disaster involved in running a company for any length of time without much box-office support, it is doubtful if it is artistically desirable. In any case established choreographers wanting to try out new ideas would probably not want to work with minor companies or with comparatively untalented dancers. It seems clear that the place for new choreography and experiment must be London.

To this it may be objected that London already has too much cultural life, too much experiment and novelty, and that even the London public cannot cope with all that is going on, especially in the worlds of theater and music. But whereas London has two resident opera companies, playing for most of the year at Covent Garden and the Coliseum, it has only one resident ballet company, at Covent Garden. Ballet performances there are given only three or four times a week, alternating with opera, and are always full or almost full. Many people have given up going to ballet at Covent Garden, either because they find it too difficult to get tickets, or because the prices are too high, or even because they do not like the slightly snob "establishment" atmosphere of the Royal Opera House.

They would go to ballet if it were more accessible, just as some people prefer opera at the Coliseum, where it is given every night of the week. The number of opera performances in London must be between fifty percent and a hundred percent more than the number of ballet performances.

In the days of the old Sadler's Wells Theatre Ballet, there was a significant regular public for ballet at Sadler's Wells, which enjoyed seeing lesser-known dancers at the beginning of their careers and trying out new ballets. Since then the London public for novelty and experiment of all kinds has grown, as witnessed by the success of various visiting American modern dance groups. London could easily support, and indeed now needs, a second resident ballet company. This could be similar to the old Sadler's Wells Theatre Ballet: essentially a classical company, with well-trained dancers and experienced artistic direction, but able to afford lots of new ballets and production ideas. This simply is not practicable at the Royal Opera House, where every new production costs a great deal; if there can be only two or three new productions a year, very few of them can afford to be flops.

An alternative method of providing more ballet performances, with more new productions, would be for the Royal Ballet to leave Covent Garden and set up in a theater of its own. There is no rule which prescribes that ballet must be in an opera house, or must alternate with opera performances; although that is the custom in Moscow, Leningrad, and most continental cities, it is not exactly the case with New York City Ballet. The Royal Ballet would undoubtedly gain in certain ways from leaving the Royal Opera House. It would be able to give more opportunities to its dancers and present a wider repertoire and it would not have to fight with the opera company for stage rehearsal time, orchestral rehearsals and the allocation of available funds. Far more has been spent on opera than on ballet at Covent Garden, although for many years it was only the ballet that attracted anything like capacity houses. It is still only the ballet that has an international reputation and constantly earns dollars on its tremendously successful American tours. Moreover sight lines at Covent Garden, though not as bad as in many continental opera houses, are far from ideal. The stalls at the Theatre Royal, Drury Lane and at the London Coliseum give a better view of the dancers' feet and the cheaper seats are more central than at Covent Garden, where many of them only have a view of part of the stage. The stage itself at the Coliseum is actually bigger than at Covent Garden, though not all of it is at present in use.

Ultimately, therefore, the Royal Ballet might well find a home in a separate theater from the Royal Opera. But economic factors are likely to make this impracticable in the foreseeable future. In any case there is also much to be said for some real competition for the Royal Ballet on its home ground, so that it should not become too complacent in its quasimonopolistic position. Moscow has competition for the Bolshoi from the Stanislavsky company, Leningrad for the Kirov from the Maly, and New York has competition between New York City Ballet and numerous other companies both American and foreign.

Companies touring the provinces have found increasing difficulty in getting engagements, because of the dwindling number of large theaters outside London, and also in getting audiences. Too many companies have been chasing each other around the country to the same small group of theaters, with very similar productions of the same ballets. The transformation of Rambert from a classical into a modern experimental company meant that it was no longer competing with the Royal and Festival, and could go to smaller theaters, where it was in competition with Western Theatre Ballet instead. One touring classical company is probably enough, and the touring section of the Royal Ballet seemed best equipped to fill this role. The very name Royal Ballet was a major box office attraction, even if it was slightly deceptive; many people imagined they were seeing the actual Covent Garden company. Still, the Covent Garden stars did dance with the touring section in rotation, and the productions were probably as near to the Covent Garden versions as was feasible in touring conditions.

Early in 1970, however, the management of the Royal Ballet decided to abolish the touring company and to integrate all the dancers in one London-based ensemble. This decision was partly economic; it was hoped to save £100,000 ($240,000) a year on touring costs. It was partly surrender to the increasing difficulty of finding suitable theaters and rehearsal facilities on tour. And it was partly an artistic decision taken by John Field and Kenneth MacMillan, who were about to succeed Ashton as codirectors of the Royal Ballet.

The plan was that the full Royal Ballet would tour the larger provincial theaters for eight to ten weeks each spring with as close an imitation as possible of the Covent Garden repertoire, while smaller-scale tours would be undertaken in autumn and winter by a group of twenty-five dancers, selected in rotation from the main company. This group will perform short ballets, including new works and revivals, but not full-length classics, classical excerpts or even classical pas de deux. It is also intended to give its own London seasons, at Sadler's Wells or some similar theater.

This decision took the ballet world by surprise and it is too early to say how it will work out and what effect it will have on other companies. There is certainly a great deal to be said for integrating members of the Royal Ballet into one group, so that none of them will be subjected to the exhaustion and strain of constant touring. Audiences everywhere should now get fairer shares of the available talent, dancers should get more opportunities, and the new scheme may well provide the much-needed showcase for new choreography. But it is extremely doubtful whether an adequate audience will be found in the provinces, even if the group includes the Royal Ballet's biggest stars, and it is not certain that there is either a theater or an audience in London to sustain long seasons of the kind envisaged. The twenty-five dancers will probably have to develop into something more like the old Sadler's Wells Theatre Ballet, with a repertoire including classical excerpts and pas de deux, if they are to win an audience of their own.

Ultimately the management of Covent Garden hopes to build a second opera house, adjacent to the present one, in the space to be vacated by the fruit and vegetable market. If this eventually materializes, it will at least make possible something like an adequate number of ballet performances, though it will extend the quasimonopolistic position of the Royal Ballet instead of providing competition for it. A new opera house, or at any rate a new ballet house, is highly desirable, but the earlier plan for an entirely separate building on South Bank still seems preferable. In any case, the new building is a long-term plan, and it may turn out to be a pipe dream. In the meanwhile, there will be no ballet at Covent Garden in April, May and part of June, and it will presumably become even more difficult to obtain tickets for the classics when they are performed.

It is ironic that one of the people responsible for complementing the decision to abolish the Royal Ballet's touring company is John Field, who has done so much over the years to give it a life and a personality of its own. No doubt he will ensure that his best dancers and productions will survive, though some will undoubtedly be lost in the changeover.

Field's codirector, Kenneth MacMillan, will of course be undertaking a great deal of new choreography, both for the large company at Covent Garden and for the new touring group. But duumvirates seldom work, and one cannot help wondering whether this one will be an exception. Field has proved that he is a skilled administrator and director of a company, and makes no claims to be a choreographer. Choreographers generally find administration a distraction and a bore. There could therefore be a clear division of responsibilities between the two men. If, however, both have overall responsibility for running the company, there could be clashes about selection of dancers and choreographers and about choice of repertoire, and the conflict could make codirection impossible. MacMillan's ideas of bringing in foreign male dancers as members of the company and of personally rechoreographing the classics, may or may not be agreeable to Field; they seem certain to rouse strong opposition in the company and among some of its most influential supporters so that one cannot help wondering whether in fact MacMillan will be able to have his way.

Indeed there is some doubt how much any director of the Royal Ballet can have his way, controlled as he is at Covent Garden by the General Administrator, the Board and various specialist subcommittees. Certainly choreographers, however distinguished, cannot always have *their* way. Cranko's *Eugene Onegin* ballet to Tchaikovsky's music and MacMillan's *Song of the Earth* were both vetoed by the Covent Garden music committee before they were successfully created in Stuttgart. Some people thought that Cranko, after his enormous success in building up and running a company in Stuttgart, would have been the obvious choice to succeed Ashton as director but it is extremely unlikely that he would have accepted all these controls and committees. The management of Covent Garden has always claimed that the ballet is given all it wants, and has no complaints, but a really tough director determined to get a larger slice of the available resources would probably soon run into difficulties.

Whoever directs the Royal Ballet, and whatever changes they may make, there is no doubt that it will continue to be Britain's major classical company. As such, it seems likely that it will continue to hold the main responsibility for providing classical ballet in the provinces, as well as in London.

All this discussion is based on the assumption that public subsidy will continue at least at its present level, even if it is not increased. The fact that it seems reasonable to make this assumption is an indication of the extent to which the situation of the arts in Britain has altered during the past twenty or thirty years. Before the 1939–45 war, public subsidy of the arts was unknown and such enterprises as the Old Vic, and the Sadler's Wells Opera and Ballet, had to struggle as best they could on shoestring budgets provided by private donors. The use of taxpayers' money to support the arts started as a daring experiment during the war with the formation of the Council for the Encouragement of Music and the Arts (C.E.M.A.) . This grew into what is now the Arts Council, which receives a government grant and is responsible for distributing it to theater, opera and ballet companies, musicians, artists, authors and poets. It is now totally accepted by the main political parties and by the mass of public opinion that this must continue because culture is a vital part of the life of a nation and because private donors no longer exist on anything like the scale needed to provide it. It is also widely accepted by people concerned with British cultural life that the extent of the money available to the Arts Council at present is quite inadequate, comparing badly with the amount of public money spent on the arts in most European countries. But it seems unlikely that Britain's economic situation will permit any great increase in expenditure on the arts in the near future any more than on any other sector of public life.

Admittedly, voices are occasionally heard protesting that opera and ballet are very expensive minority arts which do not justify the money spent on them. One reason that the Arts Council is so keen to support tours outside London and is so sympathetic to the idea of resident ballet companies in provincial cities, is to counter the criticism that an unfair proportion of the money available is spent on London. As more people get the opportunity to see good ballet, the audience for it increases and its appeal becomes less of a minority one. But none of the fine arts, in any society, are likely to win a mass audience, and that is why they have to be carefully nurtured by rich patrons or by the state if they are to survive. Luckily it is no longer necessary to argue the case for the survival of the living arts, and probably no longer necessary to argue for ballet as one of those arts.

CHAPTER VI

How It Is Done—The United States

THE AMERICAN taste for classical ballet, like the British, was first aroused by Diaghilev, Pavlova and Nijinsky; Diaghilev's company only visited the States when he was quarreling with Nijinsky and the company was consequently in a crisis and not at its peak, but nevertheless the seeds of a native ballet were sown. Ballet was developed and stimulated in the thirties by dancers and ballet masters who had worked with Diaghilev and by various forms of Ballets Russes which to some extent inherited his mantle. Sol Hurok brought Colonel de Basil and René Blum's company to New York in 1933, with the child ballerinas Baronova, Riabouchinska and Toumanova, and with many ballets by Massine, who also danced in the company. De Basil's dancers were frequently in the States during the next fifteen years, while Sergei Denham's rival Ballet Russe de Monte Carlo was based there for most of the second world war and the years immediately after it. One of Pavlova's partners, Mikhail Mordkin, also formed a company in the thirties and one of his dancers, Lucia Chase, was later to launch Ballet Theatre.

It was a Diaghilev protégé, George Balanchine, who in 1933 founded the School of American Ballet, which is the official school of New York City Ballet today. From this school grew the American Ballet, which made its New York debut in 1935 with an all-Balanchine program and remained attached to the Metropolitan Opera House till 1938. In 1936 Balanchine's business associate and principal fund raiser Lincoln Kirstein formed another company, Ballet Caravan, which joined forces with American Ballet in 1941 for a South American tour. After the war, in 1946, Balanchine and Kirstein formed Ballet Society, which in 1948 moved into New York City Center and became New York City Ballet. It was in 1950, when New York City Ballet paid its first visit to Covent Garden, that the company achieved international recognition, much as the British Sadler's Wells Ballet had done at the Metropolitan the previous year. The New York company was not then as finished and mature as the British one, but it has continued since to make rapid progress both in breadth of repertoire and in technical standards of dancing, blossoming still further after its transfer to the large and opulent State Theater in 1964. It is now without any doubt one of the world's great classical companies.

Its most important rival in America has always been Ballet Theatre, founded in 1940 by Lucia Chase and Richard Pleasant; during and immediately after the war years, Ballet Theatre was the leading American company. It was the first one to dance at Covent Garden (in 1946) and also the first to dance in the Soviet Union (in 1960). But Ballet Theatre's fortunes have fluctuated a great deal depending to some extent on Miss Chase's ability to raise money. Sometimes it has closed down altogether; and it has not developed a major choreographer or a distinctive style of its own. However it is now again in the ascendant, giving regular New York seasons at both the Metropolitan Opera and the Brooklyn Academy of Music, and it is to be resident for part of the year at the new Kennedy Center in Washington, D.C. In 1970 Ballet Theatre was provided with permanent rehearsal facilities at New York City Center.

Balletic activity started in San Francisco more or less simultaneously with New York. The San Francisco Ballet was founded in 1933 by Adolf Bolm, a Russian dancer who had also worked with Pavlova and Diaghilev. This company was taken over four years later by an American of Danish origin, Willam Christensen, the brother of the company's present director, Lew Christensen. At one time the San Francisco Ballet was regarded as one of the most important American companies and it produced a number of dancers who became stars in New York. But it seems to have declined in recent years and is no longer regularly attached to the San Francisco Opera House.

Bolm also worked in Chicago, where he choreographed for the opera ballet back in the twenties. The dancers toured independently and there is now a long tradition of Chicago opera ballet. Ruth Page—an American who worked with Bolm and with the Diaghilev company and also with the Central-European modern dancer Harald Kreutzberg—ran a series of such companies, known at various times as the Page-Stone Ballet, the Chicago Ballet, the Chicago Opera Ballet, and most recently as International Ballet. In the early days Miss Page was a pioneer of modern dance; some of the photographs of her dancing in a sack look remarkably like some of the experiments which are considered modern today. In recent years Miss Page's company has had a popular classical image, performing her danced versions of operas and operettas and employing many well-known European guest artists. She brought a large number of dancers and choreographers to the States; Flemming Flindt's *The Lesson* (based on Ionesco's play), for example, was given its first American performances by her company. In 1969, however, financial and administrative problems forced Miss Page to cancel her company's Chicago season and national tour, and the dancers dispersed. This, followed by the death of her husband

Tom Fisher, who had played a vital role in the company's business affairs, cast doubts on its future, and on the future of ballet in Chicago.

The future of ballet in New York, on the other hand, seems secure. There are three theaters which regularly provide stages for ballet, so that there are often three companies performing simultaneously in the city; in addition, the Metropolitan Opera House has occasional seasons by touring companies from abroad like the Bolshoi, the Stuttgart and the Royal, and by Ballet Theatre. Ballet Theatre also appears at the Brooklyn Academy of Music, as does the Harkness Ballet. Eliot Feld's new American Ballet Company and the modern dance companies of Alvin Ailey and Merce Cunningham are officially resident there. The only thing wrong with this charming and ambitious Brooklyn theater is that inhabitants of Manhattan and other parts of New York apparently regard a bus or subway trip to Brooklyn as more difficult or more dangerous than a flight to Washington or Boston. This baffles the visiting London critic, used to traveling similar distances to theaters in Hampstead, Stratford, Islington or Richmond as a matter of routine. The City Center, formerly the home of New York City Ballet, is a more convenient but less agreeable theater; it now houses the City Center Joffrey Ballet as well as lending its stage to various visiting modern dance companies.

Robert Joffrey has run a succession of ballet companies since 1956. From 1962 he was sponsored by the wealthy Mrs. Rebekah Harkness and the Harkness Foundation, until she formed her own company in 1964. The present Joffrey Ballet is run by a triumvirate consisting of Joffrey himself, his cochoreographer Gerald Arpino, and Alexander Ewing who mainly looks after the business and administrative sides. But all three of them share major policy decisions, which must be a unique arrangement. The Joffrey Ballet had an enormous success at the Vienna Festival in 1969.

The Harkness Ballet has also visited European festivals—at

Monte Carlo and Spoleto in Italy; in its early years, under the artistic direction of George Skibine it was seen more frequently in Europe than in the United States.

It is now based in New York, with lavish headquarters at Harkness House which is also the home of the Harkness School and until recently housed a second ballet company, the Harkness Youth Dancers. The main company has had a whole series of directors; most recently it seemed to be doing well under the joint direction of Lawrence Rhodes, its leading male dancer, and Benjamin Harkarvy, formerly of Netherlands Dance Theatre. But in the spring of 1970 Mrs. Harkness suddenly dismissed both of them, recalled the company from the middle of a European tour, and announced that it would be merged with the Youth Dancers under her personal artistic direction. Ben Stevenson, an experienced British dancer and teacher who had been running the Youth Dancers, was named resident choreographer, shortly after his successful production of Prokofiev's *Cinderella* for the National Ballet in Washington. But it is impossible to say whether the Harkness Ballet in its new form will play an important role in the American dance scene. The company's main problem has always been to find a repertoire and an image to match its talented dancers and its ample financial resources, and to suit Mrs. Harkness's wish for a basically classical company.

Eliot Feld's American Ballet Company, which made its debut at the Spoleto Festival in 1969, had a most successful inaugural season at Brooklyn Academy in the fall of the same year. It is too early to say whether it will survive, but the omens are good.

Most of these companies make extensive tours in addition to their New York seasons, though in general they now try to avoid the traditional one-night stands, which are very exhausting and make high quality performances difficult, if not impossible. New York City Ballet scarcely tours at all, though it has a summer home in a specially built theater at Saratoga Springs. Individual stars of New York City Ballet appear as guest artists with other companies, especially companies which take advantage of Mr. Balanchine's generosity in allowing them to stage his works. (The Balanchine empire is also extending into Europe; he is now personally supervising the ballet in Geneva.) These smaller companies in their turn do a lot of touring, though the demand for tours may conceivably be reduced as more and more companies are successfully established around the country.

Washington, D.C., for example, already has two companies and will have a third when Ballet Theatre is installed at Kennedy Center. The National Ballet is a fully professional group under the direction of Frederic Franklin, a British dancer who was for years the partner of the Russian ballerina Alexandra Danilova. In 1969 the National Ballet persuaded Fonteyn to tour with them most successfully in a production of *La Sylphide.* The Washington Ballet, which is amateur, is under the direction of Mary Day and is an offshoot of her school. Both companies actually perform *The Nutcracker* simultaneously at Christmas!

The Pennsylvania Ballet, under the direction of Barbara Weisberger (not to be confused with Catherine Littlefield's Philadelphia Ballet of the thirties), is also linked with her school, but it is a fully professional company which has already, in a few years, reached a remarkably high standard. Its headquarters are in Philadelphia but it also tours; for example it filled the gap caused by the demise of Miss Page's company, performing *The Nutcracker* in Chicago at the end of 1969. The Boston Ballet is also now professional and tours extensively; like most American companies, it too is linked with a school, both under the direction of E. Virginia Williams.

The Washington Ballet is the only one of these companies forming part of the growing complex known as regional ballet. This is extremely confusing for the British visitor, as in Britain "regional" is the currently fashionable euphemism for provincial, and all culture outside London is called regional. In the States, however, regional ballet is the term applied specifically to amateur companies, associated with ballet schools and normally consisting mainly of girls of high-school age. They are grouped together for advice and adjudication in the National Association for Regional Ballet and their activities are fully reported in *Dance Magazine,* whose associate editor, Doris Hering, takes a special interest in them. Inevitably, standards vary widely. Small groups of dancers who are really just students sometimes make the mistake of advertising themselves overgrandly as ballet companies; audiences cannot always be sure whether they are being invited to watch a proper professional ensemble or some enthusiastic teenagers. One tiny group of students which I saw even proudly billed four premieres in its first public performance, but I am afraid the choreography was mostly as amateurish as the dancing. In Sacramento, California, there are two "companies"; in Houston, Texas, there are about half a dozen. It is obvious that the dissipation of talent must be enormous and it seems a pity that rival schools cannot at least combine their efforts for their public performances.

In addition to regional ballet, there is also a rapid growth of ballet in the universities. Many American universities are fortunate in having large funds and admirable theaters. When the Stuttgart Ballet toured California in 1969, it appeared at the University of California at Berkeley rather than in San Francisco itself. Ballet West, the company associated with the University of Utah in Salt Lake City, is directed by Willam Christensen, who formerly ran the San Francisco Ballet. It may easily become a fully professional company and fill an important role in the West. The University of Cincinnati also has a flourishing dance department and recently engaged Miss P. W. Manchester, the well-known British critic and dance historian, and Markova, the former ballerina, as teachers. Anton Dolin is to teach and stage ballets at the University of Indiana. The University of Illinois has an ambitious project for a Foundation for the Dance, to be linked with the British Royal Academy of Dancing and to be under the active patronage of Margot Fonteyn. John Hart, a former leading soloist and then associate director of the Royal Ballet, now teaches at the In-

ternational University in San Diego, California, while Stanley
Holden, a star of the Royal Ballet until 1969, is director of
the Dance Academy at the Los Angeles Music Center. The
catalogue is endless.

Indeed the pattern of American ballet is now so elaborate,
and so rapidly changing, that it is difficult to keep track of it.
When I came to the States in 1969 I hoped to see a flourishing
professional company in Atlanta, Georgia. But I discovered that
soon after going professional it had run into difficulties and
disbanded, at least temporarily. I heard of interesting work
being done in many places: in Buffalo, New York, where
Kathleen Crofton, a British teacher, had enterprisingly persuaded Bronislava Nijinska to revive some of her ballets; in
Minneapolis where Loyce Hourlton's Minnesota Dance Theater evidently gives interesting and promising performances at
weekends; in both Houston and Dallas, Texas. In San Francisco
I saw a performance called Dance Amalgam which united West-
Coast ballet companies and modern dance groups and whetted
my appetite to see more of some of them.

It is also impossible to keep track of the different ways in
which American ballet is financed. Ballet can virtually never be
self-supporting; it must either be financed by wealthy individuals (who are becoming rarer, even in the States), by private
businesses or charitable foundations, or by various forms of
public subsidy. Both the Ford and Rockefeller Foundations
have made grants to ballet companies; in 1963 the Ford Foundation distributed about $7,750,000 to ballet, mainly to New
York City Ballet and its affiliated School of American Ballet,
but also to companies in Boston, Houston, Philadelphia, Salt
Lake City and Washington, most of which work in close association with Balanchine, staging his ballets and borrowing his
dancers as guests. In 1965 the Ford Foundation made a further
grant to New York City Ballet and the School. These grants,
which were for ten-year periods, were originally much criticized
for giving Balanchine too dominant a position in American
ballet, and particularly for neglecting Ballet Theatre. But they

were rather a recognition of the preeminent position Balanchine already held, and at least they marked a significant step forward in the semipublic patronage of ballet. The Ford Foundation has also given a substantial grant to the Joffrey Ballet.

Both the National Endowment for the Arts and the various State Councils on the Arts can and sometimes do give money to ballet, though their funds have until now always been extremely limited. Nancy Hanks, who became chairman of the National Endowment in 1969, is extremely active and seems likely to expand its activities. Soon after she took office she announced grants to Ballet Theatre, New York City Ballet and the Joffrey Ballet, and to the Brooklyn Academy of Music, and the Endowment also invited applications from choreographers for grants to help them develop new works. One form of grant which may prove particularly valuable is a contribution towards the salaries of directors of development—given to both Ballet Theatre and Joffrey—who may in their turn more than pay for themselves in improved administrative and business efficiency.

In addition to these various domestic grants, American ballet companies normally get State Department grants for their foreign tours. Such a grant came to the rescue of Ballet Theatre at one time. But of course this form of aid depends on official policy about when and where foreign tours should be made, and the State Department may also have views about what constitutes a suitable repertoire to project the American way of life.

President Nixon made it clear, in his message to Congress of December 10, 1969, that the Federal Government now fully accepts the need for public subsidy of the arts and wants to increase the amount available. While saying that Federal subsidy would not replace private support, he drew attention to "the acute financial crisis in which many of our privately supported cultural institutions now find themselves." And he specifically mentioned the dance as one of the fields to be supported. It seems likely that public subsidy of all the arts, including ballet, will eventually become as normal a part of American cultural life as it has already become of British.

But there is as yet no guarantee of this. Ballet companies must still rely heavily on their private backers and organizations of supporters, and cannot plan with any confidence very far ahead. Nobody can know whether the present American ballet boom is transitory or permanent. Some people in both Britain and the United States claim that ballet in its conventional form is outmoded, and that live performances in the theater will be replaced by television or the cinema. These certainly do seem, superficially, more practical media for bringing ballet to a much wider audience at much lower cost. But the enthusiastic audiences all over the States for live ballet, and especially for the big classical companies, do not suggest that this will happen.

There is no doubt that both the cinema and television can be extremely useful adjuncts to ballet. Film, as we have seen, can be used to record ballets as an aid to their subsequent revival. Films like those of the Royal Ballet's *Ondine* and the Bolshoi's *Giselle* (made on stage at Covent Garden, with Ulanova) give people who do not have the opportunity to see the live performances a fairly good idea of what they are missing. Individual pas de deux can be exciting and effective on the screen: cinema audiences frequently burst into spontaneous applause after the Fonteyn-Nureyev *Corsair* pas de deux in the film *An Evening with the Royal Ballet*. Dance techniques and training can be very well shown on the screen; the ballet-school sequences in the Bolshoi Ballet film, *The Secret of Success,* were particularly successful and one of the best dance films ever made is Martha Graham's *A Dancer's World,* which shows her company practicing in the studio, accompanied by a slightly pretentious but illuminating commentary by Graham herself. And of course ballets can be specially created for the cinema, using trick effects, constantly moving cameras and all the other devices at the disposal of a film director. Many attempts to do this have fallen between two stools, ending up as poor ballet and poor cinema, but one of the earliest efforts in this genre, the fantasy *Red Shoes,* starring Moira Shearer, Robert Helpmann and Léonide Massine, showed how well cinema ballet can be done.

The same things are true of television. Several stage ballets have been filmed or telerecorded and shown more or less in their original form on television. Ballets are also created specially for television: among the most notable are *The Lesson* and other ballets by Flemming Flindt and some of the ballets specially made for French and German television by Juan Corelli, who specializes in this field. One of the most successful ballet programs on British television was a demonstration of a Royal Ballet class. Because it is not necessary to see the whole studio at once, but only to concentrate on certain dancers, classes lend themselves particularly well to the screen.

The main trouble with ballet on the screen, and especially on the comparatively small television screen, is that either one is shown the general pattern and shape of the ballet, without being able to recognize individual dancers or see their facial expressions, or one finds oneself watching a dancer's face or foot and wondering what is happening on the rest of the stage. Sometimes the dancers move so quickly that they jump out of sight. Sometimes we are shown a face when we want to see a foot, or one dancer reacting to another, when we want to see them both. We are shown dancers when we want to see the scenery and, when we *are* shown the scenery, it either looks artificial and stagy or is inappropriately realistic, out of keeping with the artificial conventions of the dance. Television is worse than the cinema: screens are smaller, so that we can see even less, sound quality is poorer so that the music sounds tinny, and many people have not yet got color sets so that the visual spectacle and three-dimensional effect are lost.

Even in the theater, of course, we have to select what we watch. We may focus on the ballerina, or on a group of the corps de ballet, or watch the stage picture as a whole. And the inspired film director, or the one who shares our particular approach, may persuade us that his choice would have been ours. Even so, a film record of a stage ballet can only be a second best for those who have seen the original. An essential part of the theatrical appeal of ballet is the element of circus excitement. The audience is always wondering, even if unconsciously, whether a dancer will fall, whether a particularly difficult feat will be pulled off, how the interpretation will vary from previous occasions. Direct contact between audience and dancers is particularly important when the dancers include a star, whose personality must make a far greater impact live than when seen through the lens of a camera. And of course the original choreographer would have arranged his ballet quite differently if he had been making it for the screen. *Swan Lake* or *Giselle* depend on their skillful exploitation of theatrical convention; nobody would ever have dreamed of making them, in that form, for the screen.

No doubt new ways of presenting ballets and other forms of dance on the screen are still to be found. Alwin Nikolais now dislikes transferring his stage works to television, pointing out that equally remarkable, but different, effects can be achieved by the fullest use of the special techniques and tricks of the camera. Objects and people can disappear, or blend into each other, or fly about unaided in the air. Television and cinema ballets can be intriguing and entertaining, but they cannot be the same as stage ballets. And those of us who love and value stage ballets, in all their forms, will therefore be determined to ensure that there are going to be theaters in which they can be performed, live dancers and orchestras to give the performances, and live audiences to appreciate them.

Part Three

THE APPEAL OF BALLET

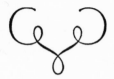

CHAPTER I

The American Scene

ONCE THE EUROPEAN VISITOR has learned to cope with the sheer quantity of American ballet, especially in New York, he can then turn to being astonished by its quality. The quality is twofold: quality of dancing, which is surprising enough, and quality of choreography, which is much more surprising. American dancers have always been thought of abroad as cool and athletic, an image fostered partly by Balanchine's use of his ballerinas and partly by ballerinas like Rosella Hightower or Lupe Serrano, who seemed happier in virtuoso pyrotechnics than in lyrical or dramatic interpretation. New York City Ballet has achieved a reputation for its quick-moving, high-kicking girls; in its early days its male dancers decidedly took second place. This has altered now, and one of the most impressive things about the company today is the strength of its male contingent.

Edward Villella, a New Yorker of Italian origin, has for some time been generally accepted as one of the world's great male dancers. His phenomenal elevation is combined with an attractive Latin personality. He also has great dramatic ability; his appearances in the title role of *The Prodigal Son* are deeply moving and hold the ballet together. Balanchine has written complicated solos for Villella in many of his recent works, and created special pas de deux, like the Danish-style *Tarantella,* for Villella and Patricia McBride, whose speed and lightness equal Villella's but who is rather lacking in stage personality. Jerome Robbins also devised a fiendishly difficult but effective solo for Villella in his *Dances at a Gathering.*

New York City Ballet's other leading male dancer, Jacques d'Amboise, used to seem a bit like an overgrown college boy. His most famous role is Apollo, in which his large muscular body and slightly narcissistic personality are particularly appropriate. But he has also now grown into a stylish classical dancer; this is very evident in the Diamonds section of Balanchine's *Jewels* and again when d'Amboise plays the Sugar Plum Fairy's Cavalier in *The Nutcracker,* making one wish that the principal male dancer had a more extended role in Balanchine's version.

A younger generation of New York City Ballet male dancers is also rapidly moving into the fore. Anthony Blum, like Villella, does some astonishing jumps and spins in *Dances at a Gathering.* John Prinz also did difficult Russian-style spins in d'Amboise's *Tchaikovsky Suite* and Hungarian-style character dancing in the last section of Balanchine's *Brahms-Schoenberg Quartet.* He was highly praised for his Poet in Ashton's *Illuminations.* But he left the company in 1970, and joined Ballet Theatre. John Clifford combines a brash, comic personality with technical strength; he has successfully replaced Villella in both *Jewels* and *Dances at a Gathering* while in his own *Prelude, Fugue and Riffs,* he proves that his show-business background has left him with a flair for something approaching revue-style dance. Peter Martins, who joined the company from the Royal Danish Ballet, has an appearance and bearing which remind many people of the young Erik Bruhn, but his dancing style is curiously lethargic and at present he makes little impact.

It is not only New York City Ballet which boasts remarkable male talent. Standards of male dancing in all the principal American companies strike me as higher than in any others outside the Soviet Union and Denmark. Ballet Theatre's roster includes Bruce Marks, a tall, thin, elegant dancer who seems equally at home in the classics and in modern dramatic works; Ted Kivitt, with a formidable technique and an exuberant manner which sometimes lead him into untidiness; and Ivan Nagy, whose style is more romantic and poetic.

In Lawrence Rhodes and Helgi Tomasson, the Harkness Ballet boasted two male dancers who would be outstanding in any company. Rhodes is handicapped by a face which is not really suited to the romantic classical roles; his powerful dramatic talent helps the modern repertoire and his technical facility is mainly displayed in pas de deux. Tomasson, who won a prize at the Moscow ballet competition in 1969, excels in light, bouncy pas de deux, though he too took a major share in the modern repertoire. In 1970 Rhodes joined the Dutch National Ballet, while Tomasson transferred to New York City Ballet. The Joffrey Ballet's Luis Fuente, with his flamboyant personality and flashy technique, obviously has a big personal following, though I found him rather too ostentatious and exaggerated in style at the few performances I attended. John Sowinski of Feld's American Ballet, on the other hand, is extremely gentle in manner but has both a strong technique and dramatic ability.

All these companies also have other male dancers among the soloists and corps de ballet who are well-trained, virile and technically strong. The same seems to be true outside New York. I was greatly impressed by the Nureyev-like Alexei Yudenich, a Yugoslav leading dancer of the Pennsylvania Ballet, in the difficult jumps and spins of the *Corsair* pas de deux, and by the dancing of Robert Rodham, the company's ballet master, in his own *Cavalier Variations*.

The emergence of so much male talent is remarkable in a country where ballet is such a new growth and where there is still quite a lot of natural prejudice against dancing as a career for boys. The enormous reserves of female talent are less surprising. Balanchine has always been thought to be more interested in choreography for women, and in particular for ballerinas who are young, strong and efficient rather than mature or lyrical. Melissa Hayden and the French ballerina Violette Verdy are the current exceptions in New York City Ballet. They bring an authority and a depth of feeling to their work which is not always present in the younger girls and their technical powers are at their peak.

Until her departure in 1969, Suzanne Farrell was dancing virtually all the leads in the Balanchine ballets and seemed destined to occupy the positions, as his wife and leading dancer, which Maria Tallchief and Tanaquil Leclerq had occupied before her. With her marriage to Paul Mejia, a dancer in the company, that prospect was destroyed and she left to freelance. Her most likely successor in the leading roles was Kay Mazzo, a very attractive and gentle dancer, yet with a strong technique, who was first noticed with Ballets U.S.A. in Robbins's *Afternoon of a Faun*. Among other young dancers rapidly establishing themselves are the sisters Johnna and Gelsey Kirkland; Gelsey when just sixteen was already dancing leading roles in Balanchine's *Monumentum pro Gesualdo* and in Clifford's *Reveries,* with a cool classical purity which recalled the young Antoinette Sibley.

Ballet Theatre's new young ballerina, Cynthia Gregory, is a skillful comic actress, as shown by her Swanilda in *Coppélia*. She dances the full-length *Swan Lake* with technical skill and fluency, but without much facial expression; if she develops an emotional range to equal her technique, she may become a ballerina of international stature. Ballet Theatre already has two ballerinas in that class, the Danish Toni Lander, who seems to dance less often nowadays but is still inimitable in *Etudes,* displaying the gracious romantic style as well as classical strength, and the Chilean-born Lupe Serrano, who can arouse an audience to frenzy with her balances and jumps but who seems to me to lack grace and interpretative ability.

It is probably just as well for New York balletgoers that they have so many companies performing for them; an exclusive diet of New York City Ballet might in time become indigestible. Balanchine and his collaborators are extremely creative; the company produces three or four new ballets every season. Nevertheless most of them are by Balanchine, and even when they are not they usually follow his favorite recipe. That is to say, they tend to be abstract, using a different team of dancers for each movement of the piece of music. We probably see some lyrical dancing, some brilliant, and perhaps some comic or character work. The ballerina in each section dances to the solo instrument, with the corps de ballet accompanying her when the full orchestra is playing; each bar of the music is usually meticulously translated into appropriate stage movement.

This formula always works well in Balanchine's hands, and sometimes brilliantly. But even with his use of widely contrasted types of music, it can pall. His three-part *Jewels*, for example, is really three separate abstract ballets, set to music by Fauré, Stravinsky and Tchaikovsky. Each section is good in its way, though not in my opinion the most original or inventive Balanchine, but the cumulative effect is not very great and scarcely amounts to a completely satisfying evening in the theater. At its best, Balanchine's method can be miraculous. Works like *Symphony in C, Ballet Imperial* and *Bourrée Fantasque*, with their strong musical and emotional contrasts between movements, provide opportunities for dancing contrasts as well, and for the display of a good deal of technical virtuosity.

There is a danger, however, in imitating the Balanchine formula. Robbins's *Dances at a Gathering* may look at first sight like an imitation, but the way in which Robbins conveys that his dancers are real people, expressing real if only half-suggested feelings, makes it less abstract than most Balanchine abstract works. But many abstract ballets do look both imitative and sterile: d'Amboise's *Tchaikowsky Suite,* for example, with its seemingly inappropriate use of mildly folksy steps. John Clifford's daring in doing a Balanchine, on the other hand, was astonishingly successful: *Reveries,* to music from Tchaikovsky's Suite No. 1, is an inventive and beautiful neoclassical ballet, which might have been the work of the master himself. Clifford is probably still seeking a distinctive style of his own; if he finds one, he may well enrich New York City's repertoire with greater variety.

Until now the company's principal alternative to Balanchine as a choreographer has been Robbins, who has at various periods been its associate artistic director. But Robbins has never been a prolific choreographer and has spent long periods away from ballet, working on Broadway or in Hollywood. The fact that he followed *Dances at a Gathering* within a year with another Chopin ballet, *In the Night,* which also got good reviews, suggests that he may be entering another creative phase. His ballets in the past have ranged from the obscure but effective *Age of Anxiety,* based on W. H. Auden's poem, to semirevue numbers like *Fancy Free.* It is intriguing that he is now working in a more classical style and it is possible that he will be able to supply a much larger proportion of New York City Ballet's repertoire if Balanchine eventually feels the need to slow down or retire.

It is also intriguing, and welcome, that so many young American dancers experimenting with choreography are now working well within the classical tradition, rather than showing off avant-garde tricks. A lot of the new choreography I saw performed in Washington, Philadelphia and San Francisco, while not particularly remarkable in itself, was at least competent and did make use of the dancers' classical training. Dennis Nahat, one of Ballet Theatre's dancers, staged his *Brahms Quintet* in New York at almost the same time as Clifford's *Reveries,* and it too was an attractive work, to Brahms's string quintet in G major and in the style of Balanchine's charming *Liebeslieder Walzer* and *Brahms-Schoenberg Quartet.* This was only Nahat's second ballet, and his first to be seen in New York, and it was sufficiently promising for one to look forward to his next.

In general, Ballet Theatre's repertoire is more varied than New York City Ballet's, and this is both its strength and its weakness. Both companies, for example, sometimes present isolated classical pas de deux, or the second act of *Swan Lake,* but New York City Ballet stages them in Balanchine's original choreography while Ballet Theatre's are sometimes by Petipa, sometimes a long way "after Petipa," and sometimes without any choreographer being credited in the program. I have no objection to flashy pas de deux to enliven a mixed program, nor to the second act of *Swan Lake* as a curtain raiser, though purists disapprove of such things and the Royal Ballet has (regrettably) given up doing them. But they are symbolic of Ballet Theatre's rather mixed image.

There is in fact a great deal to be said for Ballet Theatre's role as a living museum of American ballet of many styles and periods. Even New York City Ballet preserves a few ballets which do not seem consistent with its regular image: Tudor's *Dim Lustre,* for example, which was originally presented by Ballet Theatre and which is like a more elaborate *Jardin aux Lilas.* Conversely, Ballet Theatre has ballets by Balanchine (*Theme and Variations*) and Robbins (*Les Noces*) among the staple items of its repertoire. Without "museum" companies it would be easy to forget what a wealth of choreography has already been minted and established in the States over the years.

Ballet Theatre, for example, recently revived Tudor's *Pillar of Fire* with Sallie Wilson making a powerful effect in the part which helped to make Nora Kaye famous nearly thirty years ago. It looks a bit dated now, and its sensuality seems tame and obvious by present-day standards, but it still works in the theater and is of immense interest as an example of Tudor's work at that time. Feld's American Ballet, in its very first season, revived Herbert Ross's *The Maids,* which had only had a very few performances by Ballet Theatre in 1957, and his *Caprichos* (1950), which was once a Ballet Theatre regular.

The Maids, with John Sowinski and Bruce Marks (a guest artist) dressed up as Jean Genêt's Claire and Solange—who in turn dress up as their master and mistress—is probably more acceptable and appropriate now than when it was first seen.

The main object of Feld's company, however, is presumably to display his own works and give him an opportunity of making as many more of them as he wishes. He is both energetic and prolific, and his choreography brings a distinctive personal touch to the classical style. My favorites so far are *Harbinger* (1967), a very energetic Robbins-like abstract to Prokofiev's Piano Concerto No. 5, and *Intermezzo* (1969), reminiscent of Robbins in his *Dances at a Gathering* style but a valid and haunting series of dances in its own right, to piano music by Brahms. His *At Midnight* (1967), to Mahler's *Four Rückert Songs,* is as beautiful and moving as Tudor's *Dark Elegies* or MacMillan's *Song of the Earth,* while his *Meadowlark* (1968) is a slightly enigmatic work to music by Haydn, in which eighteenth-century dances are performed with a deliberately modern tongue-in-cheek. He and Clifford may turn out to be the most important American choreographers since Robbins.

Other competitors for this position are Robert Joffrey and Gerald Arpino. Their work with the City Center Joffrey Ballet arouses great enthusiasm and attracts a large and youthful audience, whose loyalty and sometimes extravagant applause reminded me of the early days of British ballet. The company is capable of mastering a number of styles, so as to provide another living museum. I saw authentic revivals of Ashton's *Façade* and Massine's *Three-Cornered Hat,* though the latter lacked subtle characterization and atmosphere and neither work seemed to appeal to the audience as much as the newer American offerings. My impression was that these made their impact more by their theatricality than by actual choreography.

The company's showpiece is Joffrey's *Astarte,* an exciting multimedia psychedelic work. Lights flash, colored spots range the audience, subliminal images are flashed on an enormous screen covering the whole area of the proscenium arch, and loud pop music is played by a live group. A handsome young man walks onto the stage from the audience, slowly and methodically strips down to his briefs while gazing, apparently hypnotized, at a pretty young girl, and then they dance an acrobatic and erotic pas de deux which ends with her dominating him and with him walking off alone, still stripped, into the street at the back of the stage. The choreography is slight and in any case it is very difficult to concentrate on the dancing with so many distractions in the form of film projections and lighting effects. But the total effect is tremendous. This is the *Hair* of the ballet, and puts to shame any experiments of the same kind we have yet seen in Britain.

Arpino's *The Clowns* is also very effective, though even more enigmatic. It starts with the sound of bombs and a number of dead bodies falling down on the stage. A white-faced clown heaps them into a pile, and then they all come to life as clowns, playing with transparent plastic and using it to more purpose than in most modern ballets, first making it into a beautiful long kite, then attacking the original clown and finally burying him in an enormous balloonlike sack.

The Joffrey Ballet has also revived *The Green Table,* originally created by Kurt Jooss in Paris in 1932. Jooss was one of several well-known dancers and choreographers of the twenties and thirties, when modern dance flourished in Germany. He was trained, as were Mary Wigman and Harald Kreutzberg, at the school founded by Rudolf von Laban, the inventor of Labanotation. Jooss ran his own company for many years and more recently directed a school in Essen; *The Green Table* has always remained his outstanding work. It is a powerful satire on international diplomats who sit around the green baize conference table trying to avoid war; Jooss himself used to dominate the war scenes as the figure of death. Unfortunately the ballet's message is still relevant today, and it has been a popular addition to the Joffrey repertoire.

Like the Joffrey Ballet, the Harkness Ballet has also attempted to explore the area between ballet and modern dance.

But while the repertoires of the Feld and Joffrey companies take their distinctive characters from the choreographic tastes and talents of their artistic directors, the Harkness Ballet has so far found it hard to acquire any distinctive character at all. The repertoire has been very mixed, being partly an inheritance from the company's succession of directors, partly designed to show off the specific talents of the dancers, and partly the work of Benjamin Harkarvy. His ballets are usually light essays in the classical manner, effective enough as display pieces but of no lasting value. A successful recent addition to the repertoire was Robbins's *N.Y. Export: Op. Jazz,* which looks a bit of a period piece in the 1970's but is still exciting and effective. In addition to jazz, classical pas de deux and mock-classical works, the company also performed a number of works in the modern dance style, for example John Butler's *After Eden* pas de deux, Norman Walker's abstract *Night Song,* Rudi van Dantzig's melodramatic and largely mimed *Monument for a Dead Boy,* and Stuart Hodes's equally lurid *The Abyss.* The last two dramas are highly theatrical; the first gave fine opportunities to Lawrence Rhodes or Helgi Tomasson as the boy who is shocked into homosexuality by seeing his parents making love, while the second gave equally fine opportunities to Lone Isaksen as the girl who is raped by louts in the park.

"Modern dance" is a convenient but very imprecise label for various forms of theatrical dancing which do not use classical ballet technique and which have been pioneered by Americans for the past fifty years. The frontiers between ballet and modern dance, which used to be strictly guarded on both sides, have now been broken down and the two forms constantly exchange personnel and ideas, and increasingly use each other's techniques. The general idea of modern dance is liberation from the discipline and restraint of classical technique so as to obtain a freer and more expressive dance form. It is usually performed barefoot, allegedly to give closer contact with nature and the earth, though the "earth" is normally a splintery wooden stage.

Modern dance is often an excuse for people with a bit of musicality and no technical expertise to moon around to music, to their own satisfaction if not that of their audiences. In any case modern dance does not require such a long and rigorous training as classical ballet, and the training does not have to begin so young. The great modern dancers, however, have their own disciplines and their own specialized techniques; at its best, modern dance can be an exciting and moving theatrical experience.

The first of the famous American modern dancers, and still probably the most famous of them all, was Isadora Duncan, known again to modern audiences as the subject of films and television documentaries. Argument still rages about Duncan; she was a revolutionary, preaching and practicing free love, discarding classical technique, point shoes and tights, dancing in bare feet and free-flowing draperies, on at least one celebrated occasion revealing her bare bosom, and appearing to improvise movement as the mood took her. In fact, however, most of her dances were carefully rehearsed and she had a system of movement of her own. She exerted a great fascination on audiences all over the world, and this was probably largely due to her personality and well-publicized private life. She established schools in the Soviet Union, France and the United States but they did not survive her death in a melodramatic accident in 1927, when her long scarf got caught in the spokes of her car wheel and strangled her.

Another American modern dancer of the same period was Ruth St. Denis, who gave performances of a kind similar to Duncan's with her husband Ted Shawn. Together they founded the Denishawn School. Their work was not so well known outside the United States but had more influence there than Duncan's, in particular on Martha Graham, the most famous and most distinguished modern dancer of more recent years. Shawn has also continued to play an important part in the American dance scene with his annual Jacob's Pillow festival in Massachusetts, which combines performances of classical ballet and modern dance with demonstrations, lectures and discussions.

Graham has been a leading modern dancer for the last forty years, but she only became well-known in Europe in the latter part of her career. She runs a school and a dance company, and has choreographed an enormous number of dance works, or "plays," as she prefers to call them. She has also made several films, some of her stage works and one, *A Dancer's World,* showing her dancers at work in the studio with a commentary giving her views on the nature of dance. Graham has a philosophy and her works attempt to express it; they are concerned with psychological and introspective human feelings; their titles, like *Deaths and Entrances, Errand into the Maze,* and *Cave of the Heart,* indicate their nature. She has set several of the classical Greek tragedies, and she also creates pure dance works, notable for the physical agility and beauty of the dancers—works like *Acrobats of God, Secular Games* and *Diversion of Angels.* Graham has developed a complex technique of dancing which requires considerable discipline and training, as well as emotional insight and dedication. The technique involves much use of the floor, with special ways of falling and rising again, and with "contraction" and "release" of the body which are meant to express emotional contraction and release. Graham's works are not easy to understand or to appreciate at first viewing, but they repay return visits and once one gets the message one tends to be hooked and to want to see more and more of her work.

Graham has trained marvelous dancers to perform her works, and even to perform her own roles in them after she became too old to perform them all herself. (Graham was born in 1893 and the fact that she was still performing some of her roles in 1969 must be one of the most amazing achievements in dance history.) She has also given advice and artistic supervision to the Batsheva modern dance company in Israel and her blessing and some of her teachers to the London School of Contemporary Dance, formed to train modern dancers on Graham principles. But it is not yet clear whether Graham "plays" or the Graham technique will survive without her; I am inclined to think that they need her personal faith, creative vision and intense professionalism. Works in her style by other choreographers tend to look imitative and empty, and the technique soon becomes repetitive and monotonous when it is not used to express her insight and visions.

Graham's choice of music by contemporary composers has not always been very distinguished and she has been more concerned with the visual side of her work than the aural. She herself designs the elaborate and fantastic costumes for her dancers—the long, stretchable dress worn by the women has become as much a hallmark of Graham choreography as the tutu is of classical ballet. And she has brought outside designers, especially the Japanese sculptor Isamu Noguchi, into the theater and used their designs as an integral part of the action of her works.

There are now a large number of American modern dancer-choreographers who run their own companies and develop their own choreographic styles. The best of these that have been seen in Europe are Alwin Nikolais, Paul Taylor and Alvin Ailey. Nikolais, who is of Russian origin, is now in his sixties and has been a pioneer of mixed-media theater since 1953, well before the term became a fashionable cliché, or even known. He generally uses his dancers as abstract robots, encasing them in sacks, or attaching long colored streamers to their costumes, or fixing poles to make their arms look twice their real length. The effect is that of fantastic mobile sculptures. Nikolais not only arranges the dance movement and designs the costumes, scenery and lighting effects, but also devises the sound scores, normally a collage of electronic effects, sometimes with conventional music and human voices, all prerecorded on tape. Some of his items are very short, little more than high-quality revue numbers, and his full-length *Imago* seems to me overlong and not really coherent, though there are fine things in it. His recent works *Tower* (1966), *Somniloquy* (1967), and *Tent* (1968) show a further advance.

Tower begins innocently enough, with the dancers playing with bits of tubular scaffolding, making speeches over it and funny faces at each other through it. Eventually they build it up into a tower and all talk at once, waving rival flags. It is the Tower of Babel, and it explodes in a cloud of smoke as the curtain falls. The work starts by making us smile, and ends by wiping the smile off our faces. *Tent* is a marvelous but almost indescribable work; the tent material of the title starts on the ground but is raised to form a succession of variously shaped marquees, grottoes, and threatening or protective wrappings for the dancers. Sometimes there is a love-in, sometimes an eastern meditation; light patterns are projected, and the sound effects range from the ominous buzzing of insects to the chiming of a clock. It is the modern dance equivalent of a classical ballet divertissement.

Somniloquy is an extremely ingenious display of dancers blending in and out of decor and lighting, sometimes disappearing altogether in the camouflage and sometimes emerging as individuals more distinctly than is usual in Nikolais' works. It may be significant that one of his latest works, *Echo* (1969), also seems to give the dancers more individual opportunities; in this too there is some clever shadowplay so that the dancers appear and disappear as in *Somniloquy*.

Paul Taylor is a dancer with a lively, bouncy manner and a strong sense of humor which permeates both his dancing and his choreography. Unlike some modern companies, Taylor's does not make ambitious claims to have a new philosophy; it usually sets out to entertain, and succeeds brilliantly. *Aureole,* to music by Handel, is almost a classical ballet, except that it is danced in bare feet; it has even been taken into the repertoire of the Royal Danish Ballet. The dancers move lyrically and excitingly across the stage, always in perfect accord with the music. *Piece Period* to music by various composers including Vivaldi, Haydn and Beethoven, is a series of crazy but joyous dances which are gimmicky and amusing. Taylor likes using bits of decor as part of his ballets; in *Piece Period* there is a chandelier that comes

down to the ground and goes up into the flies again for no
apparent reason, and a girl slowly and carefully distributes
buckets around the stage and then rapidly gathers them all off
again. But these zany devices are mixed with inventive and
attractive dancing, which is always extremely musical and usually theatrical as well.

There have been some recent signs that Taylor is searching
for a new and more serious or avant-garde style. One of his
latest works, *Private Domain,* was so private that I could make
little of it at first viewing. But *Churchyard,* which had its
premiere at the end of 1969, was an agreeable and sometimes
savage piece of mock-medievalism, and the same program included *From Sea to Shining Sea,* an extremely amusing bur-
lesque of various aspects of the American way of life. I cannot
resist expressing the hope that Taylor will continue to concentrate on entertainment, which he does so well, and not be
tempted toward the kind of self-expression which baffles an
audience.

Alvin Ailey's company has a number of styles, ranging from
Graham-style modern dance to Broadway or Hollywood spectacular revue. His own best work is *Revelations,* in which his
dancers mime and dance to Negro spirituals. The effect is
beautiful and exhilarating, and *Revelations* repays viewing
almost any number of times. But I am not sure that Ailey's
attempt to make his company another living museum, but of
modern dance instead of ballet, works as well in practice as it
sounds in theory. Many of the modern dance works available to
him are not sufficiently interesting in themselves. The mixture
of Negro cabaret, Ziegfeld Follies, and the more restrained
appeal of white barefoot dancing makes for curiously unbal-
anced programs, the total effect of which is often less than
that made by its individual parts.

There are a countless number of other modern dance groups
and soloists. Apart from Merce Cunningham, whose work has
already been discussed and whose company is now one of the
residents at Brooklyn Academy, most of them perform in uni-

versities, YMCA halls and small studios. The European visitor is both baffled and impressed by the number of recitals and performances of this kind. Nor is this activity confined to New York. In San Francisco I saw some of the work done by Sheila Xoregos with her Xoregos Dance Company which struck me as witty and inventive, and I had the pleasure of visiting the studio where Ann Halprin teaches and where she pioneered some of the mixed-media and total-theater styles which are now commonplace. Even more than with classical ballet, standards of modern dance vary from the impossibly pretentious and the embarrassingly amateurish to the highly proficient professional companies which have already achieved international reputations.

CHAPTER II

International Variety

ONE OF THE GREATEST ATTRACTIONS OF BALLET, to its regular followers, is the comparison of different dancers and ballets, both at home and abroad. First there is the comparison of the dancers within one's own local companies, as they take roles over from each other in familiar productions. Then there is the comparison with foreign dancers in the same roles and foreign productions of the same ballets, when companies from abroad come visiting or when one travels abroad to see them. And finally there is the comparison of the different styles of dancing, production and choreography which have emerged in different countries.

Many of the regular audience at Covent Garden go to endless repetitions of the same ballets to compare different principals in the leading roles, or even to compare the performances of the same principals on different nights. There is always some new talent to spot, as well as progress in familiar dancers to note. No two performances are ever identical, though there is of course an elusive thing called the English style which is common in some degree to all English dancers. It places great emphasis on lyricism and musicality, and is more successful in producing ballerinas than leading male dancers. The girls are generally less remarkable for facial expression and personality than the Russians, and pay less attention to arm movements, but their footwork tends to be quicker and neater. On the other hand they do not move at the enormous speed, or with the almost masculine attack, of the Americans. (It has been cruelly said that English men dance like girls, American girls like men.) English men do not jump as high or as lightly as the Russians or Danes but they tend to be of slighter build than the Russians, and therefore to be nimbler and faster. They understand the romantic and classical parts better than the Americans. English dancers are remarkable for their versatility; they seem equally at home in the classics and in the whole range of twentieth-century works, and nowadays can usually cope with jazz and modern dance as well. The Royal Ballet is thus able to present a wider and more varied repertoire than any other major company. For this reason it is the company I would choose if I were condemned to see only one company for the rest of my life; I suspect that life confined to the Bolshoi, the Kirov, the Royal Danes or New York City Ballet would become boring more quickly.

These generalizations about English dancers of course have many exceptions. The Royal Ballet's senior resident ballerina, now that Fonteyn is a guest artist, is Svetlana Beriosova, who is not English at all, but Lithuanian. She was not trained at the Royal Ballet School and started her career with other companies. Her face, with its soulful expression which is so well suited to Odette, is typically Slavonic. Like many Slav dancers she exudes personality, is notable for her bearing and her arms, and is less strong in quick footwork than most English dancers. Her gift for conveying mystery and suffering was exploited by John Cranko in his admirable early ballets *The Shadow* and *Antigone,* and also made her well suited to the leading role in his *The Lady and the Fool.* Ashton used this aspect of her personality again for Lady Elgar in *Enigma Variations,* while he used her comic abilities in *Jazz Calendar* in which she parodies the Slav tragic style. Unfortunately choreographers have not done enough to exploit Beriosova's humorous side, which used to be so evident in *Coppélia.*

Beriosova, who was born in 1932, started as a teenage ballerina, which makes many people think that she is much older than she actually is. The Royal Ballet's other leading ballerinas, Merle Park and Antoinette Sibley, are thought of as much younger, though in fact the difference is only five and seven years respectively. Park, who comes from Rhodesia, started her career as a soubrette, first in little bouncy parts like the *Giselle* peasant pas de deux, the *Swan Lake* Neapolitan Dance and the rapid arm-jerking pas de trois in *Les Rendezvous,* then as a delightful Swanilda and Lise. After her marriage to the ballet critic James Monahan, and the birth of her child, she became much slimmer, looking more like a classical ballerina and succeeding as Juliet, Giselle, and particularly as Clara in Nureyev's new version of *The Nutcracker.* At the time of writing, she has not attempted Odette-Odile and my own feeling is that she is still more suited to comic, dramatic or pure dance roles than to romantic ones, though the combined influences of Monahan and Nureyev have evidently helped her development into a versatile ballerina. My preference in romantic roles is for the fair-haired Sibley, the first ballerina produced entirely by the Royal Ballet School. She has a remarkable, lyrical quality of movement which makes classical choreography seem natural and inevitable, whether it is *Swan Lake* or Balanchine's *Ballet Imperial.* She can look like an innocent child as Juliet or Clara, but she is less of an actress than Park. Moreover she generally dances with Anthony Dowell, a good-looking boy who has a remarkable technique, light and flowing, but who is also less strong as a dramatic personality than Nureyev or David Wall.

Dowell and Wall are the Royal Ballet's most outstanding resident male dancers, younger than Park and Sibley, but probably destined to partner them in the years ahead. Until 1970

Wall spent all his time with the touring section of the Royal Ballet, which under John Field's guidance has been responsible for producing many of our best male dancers, including the irreplaceable Christopher Gable. Wall has mostly danced with Doreen Wells, a highly efficient all-rounder with an attractive appearance and a strong technique who has sometimes seemed a bit mechanical and uninspired but whose recent performances in *The Two Pigeons* have acquired just the right comedy and tenderness. He is married to Alfreda Thorogood, an appealing dancer with "Fonteyn eyes" who is ideal in romantic or comedy parts, ranging from *Pigeons* to the lonely girl in MacMillan's *Solitaire* and the mock-nervous maiden in *Knight Errant*. She is also a most promising Odette, and may become an outstanding classical ballerina, in which case there could be a new husband-and-wife partnership, in Thorogood and Wall, to rival the fame of couples like Skibine and Tallchief, or Vasiliev and Maximova.

Wall is red-haired and does not look tall on stage, and at first I thought him unsuited to the romantic leads. He combines considerable force and panache in his dancing with a powerful personality and acting skill, which make him a marvelous Franz in *Coppélia,* a remarkable Rake in de Valois' ballet, and an equally interesting one in *Knight Errant,* which Tudor created specially for him. But he has also now grown into an outstanding Albrecht, completely convincing both as a roguish aristocrat flirting with a peasant girl and then as a lover whose heart is really broken. His dancing is sometimes untidy, as he is tempted to try more than he can actually do, but when he has overcome this fault he will be a star of world stature.

Dowell is at present a more finished dancer, with a more remarkable lightness and elevation. But his manner is a bit soft and I do not find his acting of the big romantic roles particularly convincing. He is best suited to a role like Oberon in *The Dream,* which on the other hand does not suit Wall. However, Dowell too is developing rapidly; his acting is becoming more assured and his stage presence more dominating every season.

His Prince in the new production of *The Sleeping Beauty* made a real impression; the new solos suit him extremely well and so do the costumes. Both Dowell and Wall, like Park and Sibley, have their devoted admirers, and a friendly rivalry between them, and between the two ballerinas, can only be good for all four of them.

It is not possible to mention all the highly gifted dancers in the Royal Ballet. Lucette Aldous is too tiny to have much line and her face is not very expressive. But she is a ballerina of astonishing technical strength and lightness, with almost Russian gusto and sparkle. She excels as the Cancan Dancer in *Boutique Fantasque* and as Swanilda, as she used to do in Rambert's production of *Don Quixote*. Donald MacLeary, who has partnered Beriosova devotedly for years and was one of the few dancers to lift her easily and effortlessly (she is too tall for comfort), has done some fine virtuoso dancing in his own right. He is also exceptionally good-looking, but he has never been a strong actor and in recent years he has been plagued by foot injuries which have kept him off the stage for long periods and have affected his dancing. Brian Shaw has been moving over to character and mime parts after a long run as the Royal Ballet's principal virtuoso. Michael Coleman now dances the principal virtuoso roles, such as the Blue Bird in *The Sleeping Beauty* and the Nureyev role in *Bayadère,* with remarkable elevation and élan; but in roles requiring characterization, like Colas in *La Fille Mal Gardée,* his lack of stage personality is a handicap. Wayne Sleep, one of the youngest members of the company, also has great technical virtuosity, excelling in spins such as at the end of *Les Patineurs.* He has an ebullient, brash personality which always warms the house and a strong sense of humor which is particularly evident in *Jazz Calendar;* but his unusual shortness and stocky build seem likely to debar him from the leading roles in the full-length classics.

The most promising young dancer in the Royal Ballet is Ann Jenner, a vivacious and lively soubrette who has already scored as Swanilda and Lise. She has a strong and pleasant personality, is very musical, and extremely light. It remains to be seen whether she will also develop a romantic or dramatic side, and how she will fare in the more serious classics.

In addition to those already mentioned, the Royal Ballet contains several other young dancers who may well become leading stars. In particular these are Margaret Barbieri, Paul Clarke and Nicholas Johnson.

Barbieri, who comes from South Africa and is a distant descendant of the famous ballet master and teacher Cecchetti, has the advantage of looking like a romantic nineteenth-century ballerina; her long expressive face and dark hair make her ideally suited to Giselle, which she dances with just the necessary lightness and sense of drama. Her gypsy girl in *Pigeons* combines glamor and vivacity, and her artificial airs and graces in *Knight Errant* are hilariously funny.

Johnson, who frequently partners Barbieri, is half Polish and this may account for his effective stage bearing and the style and polish of his arm movements. He is slightly built, yet seems robust and manly as Albrecht; his acting is sensitive and his dancing, though not yet of virtuoso brilliance, is polished and exciting. Clarke was hampered at first by an extraordinary physical resemblance to Christopher Gable, which invited invidious comparisons, especially as Clarke took over many of Gable's roles. He is gradually developing a personality and manner of his own; he tends to overact, and to rely too much on his good looks and his dazzling smile, and his performances are often better on tour, when he is more relaxed, than in London. His dancing too is sometimes overexuberant and untidy but with his elegant, tall, slim body, which gives him good line, and with his attractive face and sound technique, he should go far. Already he has given some excellent performances as Franz, Colas, Oberon and the artist in *Pigeons*.

Other British companies have fine dancers too, though naturally not in such profusion. Festival Ballet's John Gilpin has been a major international star for years, with boyish good

Photo Anthony Crickmay

*A typical Balanchine pas de deux: Suzanne Farrell and Anthony Blum
of the New York City Ballet in* Movements for Piano and Orchestra.

Photo Fred Fehl

New York City Ballet in Jerome Robbins's
Dances at a Gathering *(front left: Violette Verdy*
and John Clifford; back left: Kay Mazzo and
Anthony Blum; center: Sara Leland and John Prinz;
front right: Allegra Kent and Edward Villella;
back right: Patricia McBride and Robert Maiorano).

Photo Martha Swope

Edward Villella of the New York City Ballet as the Prodigal
Son *in Balanchine's ballet.*

Photo von Haven

Robbins's Afternoon of a Faun *with Niels Kehlet and Dinna Bjørn of the Royal Danish Ballet.*

A typical Bournonville pas de deux: Fredbjørn Bjørnsson and Kirsten Ralov of the Royal Danish Ballet in Flower Festival at Genzano.

Photo von Haven

A typical Soviet pas de deux: Nina Sorokina and Mikhail Lavrovsky in Diana and Acteon.
Photo Houston Rogers

Photo Hans van den Busken

Hans Knill, Susan Kenniff, and Anne Haenen (the singer) in Hans van Manen's Solo for Voice 1 *(Netherlands Dance Theatre).*

Marcia Haydée as Tatiana and Heinz Clauss
as Onegin in John Cranko's Eugene Onegin,
performed by the Stuttgart Ballet company.
Photo Mira

Helgi Tomasson in the Harkness Ballet's
production of van Dantzig's
Monument for a Dead Boy.

Photo Fred Fehl

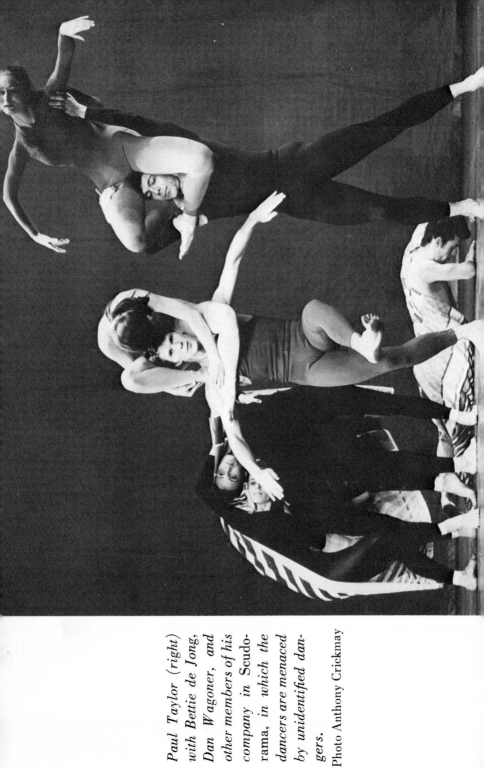

Paul Taylor (right) with Bettie de Jong, Dan Wagoner, and other members of his company in Scudorama, in which the dancers are menaced by unidentified dangers.

Photo Anthony Crickmay

Bertram Ross, Yuriko, and Robert Cohan of the Martha Graham company in Embattled Garden, *a version of the Adam and Eve story.*

Photo Anthony Crickmay

Photo Fred Fehl

*Carolyn Brown and Merce Cunningham of
the Merce Cunningham Company.*

Photo Fred Fehl

*The American Ballet Theatre's production of Petrouchka with
Bruce Marks, Eleanor D'Antuono, and Ted Kivitt.*

*Eliot Feld's Har-
binger, as performed
by the American
Ballet Theatre.*
Photo Fred Fehl

Photo Fred Fehl

(above) Balanchine's Stars and Stripes, *performed by the New York City Ballet.*

(below) Symphony in C *as choreographed by Balanchine and performed by the New York City Ballet.*

Photo Fred Fehl

Photo Fred Fehl

(above) The City Center Joffrey Ballet company's production of Kurt Jooss's The Green Table, *with Marjorie Mussman, Suzanne Hammons, Maximiliano Zomosa, and Jon Cristofori.*

(below) Trinette Singleton and Maximiliano Zomosa in the City Center Joffrey Ballet company's production of Astarte.

Photo Fred Fehl

looks, a remarkable facility for quick spinning turns and slow controlled ones, and dramatic ability which has seldom been exploited, except in *Witch Boy*. Galina Samtsova and André Prokovsky now form a regular partnership with Festival; they are both of Russian blood, but she was trained in the Soviet Union and emigrated to Canada, while he was born and trained in Paris. She has both the charm and the lyrical arm movements of the best Russian dancers; he has remarkable elevation which is all the more surprising in someone who is rather stockily built. Together, they generate much excitement from such pas de deux as their own version of the *Corsair*. Samtsova is a touching Giselle, a lyrical Odette, and a charming Aurora. Festival also has an American ballerina, Dagmar Kessler, who has a strong technique and a humorous, unclassical face; Danias, who is still very young, has great charm and an attractive soft style which holds great promise. The company's male roster, always its strength, is very international. In addition to Prokovsky, there are Alain Dubreuil, from Monaco, Robert Bestonso from France, Dudley von Loggenburg from South Africa and Jorge Salavisa from Portugal, all good-looking and talented.

Ballet Rambert's outstanding dancer is Christopher Bruce, whose personality and talent shine out of their democratic and rather anonymous-looking ensemble. His performance of the title role in Glen Tetley's *Pierrot Lunaire* is poignant and skillful, and he was hailed as a star at the Vienna Festival of 1969. It would be good to see him given more opportunities in a wider repertoire.

The leading foreign classical companies today, apart from the Royal Ballet, are the Royal Danish Ballet, the Kirov, and the Bolshoi. The Paris Opéra Ballet is probably still considered in France to be in this category, but in recent years it has lacked artistic direction and important choreographers, and its many excellent dancers have been wasted. The Stuttgart Ballet, on the other hand, is rapidly moving up into the top league under John Cranko's direction; though still comparatively small, it was hailed as a major company at the Metropolitan Opera in

1969, recalling the way in which the British Royal Ballet first won international acceptance there.

Because it lies outside the mainstream of ballet history, and because Denmark plays a smaller role on the world stage than the United States, the Soviet Union or Britain, the Royal Danish Ballet is less well-known to the general public than the other major companies, and less well-known than it deserves. It has appeared in London, Edinburgh, Paris and New York, and Danish dancers appear as guest artists all over the world. The Royal Danish Ballet is in many ways the most enjoyable of all the world's companies; the cheerfulness and exhilaration of its repertoire is unrivaled.

The company was founded in the eighteenth century, but owes its eminence and popularity to August Bournonville, who was in charge of it for half the nineteenth century. Bournonville, the son of a French ballet master resident in Copenhagen, made a large number of ballets with a dancing style and theatrical character of their own, many of which are still performed. His *La Sylphide*, as we have seen, is similar in many ways to *Giselle* but most of his other works are in happy, folksy style, and can be compared to *Coppélia* or *La Fille Mal Gardée*. Extracts from Bournonville's *Napoli* and *Flower Festival at Genzano* are now danced by other companies and in concert divertissements, but the full-length *Napoli, Kermesse at Bruges*, and *Far From Denmark* remain Danish monopolies, at least for the moment. As their titles imply, they are set in foreign countries, with plenty of opportunities for national dances, pretty scenery and simple romantic plots. There is always a lot of gentle, old-fashioned mime and a lot of fast-moving, invigorating dancing.

Bournonville's choreography has certain distinctive features, and dancers require special training to be able to perform it naturally and effectively. There are lots of light, bouncy jumps for the men, and neat, quick steps for the girls. Bournonville dancers are light, high jumpers and quick movers, and are good at expressing humor and warmth. It is a particularly valuable training for men and this is why Danish ballet has always been famous for its male dancers. It is evidently not so good for producing classical ballerinas, and the Danes are conspicuously weaker on the female side.

Since Bournonville, various efforts have been made to develop a modern Danish repertoire, but none of them have been very successful. The most influential figure was for many years Harald Lander, who was in charge of the company from 1932 to 1951. His *Etudes* (1948) is now in the repertoire of several companies. It is a magnificently theatrical display of classroom technique, building up to a bravura finale, set to Czerny piano studies orchestrated by Knudage Riisager. None of Lander's other ballets have achieved any comparable success. His other main claim to fame is as the husband of the two leading Danish ballerinas of recent years: first Margot Lander who had a great reputation in Denmark but was scarcely known abroad and then Toni Lander whose career has been mainly abroad, first with Festival Ballet and now with Ballet Theatre.

The Royal Danish Ballet is at present directed by Flemming Flindt, an outstanding dancer who started his career with Festival Ballet and then became a leading soloist at the Paris Opéra, before returning to his native Denmark as ballet master while still under thirty. In Paris, Flindt began doing choreography, originally for television. His first success was *The Lesson,* a highly effective dramatic work in which Ionesco's sinister language teacher becomes a dancing master; this ballet was subsequently adapted for the stage, very successfully, and is performed by the Joffrey Ballet, the Royal Danish Ballet, and the National Ballet of Canada. Flindt has gone on to choreograph comic and neoclassical pieces and an elaborate full-length spectacle, *The Three Musketeers,* which showed a strong French influence and has not found much favor with the international public or with critics but provided a necessary element of novelty in Denmark. Flindt's *The Miraculous Mandarin* contains more interesting characterization than most versions of this unsatisfactory and lurid story to the Bartok score.

The Danish ballet has long been extremely skillful in acquiring ballets by the world's leading contemporary choreographers. Ashton did a full-length *Romeo and Juliet* specially for the Danes in 1955; MacMillan and Robbins mounted several of their works for the company, and some of Balanchine's have also been reproduced. Robbins' *Fanfare* has become a Danish specialty, as have David Lichine's *Graduation Ball* and Roland Petit's *Carmen*. All these ballets exploit the Danish flair for character dancing and humor. The Danes have also been very successful with dramatic works by the contemporary Swedish choreographer Birgit Cullberg; her *Miss Julie,* based on the Strindberg play, gave Erik Bruhn an outstanding part as Jean the Butler and *Moon Reindeer* gave first opportunities to several delightful young dancers. On the other hand the Danes have not yet aroused much enthusiasm with their attempts to do the Petipa classics. And Danish dancers and audiences get bored with the fairly restricted and very old-fashioned Bournonville repertoire, and yearn for something new. Flindt has adopted a wise policy of staging new productions of the Bournonville works, with new decors and costumes, to revive interest among local audiences and the company itself, and to make sure that the works do not stagnate, are carefully rehearsed, and are in good condition to show to foreign visitors, many of whom come to Denmark specially to see Bournonville.

The best time to visit Copenhagen for the ballet is during the annual festival in the last fortnight of May. A wide variety of ballets is presented within that period, including a selection of Bournonville works. (It is also one of the best times to visit Copenhagen in any case, as the Tivoli pleasure gardens have just opened and it is often warm enough to bathe and sunbathe on the excellent beaches just outside the capital. There is normally no ballet after May until the beginning of September, another good time to visit both the Royal Theatre and Tivoli.)

The Danes constantly produce a stream of first-class male dancers. The best known is the internationally celebrated Erik Bruhn, widely acknowledged as the world's outstanding classical stylist. He combines virility, good looks, and precise technique with remarkable elevation. Bruhn rarely dances in Copenhagen now, but he is in charge of the Royal Swedish Ballet and also dances frequently in New York, where his partnership with the Italian ballerina Carla Fracci is almost as celebrated as that of Fonteyn and Nureyev. The leading classical dancers resident in Copenhagen are Flindt himself and Henning Kronstam. Flindt has the stronger personality and is a better actor, Kronstam is perhaps more elegant and pure in style but a bit lacking in attack. For many years my favorite Danish dancer was Fredbjørn Bjørnsson, who specialized in comic and character parts— a kind of Danish Alexander Grant. In his youth he had all the necessary bounce and joie de vivre for *Coppélia* and the Bournonville ballets; now he is a hilarious smuggler in *Carmen,* and a General with the twinkle of youth in his eyes in *Graduation Ball*; he gives a remarkable psychological study of the ballet teacher in *The Lesson.* His successor as the Danes' "cheeky chappy" is Niels Kehlet, who has phenomenal elevation and speed, but who can also bring great elegance and tenderness to *Afternoon of a Faun.*

Until recently the leading Danish ballerina was Margrethe Schanne, whose lightness and quizzical face made her ideal for *La Sylphide.* Her successor seems likely to be Anna Laerkesen, a romantic dancer a bit like Beriosova who still seems to show more promise than actual fulfillment. The Royal Danish Ballet always includes a number of very competent female soloists, each specializing in particular roles, but very few of them seem to develop true ballerina quality.

Like the Danes, the two principal Russian companies—the Bolshoi and the Kirov—are of course state controlled, with all the advantages of security, large subsidy and continuity of tradition. The tradition of teaching has continued unbroken since Tsarist times, although the Maryinsky of St. Petersburg is now the Kirov of Leningrad and the ballet at Moscow's Bolshoi Theatre is now officially the more important. Many of the best Russian dancers, including Ulanova and Nureyev, still seem to

be trained in Leningrad and, despite various revolutionary experiments and manifestoes, the nineteenth-century classics have
remained the basis of the repertoire, with the outstanding
Soviet ballet, Lavrovsky's *Romeo and Juliet,* descending from
them by evolutionary rather than revolutionary progress.

There are disadvantages in state support: bureaucracy can
stifle individual enterprise and experiment, and a strict sense of
hierarchy often means that roles are taken by dancers because of
their seniority or importance in the company rather than on
pure merit. This tends to happen to some extent in all large,
well-established companies. Flindt has broken down the rigid
regulations by which only senior dancers of certain grades could
dance leading roles in Denmark; Soviet companies visiting the
West often seem hidebound by unwritten rules of this kind. The
Bolshoi's London season of 1969 opened with Nina Timofeyeva
in *Swan Lake* although neither the production nor the ballerina had been particularly admired on the company's previous
visit, and despite the fact that the younger ballerina Natalia
Bessmertnova, whom Londoners were eager to see, was available
and danced on the second night.

The appeal of Russian ballet today is largely the dancers,
rather than what they dance. Both the Bolshoi and the Kirov
productions of the classics tend to be conventional, with pretty
but unoriginal decor; their new ballets, with the exception of
Romeo and Juliet and to some extent *Spartacus,* have found
little success in the West. The new items presented in divertissement and mixed programs are usually either music-hall
acrobatic numbers or gentle sentimental ones. They have little
artistic value but are designed to show off the virtuosity or
charm of the dancers. And these are qualities which Russian
dancers have in abundance. The male dancers are perhaps the
more celebrated, because of their virility, their high leaps, their
quick spins, and the special Russian crouching steps which are
part of the legacy of Russian folk dance. The men look like
men, not boys, and dance like men. One reason for their popularity in the West is that it is only recently that Western coun-

tries, apart from Denmark, have begun producing male dancers who are at all comparable.

But Russian women dancers are equally remarkable. The Russian schools have no difficulty in producing ballerinas who can fill the leading classical roles with charm and personality as well as technical skill. What is even more striking is that the ladies of the Russian corps de ballet all have charm and personality of their own as well. Too often our Western peasant girls and swan maidens look like blank automata, going through the motions required of them efficiently enough but apparently not knowing or caring why. The Russians look like people who actually enjoy dancing, and that enjoyment is communicated to the audience.

Technically there are certain steps which have become trademarks of modern Russian ballet. They seem to have invented a number of exciting lifts, in which the girl is balanced on one hand by her partner, and jumps in which the girl hurls herself at him like a cannon ball, virtually horizontally. There is a "Soviet style," associated with bent knees, legs deliberately turned inward rather than outward, serpentine arms, and "broken" wrists. These devices are particularly apparent in *Swan Lake,* where they are used to enhance the swanlike effect but can easily look like a caricature of classical style. The Russians pay great attention to the arms, shoulders and carriage of the back; they also pay great attention to lightness. Their swan maidens do not go tapping across the stage, as ours too often do, in noisy heavily blocked shoes. Even the Bolshoi's unatmospheric *Chopiniana* (*Les Sylphides*) at least reminded us that sylphs should be seen and not heard. Their princes do not land on the stage with a deafening crash after a jump, but softly, with plenty of plié—that is, bending the knee and landing with "give." These seemingly minor points make a great difference to the effectiveness of a performance in the theater.

The difference between the Bolshoi and Kirov styles may be partly the result of history. Before the Revolution St. Petersburg had the best teachers and the élite audience, Moscow was regarded as bourgeois and provincial. In Soviet times, the Bolshoi has had to cater for workers' delegations from all over the Soviet Union, and for visiting groups from abroad, who could not be expected to appreciate the finer points of ballet but would be more likely to respond to obvious and melodramatic effects. The Kirov, on the whole, plays to a regular Leningrad ballet audience, with fewer casual visitors. However the Bolshoi does now seem to be moving closer to the Kirov, and to what we in the West regard as pure classical style. The dancers are not as heavy as they were, and footwork is much more clean and precise. Under its new artistic director, Yuri Grigorovitch, this trend seems likely to continue and the prospects are that he will enrich the Bolshoi repertoire with revised versions of the classics and with theatrical new ballets.

His new production of *Swan Lake*, first seen in Moscow in 1969, was not brought to London as apparently it was thought to be too radical for export; some reports from Moscow, however, suggested that it was Grigorovitch's best work so far. Certainly his *Nutcracker*, which has been seen in both London and New York, is admirable; the story is told in simple children's storybook manner, with Drosselmeyer portrayed as a conjurer and the adults caricatured, but not excessively. The choreography for the divertissement in the second act is both amusing and inventive. (The pastoral dance, with the shepherd and shepherdess towing a toy lamb on a string, was too coy a joke, but the general conception of all the national dancers as dolls was delightful and well sustained.) The pas de deux were not perhaps as lyrical and effective as in Nureyev's version, and some people felt the big final pas de deux was spoilt by Grigorovitch's use of the supporting corps de ballet. Men holding candelabra posed behind the ballerina and her partner, who at one point were held up in the air, leaning slightly towards each other. These big spectacular effects are obviously essential at the Bolshoi, both because of the size of the theater and the nature of the audience, and we should not expect exactly the same style or sense of taste from the Bolshoi (or any foreign company) as we do from our own. Personally I felt that Grigorovitch had found an admirable way of combining showmanship and spectacle with choreography which showed off the skill and charm of his dancers.

His biggest success, however, during the London season, was undoubtedly *Spartacus*. This ballet, to an excessively long score by Khatchaturian, had been staged by several previous Soviet choreographers but Grigorovitch's version was evidently the first to win any real popularity. It was also the first to be seen in London, though Lavrovsky's version was shown in New York, where it was laughed off the stage. Grigorovitch persuaded Khatchaturian to shorten and rearrange the score, though the ballet still lasts three and a half hours, with two intervals. At first hearing, the music seems almost unbearably loud and repetitious, with martial heroic themes and sugary sentimental ones alternating and repeating in best Hollywood extravaganza style. But the whole conception is rather a Hollywood-spectacular one (there is of course a successful Hollywood film of the Spartacus story) and music of this kind was probably essential—strangely enough, it does not become unbearable with repetition, and if anything one grows to like it, or at least to accept it.

Grigorovitch has told the story of the slave revolt against Roman despotism in a series of big crowd scenes linked by "monologues" or soliloquies for the principal characters. This device works well; the action freezes, one of the principals is spotlighted while the rest are blacked out, and then dances a solo intended to reflect his mood and feelings. The solos and pas de deux are actually less remarkable than the crowd scenes. The Roman troops, goose-stepping across the stage, make the obvious parallel with Hitler, though for a Russian audience there must also be an immediate link between the tyrant Crassus and Stalin. Crassus' wife Aegina actually organizes Spartacus' defeat by leading a party of whores to seduce the slave army, just the kind of dedicated patriotism which appealed to Stalin, but presented in an unfavorable and tawdry light in this production, in which Aegina evidently enjoys her crude erotic tactics. The ballet opens strikingly with Crassus borne aloft behind the shields of his troops and ends equally effectively with Phrygia mourning over the bier of Spartacus, her husband. Some people felt it should have ended earlier, with the dramatic tableau of Spartacus impaled in the air on the Roman spears, but Grigoro-vitch clearly wanted to show Crassus' uncertainty after his victory and to imply, through Phrygia's mourning and courage, that the spirit of resistance would continue. This ending, and indeed much of the ballet, is surprisingly similar to Cranko's antidespotism ballet *Antigone*. Both choreographers tell their stories through dance and spectacular crowd scenes without resorting much to mime.

It is difficult to imagine a non-Soviet company carrying off *Spartacus* with anything like the necessary conviction and larger-than-life heroics. Probably it would suit only the Bolshoi, though versions of *Spartacus* are performed by the Kirov and most Soviet and Soviet-satellite companies. The dances for the male chorus had the dynamism and impact which the *Prince Igor* dances must have had when first performed by Russians in Paris. And it is difficult to think of any Western dancer who could attempt the strenuous and lengthy title role.

The best known dancer in Soviet ballet was for many years Galina Ulanova, Stalin's favorite ballerina and a great Giselle and Juliet. We saw her in the West only toward the end of her career, but even then her dramatic and lyrical talents were very apparent. Like Fonteyn today, she could still transform herself into the young Giselle or Juliet when she was approaching fifty. Her successor as prima ballerina of the Bolshoi is Maya Plisets-kaya, a controversial dancer who is most famous for her Odette-Odile in *Swan Lake*. She has a very strong personality and a highly dramatic style; her Odette is cold, aloof, and terrified of contact with the Prince, only warming at the arbitrary Soviet happy ending, and her Odile is flashy and brilliant, but bearing little or no resemblance to her Odette. She has developed an undulating arm-style which is effective at first but becomes monotonous and does not really look much like a swan. I prefer her in spectacular show-off roles like Kitry in *Don Quixote* or when she is being humorous, as in *The Little Hump-backed Horse*.

Unfortunately she seems to have very little taste or judgment about what roles she should dance. During the Bolshoi's 1969 visit to London, she appeared only in six performances of *Carmen Suite,* a ludicrous little ballet by a Cuban choreographer, Alberto Alonso, to a ghastly travesty of Bizet's music arranged for strings and percussion instruments by Plisetskaya's husband, the composer Rodion Shchedrin. Her contribution consisted mainly in high kicks to some interpolated drum rolls and vampish grimaces over her shoulder at Don José, the Toreador, and the audience.

The Bolshoi ballerina who has been most popular in Britain after Ulanova is Raissa Struchkova, who appeared as Ulanova's alternate in *Romeo and Juliet* and *Giselle* in 1956 and as second ballerina to Plisetskaya in 1963. She had great natural warmth and charm, and her range extended from the tragic roles, through *Cinderella,* to flashy acrobatic pieces like the *Moszkowski Waltz* and the Walpurgis Night scene from Gounod's *Faust.* She is presumably approaching retirement.

Her place in British affections is now being taken by the young ballerina Ekaterina Maximova. She and her husband, Vladimir Vasiliev, were the undoubted stars of the 1969 visit and look like being top stars of the Bolshoi, and of world ballet, for many years to come. Maximova is petite and charming, with a very strong technique. Her Masha (Clara in most versions) in *The Nutcracker* is a completely credible little girl, and her final scene, reawakened from her dream and reunited with her doll, is extraordinarily touching. Her Kitry in the *Don Quixote* pas de deux is sparkling and the touches of virtuosity are carried off with an amused air; she suddenly holds some balances in the middle of her solo variation with a daredevil air of slightly mocking the whole affair. Her Giselle is beautiful to watch and completely convincing, but it is the broken heart of a disap-

prologue had the lyricism and technique to make the chore-
pointed little girl rather than the tragedy of true first love.
Tragedy is not yet Maximova's forte, as we saw in *Spartacus*
where her Phrygia was frail and appealing but lacking the self-
sacrificing grandeur of Bessmertnova's interpretation.

Vasiliev is one of the world's greatest male dancers, in the
same small select band as Nureyev and Villella. Like them, he
combines virtuoso technique with a strong and distinctive personality. In *Don Quixote* he performs a whole series of difficult
and unusual steps and jumps without any sign of strain and in
Spartacus he becomes the determined hero and fighter for freedom. His unusual face, with its strong features, especially the
chin, helps him to look heroic; he is blond and handsome, and
his partnering of Maximova is so effortless that like some other
husband-and-wife teams, they seem to dance as one.

The other dancing partnership which proved very popular in
the 1969 visit was that of Natalia Bessmertnova and Mikhail
Lavrovsky. Bessmertnova, who is married to Grigorovitch, has
the dark hair and long, romantic face for Giselle, which she
danced in nineteenth-century period style, looking remarkably
like prints and photos of earlier ballerinas in the part. She
relied rather too much on her appearance and on mime, not
enough on dancing, though she showed in *Nutcracker, Swan
Lake* and *Spartacus* that technique is no problem for her. More
than Maximova she has the mannerisms we associate with the
Bolshoi, for example "broken" wrists, which often draw attention to the artful and rather artificial use of the hands. Her best
role was Phrygia in *Spartacus*, where her tragic nobility served
as a support and an equal partner to Lavrovsky's hero.

Lavrovsky is the son of the late Leonid Lavrovsky, who was
artistic director of the Bolshoi and the choreographer of the
celebrated *Romeo and Juliet*. He first bounded onto the London stage as the Prince in *Cinderella* in 1963; by 1969 he had
gained a little weight (always a danger with Russian male
dancers, perhaps because of all the complicated lifting they
must do), but still both his Prince in *Swan Lake* and his
Spartacus showed off his remarkable technique. Spartacus is

But the revelation of the season was the charming twenty-two-year-old Mikhail Barishnikov, who seemed equally at home in probably the longest and most arduous male role in all ballet, leaping and spinning almost continually through the three hours of the work; neither Lavrovsky nor Vasiliev ever flagged. Lavrovsky also succeeded in conveying a sense of doom; his hero struggled but knew that he was likely to be beaten in the end. In the classical parts, however, Lavrovsky seemed conventional and comparatively uninteresting.

Maris Liepa, another male star of the Bolshoi, was suffering from an injury during the 1969 season, and said to be dancing at about half his usual strength, but even so his dancing would have seemed outstandingly athletic and agile in any other company but that of Lavrovsky or Vasiliev. His tyrant Crassus, in *Spartacus,* with wandering glassy eyes, bored at his own orgy till suddenly enlivened by the fight to the death of two blinded gladiators, and aware of his own emptiness after his defeat of Spartacus, is an outstandingly powerful and subtle characterization.

Another Bolshoi husband-and-wife team, Nina Sorokina and Yuri Vladimirov, who specialize in flashy pas de deux, did not come to London in 1969, nor did some of the company's other ballerinas, like Marina Kondratieva and the young Elena Ryabinkina, though we have seen some of their work, and been charmed by it, in earlier seasons. The Bolshoi company is so enormous ("Bolshoi" means big, and although that refers to the theater in Moscow, it could equally well apply to the company) that it contains more talent, and more nontalent, than any other company; we only see a small proportion of the full ensemble when the Bolshoi comes abroad.

The Kirov, on the other hand, is smaller and more homogeneous. When it first came to London, in 1961, we had the revelation of pure classical dancing we had expected but failed to find on the first Bolshoi visit. The Kirov's appeal was less obvious: their scenic effects were simple and unobtrusive, their dancing was not so flashy and acrobatic as the Bolshoi's. But when they performed *The Sleeping Beauty,* every fairy in the

meaningless virtuosity. On their second visit, in 1966, *Chopiniana,* even without decor and with the inappropriate Polonaise
played as an overture, had such style, feeling and musicality that
many of us felt we were seeing the true *Les Sylphides* for the
first time. And *Cinderella,* in Konstantin Sergeyev's version,
emerged as a continuous piece of superb dancing, without much
concentration on story or humor, and without interruption
for mime or slapstick.

Sergeyev and his wife, Natalia Dudinskaya, who was the
Kirov's leading ballerina for many years, now run the company
jointly. It is significant that Sergeyev, like Grigorovitch at the
Bolshoi, seems to be concentrating on revised versions of the
classics which stress the dancing at the expense of story and
mime. This is of course a return to the old Russian tradition,
and a move away from the earlier Soviet insistence on an uplifting plot as the most important element in a ballet. The
leading ballerina on the Kirov's London visits was Irina Kol-
pakova, an attractive blonde with a brilliant technique and a
slightly hard manner, which made her ideal for the flashy and
acrobatic extract from *The Nutcracker,* in which the ballerina
was hurled in the air from partner to partner, but less suited to
the roles of Aurora and Giselle. However on the first visit Alla
Sizova enchanted us with her youth, gentleness and charm; she
was dancing her first ballerina roles at that time and there was
great sorrow that she was too ill to come with the Kirov on their
second visit. That time the most popular ballerina was Natalia
Makarova,* a tender and charming stage personality whose particular success was as Giselle. Yuri Soloviev, the blond peasant-
like boy who had excited audiences so much with his leaps and
his fresh personality, seemed to have got a bit heavy on the
second visit, but Sergei Vikulov had grown into a handsome
and brilliant virtuoso. When the Kirov came to London for
the third time, in 1970, Soloviev was again dancing superbly.

---

* In September 1970, during the Kirov's London season, Makarova decided
to follow Nureyev's example and stay in the West, saying she needed greater
artistic freedom than she could obtain in the Soviet Union. She is likely to be
an outstanding new star in the western ballet scene.

every classical step, with exemplary pacing, musicality, and outstanding elevation.

The Kirov has always had "Bolshoi-style" dancers and vice versa. The two companies share a common heritage of the Russian classical repertoire and training, and of the more recent Soviet works, and many of the same faults and virtues. In general their performances can be relied upon to be interesting and worth watching.

Virtually every capital in the Soviet bloc now has a flourishing ballet company, heavily influenced by Bolshoi and Kirov methods of teaching and styles of production and choreography. Russian producers, teachers, and dancers visit the satellite capitals; dancers from the East European countries go to train in Moscow and Leningrad, and sometimes dance at the principal Soviet theaters as guest artists. In a very similar way, the British Royal Ballet has increasingly come to serve as a training ground and source of guidance for ballet companies in Western Europe, the countries of the Commonwealth, and even Asia. Dame Ninette de Valois has frequently been asked to advise on the formation of new companies, and to send out teachers and producers to guide them. The Australian Ballet was formed, in its present incarnation, by Peggy van Praagh, who previously danced with the Sadler's Wells Ballet and became director of the Sadler's Wells Theatre Ballet. Now, as Dame Peggy van Praagh, she shares the direction of the Australian Ballet with that distinguished Australian alumnus of the Royal Ballet, Sir Robert Helpmann. The National Ballet of Canada, based in Toronto, has been directed since its foundation by Celia Franca, another former Sadler's Wells soloist. Yet another one, Alan Carter, has directed various ballet companies in Germany since the war, and was also for a spell director of the ballet in Tel Aviv. The most distinguished ballet company in Germany, in Stuttgart, is directed by John Cranko, who gained all his early experience as a choreographer in London. Although comparatively small, his company has an enormous range, and can produce the full-length classics in a way to challenge, and ography of the solos seem inevitable and not a display of meet, comparisons with any other company. It has already developed some outstanding dancers; Marcia Haydée, its Brazilian-born ballerina, is one of the best Giselles and Juliets of our day; Richard Cragun, its American leading male dancer, was chosen by Fonteyn to partner her in *Swan Lake* in 1968 and 1969, and caused a stir with his sensational turns in the air and his virile personality; Egon Madsen, the company's other leading male dancer, who is Danish, is unequaled in virtuoso roles like the Jester in Cranko's *Card Game* and he also makes a fine romantic Lensky in *Eugene Onegin*.

In 1970 Cranko made a ballet, *Poème de l'Extase,* to Scriabin's music, specially for Fonteyn. She played the part of an aging hostess recalling her past lovers, led by Cragun, and finally rejecting her latest young suitor, Madsen, preferring to remain with her memories. The ballet was an enormous success for Cranko, Fonteyn and the company and it may well be that Fonteyn will dance more frequently with the Stuttgart company before she retires, perhaps joining them on an American tour. Her presence in Stuttgart, and the successful 1969 tour of the States, certainly helped to consolidate the status of the Stuttgart Ballet as one of the world's major companies.

When Kenneth MacMillan went to West Berlin as director of the ballet in 1966 it was hoped that he would build up a company to equal the one Cranko had already developed in Stuttgart. In his three years there, MacMillan did raise the company's status considerably, winning it praise from German and British critics, and successfully taking it to the Vienna festival of 1969. He choreographed several new ballets for the company, and staged revised versions of the principal classics. But perhaps the management of the Deutsche Oper, Berlin, did not attach as much importance to ballet as the Württembergische Oper, Stuttgart, and so was not prepared to allocate as much money and rehearsal time for new productions. Or perhaps MacMillan is not such a dynamic administrator and skillful diplomat as Cranko. His stay in Berlin was punctured by frequent rows and threats of resignation, culminating in his actual resignation in 1969, a year before he was due to take up codirection of the Royal Ballet with John Field. The Berlin ballet is now supposed to have the artistic guidance of Balanchine, but it remains to be seen how this will work and what will become of the company without a distinguished resident choreographer.

While it is not clear how much time Balanchine intends to give to Berlin, in 1969 he took over personal responsibility for the ballet in Geneva, Switzerland. He appointed Alfonso Cata as ballet master, and Patricia Neary, formerly of New York City Ballet, danced regularly during the first season. An all-Balanchine program was presented at the end of the year and another in early 1970. It seems possible that the Geneva ballet may rapidly grow in importance and become Balanchine's European shopwindow.

Switzerland also has large ballet companies in Zurich and Basle. The Zurich one is directed by Nicholas Beriosoff (Svetlana Beriosova's father) and has an English ballerina, Gaye Fulton, and a talented Dutch premier danseur, Ben de Rochemont. The company in Basle is directed by Vaslav Orlikowsky, a choreographer with a penchant for spectacular, revue-style effects. He divides his time between Basle and the Vienna State Opera, where the ballet company is eclipsed by the immense prestige of the opera. Nevertheless, it has produced one distinguished male dancer, Karl Musil, who has appeared as a guest artist with many of the world's leading companies, including the Royal Ballet, and another, Michael Birkmeyer, of great promise.

All the opera houses in Germany now have ballet companies, a remarkable development in a country where classical ballet was virtually ignored twenty years ago. Most of them employ foreign dancers (Cranko's company is very cosmopolitan) and directors; the directors are generally expected to choreograph their own ballets, so that innumerable rival and inferior versions of the classics can be seen in the various German cities. There seems to be a deep-seated preference in Austria and

Germany for new choreography, even when this means an inferior version of a ballet which could have been staged in its original and superior form.

Sometimes, however, this desire for new choreography provides opportunities for surprisingly successful new versions of standard works. John Neumeier, a young American dancer and choreographer who became director of the ballet in Frankfurt in 1970, launched his regime with a new version of Stravinsky's *The Firebird* in a science-fiction, outer-space setting. The translation of the wicked Kostchei from a sinister Russian magician into an enormous robot with a television screen for a face, and of the hero from a peasant-prince into a white-suited space explorer, gave the ballet a new life, creating much the sort of shock and naïve fantasy effect which the original Fokine-Golovine production must have had in Paris sixty years ago. Neumeier, who is still in his twenties, resembles John Clifford in his versatility as a choreographer (he has also done an abstract Bach ballet for Frankfurt) and as a dancer (he replaced Richard Cragun in Cranko's difficult Webern ballet, *Opus 1*). Perhaps he will succeed in building up the Frankfurt ballet into another important German company.

The renaissance of ballet in Germany has occurred almost simultaneously with the decline of ballet in France. From 1932 to 1958 classical ballet in France was dominated by Serge Lifar, who was for most of those years leading dancer at the Opéra and also the chief choreographer. His ballets never found much favor outside France; the best known is *Suite en Blanc* (1943), later titled *Noir et Blanc,* an abstract work to music by Lalo which includes some exciting displays of virtuoso technique but which is on the whole less musical and coherent than Lander's similar *Etudes.* Lifar's choreography always seems limited in invention, and poorly related to the music. But his reign at the Opéra ensured that ballet held a place of importance there, and his company included ballerinas of international renown like Yvette Chauviré, Lycette Darsonval, Liane Daydé and Nina

Vyroubova and male stars like Michel Renault, Vladimir Skouratoff, Alexandre Kalioujny, and Youly Algaroff.

Since Lifar's departure from the Opéra, the school attached to it has continued to produce good dancers, but there has been even less of any value for them to dance. For a time George Skibine was ballet master, with his wife Marjorie Tallchief as a principal ballerina. He was succeeded by the young French ballet master Michel Descombey whose style was closer to revue and jazz than to classical ballet. His production of *Coppélia,* for example, even had Swanilda doing a kind of striptease in the first act!

In the summer of 1970, the situation at the Opéra, like most things in France, was still in a state of flux. John Taras, an American who has worked a great deal with Balanchine and with the old Cuevas company, was dismissed after only a year in charge of the ballet. Roland Petit was appointed director of the dance but resigned before actually taking up the appointment. Negotiations with Maurice Béjart, a previous choice for this post, broke down in 1969. Whoever is finally put in charge will have a hard task to restore the ballet at the Opéra to its former importance, and make it one of the world's leading companies again. There are still plenty of good dancers, however, especially among the men. Attilio Labis has several times partnered Fonteyn with the Royal Ballet; he has an exciting flamboyant style and personality. Cyril Atanasoff is rapidly emerging as an elegant classical dancer; he partnered the Bolshoi ballerina Maximova in *Swan Lake* Act 2 at the Opéra and also had a success in London as a guest artist at a Festival Ballet gala. Jean-Pierre Bonnefous is perhaps the most highly regarded of the young French male dancers; very good-looking, he too has a remarkable virtuoso technique and a strong personality. Patrice Bart and Georges Piletta are regarded as having great promise. Both Bonnefous and Piletta have successfully appeared as guest artists with the National Ballet of Canada, and Bonnefous has now left Paris to join New York City Ballet.

Immediately after the 1939–45 war, France had a number of small companies which did remarkable work in staging new ballets and pioneering new styles. The most famous director and choreographer of this period was Roland Petit, who left the Opéra and set up his own company, Les Ballets des Champs-Elysées, in 1945. This company boasted a sensational male star in Jean Babilée, the first outstanding Blue Bird to appear in London after the war and a remarkable gamin personality in Petit's modern-style *Le Jeune Homme et La Mort* (1946). This ballet, with scenario by Jean Cocteau and danced to music by Bach, was a melodramatic tale of a young man's encounter with a woman who turns out to be death, ending with a horrifyingly realistic hanging. The atmospheric and sleazy attic decor by Wakhévitch, with a rooftop transformation at the end, played an important part, too, in the ballet's success. Les Ballets des Champs-Elysées had a very catholic repertoire; for example it also revived *La Sylphide,* which was danced by Nina Vyroubova and Irène Skorik. Later Petit formed various other companies including Ballets de Paris, for which he made a version of *Carmen* (1949) to extracts from Bizet's opera, which had a sensational success and which has now found a permanent place in the Danish repertoire. The original Carmen, Petit's wife Renée (Zizi) Jeanmaire, went on to sing as well as dance and became a star of music hall and cabaret. Petit's effective dramatic ballet *Le Loup* (1953), which is also now in the Danish repertoire and in that of the National Ballet of Canada, gave one of her first opportunities to Violette Verdy, who has become a ballerina of New York City Ballet; Petit also lured Fonteyn to Paris in 1949 to star in his *Les Demoiselles de la Nuit* in which she considerably broadened her range, playing Agathe the cat. She also began a long-standing friendship with Petit, which eventually led to his later creations—*Paradise Lost* (1967) and *Pelléas et Mélisande* (1969)—for her and Nureyev.

These and other ballets which Petit now makes for various companies seem to show that he has lost much of his original creative flair. He is now obsessed with acrobatics, with making dancers writhe on the floor instead of dancing, and with elaborate and gimmicky decorative effects, so often a sign of lack of choreographic inspiration. At the end of 1969, Petit took over the direction of the Casino de Paris theater and was planning to stage revues and ballet there.

Other interesting small companies in France during the postwar years included one formed by Janine Charrat, a dramatic dancer who scored a success with *Les Algues,* a ballet set in a lunatic asylum. More recently companies of this sort have been less important. Joseph Lazzini created a number of ballets which were highly regarded by French critics during his period as ballet master in Marseilles, and he left in 1969 to form a company of his own. He was succeeded by Rosella Hightower, who also runs a very successful school in Cannes. She intends to build up a more classical repertoire. The company at Strasbourg has had some good dancers, such as the remarkable young Spaniard Jean-Claude Ruiz, and some interesting productions, especially a few years ago when it was under the direction of Jean Combes. A company called Ballet Théâtre Contemporain was formed in 1968 at the new cultural center at Amiens, to perform there and at other cultural centers throughout France. A powerful group of dancers was assembled, including Babilée and a new French male dancer, James Urbain, the well-known ballerina Colette Marchand, and three highly regarded East European dancers—Magdalena Popa from Rumania and Krassimira Koldamova and Itchko Lazarov from Bulgaria. The company had new ballets by Skibine, Descombey, Lazzini and others but has not as yet succeeded in creating a new ballet distinctive enough to put it firmly on the map.

France is still remarkably rich in dancers, partly because of its own long dance tradition and partly because of the large number of Russian teachers who settled in Paris after the Russian revolution. There is a recognizable French style of dancing, often more deliberately angled at the audience and with more conscious salesmanship by the dancers than is usual with Russian or English dancers, but usually with very strong technical skill. It is certainly to be hoped that France may soon again produce a ballet company of international importance.

Ballet in Italy has been in decline for much longer, though there are permanent companies at the three main opera houses —Milan, Rome and Naples. La Scala, Milan, produced the lovely romantic ballerina Carla Fracci, who does most of her dancing abroad, and the talented male dancer Paolo Bortoluzzi, who is in Béjart's company in Brussels. Nureyev has staged several full-length classics for the company, and danced there regularly. The Rome ballet is once again under the direction of Aurel Milloss, a prolific choreographer whose work is not sufficiently original to win a place in the general repertoire. Both Rome and Naples have some good dancers who could no doubt do more if given the opportunity. Their main function is the thankless one of appearing in opera ballets.

A theatrical art akin to ballet which grew up in Italy and now flourishes in France is pantomime, usually referred to nowadays in the West simply as "mime," perhaps to distinguish it from the traditional British Christmas pantomime, a very different form of entertainment. Pantomime in the true sense is of course a dumb show, derived from the old Italian commedia dell' arte, the harlequinade, and from the slapstick of the music hall. The old harlequinade plays, with the ebullient Harlequin, the sad, put-upon Pierrot and the flirtatious Columbine constantly reappearing in slightly varied plots, can still be seen delightfully performed in the open-air "peacock" theater in the Tivoli gardens, Copenhagen. They include a little dancing but rely more on broad, easily understood gestures, facial expressions and knockabout humor. This was the humor used too in the great comic silent movies by artists like Charlie Chaplin, who himself derived his technique from the music hall. Pantomime in this sense has been developed recently in France; Jean-Louis Barrault and his company performed a complete mime play in the film *Les Enfants du Paradis* and Marcel Marceau is now the most famous exponent of mime in the Western world.

Marceau sometimes presents a solo performance and some-times surrounds himself with a company. The solo performance is more celebrated and has had many imitators and followers. His technique is remarkable; we see him walking against an imaginary wind, or transforming himself from a big bully to a timid little man and back again so as to present a fight while remaining alone on the stage. His items are short, each intro-duced by a caption held up on a board, and the total effect of a whole evening's program is a bit scrappy. Reactions alternate between admiration and occasional bafflement. Watching Mar-ceau is like a sophisticated game of charades. It is technique at the expense of content, and finally one is left feeling rather empty.

Some of Marceau's followers have experimented with various devices to widen the appeal of this kind of performance. The Swiss mime Pierre Byland sometimes uses words as well as dumb show; the American Adam Darius has introduced occasional nudity and more realistic sound effects. But the appeal remains limited.

A different style of pantomime has developed, independently, in Czechoslovakia and Poland. Ladislav Fialka in Prague and Henryk Tomaszewski in Warsaw have built up companies which present full-length mime plays lasting a whole or half an evening. They rely less on making an audience marvel at their technique and more on theatricality and, in the case of Fialka, social comment. Fialka weaves a number of short sketches, comic, poetic and satirical, into an ingenious whole, so that the evening gains coherence. He frequently turns a slapstick item into a bitter comment on life; a circus is shown as a parallel of the circus of life, with its rat race, a clown's search for his lost button is shown as man's search for happiness. Music, sound effects and lighting are skillfully used. Fialka is not above pure slapstick. *The Fools* contains musical clowning, with larger and larger French horns lowered on a rope to be played by Fialka, and then removed by jealous fellow clowns. Finally, however, he is left without a horn to play, and appears to be dead. It ends with a Kafka-like item in which Fialka climbs up a rope ladder into darkness and emptiness.

Tomaszewski's work is less poetic and relies largely on erotic and spectacular appeal. One item is an imitation of a Japanese Kabuki drama, complete with a man impersonating the wronged wife, a vicious fight between the husband and his apprentice, a chase and the bloody stabbing of the apprentice, followed by the wife's killing of her husband and her own suicide. Another item is an old Eastern legend about the love between a warrior king and a golden shepherd boy, their defeat of a dragon-monster, and the king's triumph followed by his downfall and death. The style of movement is often acrobatic, with the leading characters and the male chorus displaying their lean, muscular bodies in what almost amounted to a male equivalent of the Folies Bergère. There are striking groupings and some effective scenes, like the bathing of the near-nude hero in asses' milk.

If Marceau suffers from too much technique at the expense of theatrical content, these Central European companies perhaps suffer from too much theatricality, without any precise technique. My personal preference is for the latter. But it remains to be seen whether either of these forms of pantomime, or the various forms of modern dance, will attain anything like the popularity of the more disciplined art of classical ballet. This seems unlikely and certainly there is no sign yet of either modern dance or mime spreading all over the world and finding an enormous public in the way that ballet has spread in recent years from Russia, Britain and the United States.

Ballet is now so popular and so fashionable that every country with pretensions to cultural respectability wants to have its own company. And countries with long-established traditions of ballet which had been dying, like Italy and Sweden, are trying to revive and reinvigorate them. The Royal Swedish Ballet, which is almost as old as the Royal Danish, has long been eclipsed by Bournonville and by Danish dancers, but it is now itself under the direction of the Danish star Erik Bruhn. The company usually has some fine dancers; Caj Selling made a good impression at Covent Garden when he partnered Beryl Grey, and recently the young Nils-Åke Häggbom has been earning golden opinions for his appearance and technique. Annette av Paul is known to American audiences from her seasons with the Harkness Ballet. The well-known Swedish ballerina Elsa-Marianne von Rosen has from time to time formed small touring companies of her own, and she has also choreographed for television and for the Royal Danish Ballet, as well as mounting Bournonville's classics abroad. Birgit Cullberg also recently formed a company mainly to perform her own choreography, which visited the Paris festival in 1969. Norway too has been trying to develop its own ballet company, under the direction of the Bulgarian-born ballerina Sonia Arova, who used to dance with Nureyev, while Finnish ballet leans heavily on the Soviet Union for producers, teachers and guest dancers.

All the ballet companies in Eastern Europe naturally tend to follow Soviet styles and methods, but Poland and Czechoslovakia have also developed avant-garde and experimental groups. Ballet Prague, which visited London in 1969, has found a happy way of combining dancing skill, entertainment and social message. One of their works, *Black Collage* by Pavel Smok, the company's director, seemed a daring comment on the Soviet occupation. Several of their ballets were very amusing parodies of classical styles and mannerisms.

Classical ballet companies have been established in recent years all over the world, in Turkey, Israel, Iran, Japan, South America and the Commonwealth. Alicia Alonso, who is Cuban but made most of her career as a ballerina in the United States, returned home to form the Cuban National Ballet, which has already appeared in Paris and Brussels with some success. Brazil, in addition to providing some of Fonteyn's ancestry and Stuttgart's ballerina Marcia Haydée, also has its own classical company. In North America, Canada has three major companies. The National Ballet of Canada, based in Toronto, is run by Celia Franca; it has a large repertoire and a good school; it is modeled on the Royal Ballet but lacks star personalities. Most of the performances during the week I spent in Toronto in 1969 depended for their success on international guest artists. This company has no very specific character of its own, which is probably mainly because it has not been able to develop a choreographer of its own. Its repertoire is almost too eclectic; it seems doubtful whether Petit's arid and gymnastic *Kraanerg,* for example, is really suitable for a company at this stage of its development, let alone for its comparatively unsophisticated audiences. The Royal Winnipeg Ballet has toured the Soviet Union and been seen in Paris, London and Italy; it is a very likable but slightly lightweight group specializing in works with a distinctly Canadian flavor. Its director, Arnold Spohr, devotes a lot of time to seeking out new dancers and studying other companies and their methods of training. As a result he has achieved a surprisingly high standard of dancing. The company's regular choreographer, Brian Macdonald, whose works are mostly pleasing but lightweight, was for several seasons director of the Harkness Ballet. Les Grands Ballets Canadiens (based in Montreal) was founded and is run by Ludmilla Chiriaeff, a dynamic lady of Russian origin who trained in Berlin, Paris and Switzerland. Her company is perhaps overambitious, attempting Balanchine and Petipa as well as modern dramatic works. But the Vic-Wells Ballet also started in this way, running before it could walk, and it may turn out to be a recipe for success once again.

Many of the world's ballet companies are the result of the drive and determination of tenacious, single-minded women: de Valois and Rambert in Britain, Chase and Harkness in New York, Franca and Chiriaeff in Canada, van Praagh in Australia, Arova in Norway and Gaskell in Holland. Most of these women are foreigners in the countries where they work. It is further proof of their tenacity, and of the receptivity of their host countries, that they were able to establish ballet where, for the most part, it had not previously existed, often in the face of skepticism, chauvinism and harsh criticism.

Ballet *had* previously existed in Australia, in the shape of the

Borovansky company; Edward Borovansky had been a member of Pavlova's company and of de Basil's Ballets Russes, and he brought Russian-style ballet to Australia. The company collapsed after his death and was transformed by Peggy van Praagh into the Australian Ballet, a company much more like the Royal Ballet and using a lot of British-trained dancers and choreographers. Its repertoire now includes many of the full-length classics and new works, including some by Robert Helpmann with an especially Australian or Asian flavor.

Ballet had also previously existed in Holland, but in the form of several rival companies, all small and comparatively unimportant. Sonia Gaskell fused several of them into the National Ballet, overcoming numerous jealousies and rivalries in the process, and also contending with a certain amount of Dutch opposition to a foreigner (like Chiriaeff, Gaskell is of Russian origin). On her retirement the company was taken over by Rudi van Dantzig and Robert Kaesen, young Dutch choreographers who had worked with her, and in 1970 they were joined by the American, Benjamin Harkarvy. It is a very large company with an enormous repertoire covering all periods and all styles, and, like the National Ballet of Canada, with no very distinctive character of its own. But performances are generally enjoyable and technical standards high, largely because of the unrestricted use of dancers from the United States, England, Germany and Switzerland. Two of the company's leading male dancers, Sylvester Campbell and Lawrence Rhodes, are Americans.

Van Dantzig's best-known work is *Monument for a Dead Boy*, which has been danced in Holland and London by Rudolf Nureyev and was also one of the most successful works in the repertoire of the Harkness Ballet. It is a powerful theatrical work—the choreographer's second ballet on a daring homosexual theme. It grips its audience at least as much by its subject matter, its psychological interest and its skillful staging as by its dance content. The scenes in which the hero sees his parents making love and imagines his own birth, and in which he is almost raped in the locker-room at school, are particularly effective. Van Dantzig usually works with electronic scores and his choreography is generally modern in style. In 1970 he staged *Ropes of Time* for Rudolf Nureyev and the Royal Ballet, but it was not very successful, either in London or New York.

The other Dutch company, Netherlands Dance Theatre, has always relied very heavily on American talent. Hans van Manen, who was a principal choreographer and artistic director till 1970, is Dutch, but Benjamin Harkarvy was his codirector for many years. Harkarvy's successor, Glen Tetley, and the ballet master Scott Douglas are also Americans. In 1970 Jaap Flier took over as director of the company, but it seemed probable that its character would remain more or less unchanged. The company's style is midway between classical and modern dance, and its most remarkable characteristic is its creativity: it stages about half a dozen new works each year. Most of them are semiabstract, using gymnastic movements and being heavily preoccupied with various forms of sex, often in its more obscure or perverted forms. The company is much admired by many critics and its dancers form a coherent ensemble, well suited to the works they perform. But it lacks star personalities and its ballets strike me as too much alike, and on the whole lacking in sufficient dance interest. Tetley, who has also choreographed extensively for Rambert, seems to me to waste dancers' special training and techniques and use them as gymnasts or acrobats, to no great avail.

Most of the European companies are attached to opera houses and subsidized by the state or municipality or both, and most of them also, apart from the big five, are very cosmopolitan in their membership. Diaghilev, de Basil, Mona Inglesby, the Marquis de Cuevas and Julian Braunsweg could run more or less private companies, raising money from their own pockets or from other private sources as occasion required. No doubt great wealth still exists in Europe; one day an Onassis or a Niarchos may decide to run a ballet company. But in general, governments and municipalities must finance the ballet companies now, either as part of their grants to the opera houses or directly.

The world's five big companies—the Bolshoi, the Kirov, the Royal Danes, the Royal and New York City—on the whole stick to dancers of their own nationalities. There are exceptions: the Danes now hold regular auditions for foreign dancers, while New York City Ballet has engaged principals like Peter Martins, André Prokovsky and Violette Verdy as regular members of the company. The Royal Ballet is even reluctant to have foreign guest artists, though it does sometimes do so. Nureyev ranks as a guest artist. All members of the company, including the former ballerina Violetta Elvin (née Prokhorova) and Svetlana Beriosova, are British subjects.

When Kenneth MacMillan said he would import German male dancers when he became director of the Royal Ballet in 1970, many people were outraged by the idea of diluting the British national ballet with foreigners. It was suggested that the unity of style which the Royal Ballet has achieved over the years would be jeopardized and that it would be more sensible to import foreign teachers for the Royal Ballet School, if British standards of male dancing were really lagging behind those of the Continent.

It is not necessarily true that a company must be all of one nationality to have a unified style. A strong choreographer-director can impose his style and personality on a company, as Cranko has done on the very international company in Stuttgart. The style of the Royal Ballet probably has more to do with the combined personalities and tastes of Ninette de Valois and Frederick Ashton than with British nationality. The Royal Ballet School imposes its style on its pupils, irrespective of nationality, and outstanding foreign pupils are often lost to the Royal Ballet simply because of the rules about nationality. Even South Africa, which used to provide a great deal of outstanding talent for the Royal Ballet, including Cranko and such dancers as Nadia Nerina, Patricia Miller, Johaar Mosaval and David Poole, is now debarred because it is no longer in the Commonwealth. The time is coming when the Royal Ballet and Equity must revise their ideas about this.

The situation is especially anomalous as most continental companies are happy to accept British dancers. British graduates of the Royal Ballet School who do not get places in the Royal Ballet are regularly engaged by the innumerable German companies, in Norway and Sweden, and even further afield. In ballet, as in trade, one-way traffic is unlikely to be possible indefinitely; either everyone will raise protective barriers or we must all allow free interchange. We should all gain by choosing talent irrespective of nationality and by the possibility of a wider range of temperaments and personalities.

On the other hand, it probably would be dangerous to engage too many experienced dancers from abroad to join a national company, as distinct from employing dancers straight from school, when they can still be molded into the company's style. Nevertheless I think the Royal Ballet has been too coy about guest artists in recent years. In the past Danilova and Franklin, Markova and Dolin, Fracci and Flindt, were engaged for occasional performances with much benefit to the company and the public. There are inevitably times when the company is short of ballerinas or male dancers, and when a season could be enriched by some guest appearances. Ballet Theatre has gained immeasurably from the regular guest appearances of Carla Fracci and Erik Bruhn. The Paris Opéra has frequently invited Soviet dancers to appear with its own company. Covent Garden audiences would surely welcome the opportunity of seeing stars from Moscow, Leningrad, Copenhagen, New York and Stuttgart more often than it is possible to arrange visits of the full companies. The Royal Ballet is now so well established that it need not fear the competition, and visits could be arranged on an exchange basis, so that British stars would get the stimulus and the pleasure of more foreign trips. Moreover the management of Covent Garden has a duty to display us the top international stars of the dance, just as they try to present the top international singers.

The only other ways we can see what is going on elsewhere in the world of ballet are by exchange visits of companies, or by traveling to ballet centers. The trouble about going to Moscow, Leningrad, Copenhagen, Stuttgart or London to see the ballet, even if one can afford the time and money, is that only a very small proportion of the repertoire can normally be seen in a week or even a fortnight. At Covent Garden the same ballets tend to be repeated for several performances, and, as in all these cities the ballet alternates with the opera, the number of performances in a week is limited. One solution is the festival, or special ballet season. The Royal Danish Ballet has a festival every year during the last fortnight of May, when a much higher proportion of the repertoire can be seen than in any ordinary fortnight. Stuttgart, Munich, and recently Berlin too, hold special ballet weeks with performances every night. There are winter festivals in Moscow and Leningrad. The Royal Ballet might well introduce some similar season in London, primarily for foreign visitors.

There are also some summer festivals at which ballet can be combined with sun or seaside holidays. The festival at Nervi, just outside Genoa in Italy, was started in 1955 and was originally biennial but in recent years it has become annual. It is sponsored by the Genoa tourist board. Performances take place on a large open-air stage in a charming park near the sea; passing railway trains and various insects interrupt the music but all open-air performances are subject to similar distractions. The performances start after dinner (which can be taken in the nearby gardens of the two best hotels) and end around or after midnight. The festival is usually organized by Dr. Mario Porcile, who has succeeded in attracting many of the world's leading companies and individual dancers. He frequently arranges a special group—for example in 1969 there was a four-hour divertissement including American, French, Soviet, and Italian dancers, a ballet created for the occasion by Serge Lifar, and Luisillo and his Spanish folk-dance company. In 1958 there was a special homage to Cecchetti and Bournonville, and in 1957 four international ballerinas danced Dolin's *Pas de Quatre*. The Royal Ballet and Festival Ballet have visited Nervi several times. Modern dance groups have appeared there and there are occasional showings of dance films. Standards of performance, as at all festivals, have been variable, but at least the holiday-maker can reckon to see two or three different ballet companies within a fortnight. Unfortunately the festival is not well pub-licized, and programs are rarely available much in advance; if these things were remedied Nervi could easily become a major international gathering place for balletgoers. At the moment audiences are mostly local people and holidaymakers who are on that coast by chance; audience reaction is therefore not very discriminating.

A similar open-air festival is now held at Monte Carlo, though some of the performances are given in the beautiful Opera House. The money available in Monte Carlo makes it possible to bring companies over specially from the United States; in 1967 the Harkness Ballet and in 1969 New York City Ballet made exclusive European appearances there. The festi-val usually includes only one or two companies, with a gap in between, but again the holidaymaker can choose a week which will have ballet performances almost every night. Seats in the Opera House, which is very small, are sometimes hard to obtain, but the open-air performances, as at Nervi, have an enormous seating capacity and it is usually possible to get in without advance reservations.

The Festival of Two Worlds at Spoleto, in the Umbrian hills north of Rome, which was founded by the Italo-American composer Gian-Carlo Menotti, includes a fair amount of ballet, though opera is the main attraction and concerts, drama, films and art exhibitions are also featured. There are two charming theaters, and experimental programs of modern dance are also given early in the evening in a small hall. Spoleto saw the debuts of Jerome Robbins' Ballets U.S.A., and of Eliot Feld's company. Nureyev first staged the full *Raymonda* for the Royal Ballet in Spoleto, and the Stuttgart Ballet, the Harkness company and Ballet Rambert have also appeared there. Spoleto is not an ideal summer holiday place—being right in the center of Italy it is inclined to be very hot and to suffer from water shortages—but the performances are varied and usually of considerable interest. The town itself is historic and full of atmosphere, and conveniently close to Perugia, Assisi and Gubbio. A long weekend there is usually sufficient to see most of the festival's attractions, as the programs are very intensive, with informal chamber-music concerts in the mornings, major performances in the afternoons and evenings, and fringe events in the early evenings and late at night. Accommodation in Spoleto is very hard to find, and should be booked well in advance, probably before the programs for the festival are available! Tickets for weekend performances should also be booked as soon as details are published.

Ballet festivals are spreading. Paris has held one every autumn in recent years, privately organized by the impresario Jean Robin at the Théâtre des Champs-Elysées. A ballet festival was held in Rome for the first time in 1968, and the Vienna Festival of 1969 made a special feature of ballet, with the Kirov, West Berlin and Joffrey companies among others. New York in autumn and spring is often like a permanent dance festival, because so many ballet and dance companies appear there. It is surely only a matter of time before some enterprising impresario organizes a ballet festival in London, a city which does very badly, compared to Paris or New York, in terms of foreign companies and dancers.

A foreign tour by a full ballet company is, of course, an expensive and complicated undertaking. It must be arranged well in advance, and usually depends on government grants towards the enormous cost of transportation. The Covent Garden section of the Royal Ballet has recently visited the United States every year and has come to be regarded by New Yorkers at least as virtually one of their own home companies. New York seasons and extensive American tours have been profitable dollar-earning ventures organized by the American impresario

Sol Hurok, but rising costs may make these tours less practicable in the future. The Stuttgart Ballet toured the United States for the first time in 1969, under Hurok's management, and being a smaller company than the Royal it may prove more economical for it to undertake most of Hurok's tours in the future. The Bolshoi and Kirov companies, or sometimes sections of them, visit Western countries frequently and the principal American companies visit both West and East Europe, and the Far East. Large companies are rarely seen at their best on tour, as their productions have to be modified for different stages and the dancers usually dance less well on an unfamiliar stage. The Bolshoi, with their enormous spectacular productions and their dancers accustomed to leaping across a very wide and deep stage, suffer particularly. The dancers of New York City Ballet kept falling down the first time they appeared at Covent Garden, because they were unaccustomed to the raked stage. On the other hand, the Royal Ballet is always said to dance better in New York than in London. In any case it is obviously much better to see a company in slightly adverse conditions, away from its own home, than not to see it at all.

It might seem that every foreign tour or exchange visit is obviously desirable, and that there could not be any objection on principle. This may be so, but it is not quite as self-evident as it may appear; there do sometimes seem to be good political reasons for cultural boycotts. The arguments are similar to those which apply to trade; if we strongly disapprove of a political regime, whether it is Soviet, fascist or racialist, we do not want to encourage or support it in any way. We may even think that a refusal to trade with it, or to recognize it diplomatically or culturally will help to bring about its downfall. History scarcely supports this attractive idealistic notion but even if we realize that sanctions or a boycott will have no practical effect, we may still want to indulge in it for the sake of our own consciences, to keep our hands clean.

My own inclination is to think that cultural exchanges should continue regardless of politics. But there are times when political and moral senses are so outraged that this becomes impossible. The obvious example is wartime; nobody would have suggested cultural exchanges with Nazi Germany between 1939 and 1945. And it is doubtful whether British artists should have performed in Germany in the years just before the war. German artists who performed for Hitler came under considerable criticism, while those who became refugees were admired. The great Spanish cellist Pablo Casals has consistently refused to play in Franco's Spain, or even in countries which recognized Franco.

The first visit of the Bolshoi Ballet to western Europe was in Paris in 1954. The first night was canceled at the very last minute by the French government because of the fall of Dien Bien Phu, and the company then returned to Russia without giving any performances. Many of us thought that the appearance of a Soviet orchestra at a BBC Promenade Concert in London on the night the Soviet Union invaded Czechoslovakia should have been canceled. And some people suggested that all performances by Soviet artists should be boycotted while the Soviet occupation of Czechoslovakia continued, a gesture requested by many Czechoslovaks.

There is certainly a greater moral problem about cultural exchanges with the Soviet bloc than with any other country, if only because all Soviet companies and all Soviet artists are employed by the state. The Soviet Government treats its cultural exports as propaganda events, and in its turn threatens to cancel cultural exchanges when it wishes to express displeasure with another government. The Soviet anthem is usually played, and the Red Flag often displayed as decor, at performances where such things are out of place.

My personal aim is to separate, as far as possible, the artists and their art from their governments and political systems. Individual Russian dancers may be as anti-Soviet as I am; no doubt many of them are. It is marvelous for any Soviet citizen to be able to get out of his own country and enjoy, even partially and temporarily, the greater freedom and the far higher standard of living to be found in the West. It is also highly desirable that as many Soviet citizens as possible should see conditions in the West for themselves, and hear what we think of their regime, so that they should not be wholly susceptible to Soviet propaganda. Admittedly our admiration for the Soviet musicians who were in Britain at the time of the invasion of Czechoslovakia would have been greater if one of them had spoken out against the invasion; some were such famous celebrities that just conceivably they could have taken the risk. The cellist Rostropovich cried at one concert, and asked his audience to pray for peace at another, but those gestures are not as conclusive as Casals' breach with Franco. However those of us who live safely in free countries cannot tell those who have to endure totalitarian systems what protests they should make.

The advantages both to the Soviet artists and to ourselves, and possibly in the long term to the people of the Soviet Union, of encouraging as much exchange of people, ideas, and culture as possible seem to me to outweigh those of a boycott on moral principle. At the same time we must always be careful to make clear that our admiration for Russian dancers or musicians is not to be construed as admiration for the Soviet system. Some people seem to imagine that any achievement by the Bolshoi or Kirov ballets is in some way an achievement for the Kremlin, an idea eagerly propagated by the Kremlin and its stooges. It is true that the Soviet Government has vastly expanded the quantity of ballet, financing ballet companies in virtually all provincial cities. It is equally true that the vulgarization of taste and many of the crude propagandist ballets which have been staged by the Bolshoi are the result of Soviet ideological pressure, of having to perform for endless delegations of factory and collective farm workers and foreign sympathizers, rather than for genuine ballet lovers. It is also true that the isolation in which Stalin kept Russia for so many years cut the ballet off from foreign influences and kept it in a conservative rut. But the artistry of the ballerina Ulanova or the violinist Oistrakh, like those of their predecessors Pavlova and Heifetz, is a Russian rather than a Soviet achievement, and it is as such that we can applaud them.

On the other hand I see no reason why those of us who oppose the Soviet system should stand up for the Soviet anthem, which is not a traditional Russian patriotic hymn but a postwar Soviet invention. My practice is to sit through it, as a small silent protest, except when I have been given complimentary tickets by the management, in which case I wait outside the auditorium until the anthem is over. This is a simple and non-violent way of showing one's feelings. If more people did it, the distinction between the artists and their political system would be clearly made.

CHAPTER III

The Appeal of Ballet

WHEN I ASK PEOPLE if they like ballet, they often say apologetically that they quite like it but do not know much about it, or do not understand it. I always reply that it is not necessary to understand. Most people know straight away whether they like ballet or not, the first time they see any. It is true that some people start by liking the classics, and only come to enjoy more modern works later, while others start with contemporary dramatic works and come to appreciate the classics later. Therefore it is wise to try say *Swan Lake* and a modern mixed program of short ballets before deciding whether one is hooked by ballet or not. And I really do mean hooked; ballet is like a drug—once people decide they like it, they generally want to see more and more.

Some preparation for going to a ballet is probably desirable, but this is not a matter of technical or historical knowledge. With a story ballet, it is helpful to read the story beforehand, at least allowing time to read the synopsis in the printed program at the theater. What is more important is to be in a state of receptivity. This involves having some idea of what to expect, whether the ballet is going to depend for its appeal mainly on its story, its decor, its music, its dancing, its beauty, its humor or what. At the same time, one has to try to keep one's mind reasonably clear and unprejudiced. The same work may strike different people in different ways and a newcomer may be more impressed by the actual dancing, for example, than someone who has seen the ballet many times before and is mainly interested in the new decor. It is important to be in a state of expectancy, and to clear one's mind of other, irrelevant thoughts. I normally arrive at a theater well before the performance to make sure of being in time but also to get away from the problems of the outside world and to soak up the indefinable atmosphere which permeates a real theater or opera house. That is why I am horrified when I see people reading a newspaper until the very last minute before the curtain rises, or during the interval, and is one of the reasons why people should not go on discussing their marital problems or their dinner menus during the overture.

The slightest noise in the auditorium can be very distracting during a performance and people who cannot resist comments to their neighbors, or unwrapping or chewing sweets, or who have to laugh extra loudly when nobody else does, are a menace. I was once even reprimanded for applauding a dance too loudly, as my neighbor said it was distracting.

The common American (and Danish) practice of applauding during the dancing, as soon as any skillful technical feat has been accomplished and while the music is still playing, is even more distracting. Fokine would have been particularly outraged by the audience which did this during a Ballet Theatre performance of *Les Sylphides*. The program should be studied before and after the performance, not during it; similarly comments and questions should be saved till after the last note of music, and preferably till after the applause. People who start chattering during the curtain calls (which are often a performance in themselves) are almost as irritating as those who do so during the overture.

All this may sound very harsh and puritanical. We go to the theater to enjoy ourselves, many people say, and why shouldn't we chat, or eat chocolates, or play with our bangles, if we want to? But all these things have an adverse effect on the people around and disturb the audience's complete concentration on what is happening on the stage. Discipline is necessary in a theater audience, as in all social activities. We can only fully appreciate a ballet (or an opera, play or concert for that matter) if we give it our full attention. I am therefore firmly on the side of those who say "shush," and complain about outsize hats, noisy jewelry, and critics who make clever comments. It therefore goes without saying that I am totally against the admission of latecomers, which should never be permitted during a ballet, and against people leaving the auditorium during a performance. However bad a ballet may seem, it is probably giving pleasure to other members of the audience.

No two people see quite the same performance. Our enjoyment obviously depends on our personal tastes, our degree of experience and sophistication, and our mood of the moment. Moreover no two pairs of eyes are physically the same, and no two seats in the theater give exactly the same view. Being both myopic and astigmatic, I always have opera glasses in the theater, using more or less powerful ones depending on where I am sitting. This means that I see less of the general pattern on the stage and less of the corps de ballet than most people, but also that I probably see more of the facial expressions of the principals and more detail of their arm and footwork. The same is true of people with normal sight who always sit very close to the stage. They cannot know the beautiful patterns formed by the swans or the sylphs, but they do know that the ballerina made an awful face as she jumped. People sitting in the higher tiers of the theater get a much better impression of the overall picture. Jumps look higher from the orchestra and footwork tends to sound less noisy. Regular balletgoers, and critics, should try to move around to different parts of the theater for different performances. It is astonishing how different the same ballet can look; indeed, some ballets definitely look better from the top tier, while others lose their effect and should always be seen from close quarters. In general the classics and pure dance works are better seen from a distance; dramatic works make a stronger impact at short range, or in a smaller theater.

Just as no two people see exactly the same performance, so no two people watch for exactly the same things. It is virtually impossible to take in all the various ingredients of a ballet, though with experience one learns to assimilate more and more. The newcomer to ballet may be so moved by the dramatic experience, or so excited by the visual spectacle, or so impressed by the sheer virtuosity of the dancers, that he notices little or nothing else. When I first went to ballet, I was not at all interested in scenery or costumes, and I rarely paid attention to facial expressions or arm movements. It was movement to music that excited me, and in particular various kinds of intricate footwork. I still find small precise beats of the feet, whether on the ground or during a jump in the air, very satisfying, especially when performed precisely to suitable music. But gradually I have learned to assimilate other aspects of dancing as well and even, by making a conscious effort, to respond to decor and costumes which remain, for me, the least important part of a ballet.

Even if one concentrates on the dancing, there are many ways of looking and judging. An attractive body with good proportions, an interesting or pretty face, elegant line, high elevation, precise and soft footwork, good posture, fire and personality—all these are important but their relative importance varies for different spectators. Some people are so irritated by a dancer who constantly stops in the middle of a solo to prepare for a difficult series of turns or jumps that they grudge praising the actual dancing, however well done. Others will readily forgive this sort of thing, and any amount of unmusicality, if the dancer's personality and technique are sufficiently striking. Illogically, I sometimes find myself condemning one dancer for landing heavily or breaking up the steps unmusically when I will readily accept the same thing from another dancer. But in general, movement out of time with the music, turns which are not properly finished to face the audience, hard, athletic movement in lyrical roles, and noisy dancing by ladies in blocked shoes or by men crashing down from jumps are the things which particularly irritate me. I can easily ignore the fact that a dancer does not jump very high, just as I can respond to an attractive or interesting face even if it is inexpressive. Over the years, however, I hope I have learned to attach less weight to my own particular tastes and prejudices and to assess all the aspects of a dancer's performance. Every balletgoer must go through the same process, starting subjectively with personal likes and dislikes and gradually learning to distinguish good from bad by more objective criteria.

The best way to learn about ballet is by watching it. Standards are built up by invidious but inevitable comparisons. By reading the critics, people discover what varied opinions even professional observers have of the same performance. They also discover that the critics spotted things which they missed. In addition they may read the specialist ballet magazines, and books on the history and technique of ballet. But it is perfectly possible to enjoy ballet, and to tell a good performance from a bad one, without any knowledge of history or of the technical terms involved. I am delighted that ballet in Britain has now attained the respectability of a school examination subject, but I hope that studying it for an examination will not kill anyone's love for it. Much of the detailed history and technical knowledge required is really useful only to a choreographer, or just possibly to a critic.

Of course it helps to understand some of the conventional sign language of classical mime, though little is used nowadays. The Prince's mother in *Swan Lake* points at the ring on her finger to indicate that he ought to get married; the Prince later swears his devotion to Odile by raising his right hand in the air straight above his head and holding his left hand to his heart; the conventional signal representing dancing, much used in the first act of *Giselle,* is the two hands rotated around each other above the head; the indication of a pretty face, used by the Lilac Fairy and Carabosse when casting their rival spells in the pro-logue of *The Sleeping Beauty,* is the hand circling around a smiling face. These are the commonest conventional signs; their meaning, like that of most other mime, is usually self-evident.

Some technical vocabulary is inevitably acquired by regular balletgoers: it is much easier to discuss performances by re-ferring to at least some of the steps by their correct names. (Attempts to describe complicated steps in technical terms often go awry, as writers and critics use the wrong names and even dancers and teachers frequently disagree about correct terminology.) It is useful to rocognize good "turn-out" and the five basic positions of the feet. "Plié" is the way the dancer bends the knees to take off for a jump and to land lightly after it. "Elevation" refers to movement in the air as opposed to "terre à terre," steps on the ground. "Ballon" is the quality of bounciness or springiness which some dancers have. A "jeté" is a jump from one foot to the other—"grands jetés" are those big scissorlike jumps which can bring dancers diagonally across a huge stage at rapid speed. The "entrechat" is a vertical jump with the legs and feet crisscrossing; it is included in most classical male solos and some female ones and if neatly done, with a high jump, is one of the most exciting steps in ballet. Another is the "tour en l'air" in which the male dancer spins right around while in the air, possibly two or three times and possibly repeating this feat several times in quick succession. This is most commonly done vertically, while the dancer re-mains on one spot on the stage, sometimes landing on one knee at the end, but it is even more exciting when done by a virtuoso dancer traveling around the stage, turning in the air while holding a posed position. A "fish dive" ("temps de poisson") is the exciting jump done by a ballerina in the last pas de deux of *The Sleeping Beauty.* Her partner catches her and holds her with one arm with her head down, almost touching the stage. (This depends on skillful partnering; if the Prince missed her, Aurora would fall flat on her face.)

One of the best-known steps on the floor of the stage is the "pirouette," a spinning turn on one foot with the other foot raised, a step done by both men and women. The "fouetté" is a particular type of pirouette, normally performed by women, in which the raised leg is whipped around the other knee in a circular movement while the dancer spins on the balancing leg. (Strictly speaking this should be called a "fouetté en tournant," the simple fouetté being the whipping motion without the turn.) The whipping motion is one of the many beaten steps, grouped under the name "batterie," which range from small beats of the foot on the ground or in steps of elevation like the entrechat to large beats in aerial steps like the "cabriole." "Bourrée" is now generally used to describe a girl dancer moving across the stage in small steps on her points, though this is sometimes called a "couru"; "pas de bourrée" also has many other meanings. There are various posed positions on the stage, of which the best known is the "arabesque" in which the body is balanced on one leg, with the arms outstretched to give a balancing line.

The technical vocabulary of ballet is nearly all French, and not all these technical terms are translatable, though English equivalents like "turns" and "beats" are used for some of them. Many of the terms are long and complicated, attempting to describe equally complicated combinations of steps. There are also French words ("de face," "croisé," "écarté," and "effacé") for the four possible positions of a dancer in relation to the audience—facing or oblique at various angles—and for the various grades and types of dancer.

The principal male dancer is often called a "premier danseur" and if he is the distinguished-looking type who plays princes and poets he is called a "danseur noble." Dancers who appear in groups of three or four, coming in rank between soloists and corps de ballet, are called "coryphées." A "demi-caractère" dancer uses classical technique in roles of a less noble or romantic kind, roles which require comic or other strong characterization. Massine's ballets are full of such roles, and so are Tudor's, but the term itself is not so commonly used nowadays. The full character dancer (as distinct from demi-caractère) specializes in mime and national folk dances, as in the Petipa divertissements, rather than in classical technique. Alexander Grant's part of Alain in *La Fille Mal Gardée* is demi-caractère; Stanley Holden's Widow Simone is full character. But, I repeat, one does not need to know any of this to appreciate the performances.

The appreciation and enjoyment of ballet is primarily an emotional and aesthetic thing, not an intellectual one. That is why neither historical nor technical knowledge is necessary and it is also why the intellectual content of a ballet is irrelevant to its success. Some people write as if intellectual or dramatic content, or relevance to contemporary life, were one of the prime requirements of a ballet. Those things are incidentals, which may be present in a bad ballet and absent in a good one. But this does not mean, as ballet's opponents appear to think, that ballet is therefore unimportant, and unworthy of serious consideration or public subsidy. It means that ballet is akin to music, painting, sculpture and athletics, not to drama or literature. The mistake is to look at ballet as a play without words; it is an obvious mistake but one we all make from time to time, for example when we start looking for a meaning that can be expressed in words in what is really an abstract ballet. The choreographer may well have a point of view, about life or love or the nature and use of the human body, but we should no more expect to be able to translate it into words than we can translate a Rodin or a Barbara Hepworth, a work by Bach or Britten, Rembrandt or Picasso, or the excitement aroused by an athlete or sportsman. Nevertheless, just as some of these can be described or analyzed in words, so some good ballets can also be described and analyzed and their content discussed—but that is not why they are good.

Ballets are good if they work in the theater. And when they do, they can work even more strongly than other branches of theatrical art. Anybody who has seen and heard the audience at a performance by Fonteyn and Nureyev or at a Bolshoi divertissement will know what this means; the audience is held, almost electrically, by the performance and its release when the curtain falls is signaled by prolonged and deafening applause, cheers and shouts. The only comparable occasions in the theater are operatic performances by the greatest singing actors, like Maria Callas, Tito Gobbi, Boris Christoff, or exceptional interpretations of the classic tragedies, like Laurence Olivier's Oedipus or Othello. The audience reaction to a favorite dancer in a new role, or making a farewell, to the first or last night of the Bolshoi or the Kirov, and to almost any performance by Fonteyn and Nureyev, Carla Fracci and Erik Bruhn, or Antoinette Sibley and Anthony Dowell is often more like the reaction to a big sporting event, such as the Cup Final. Flowers are thrown, dancers' names are shouted, the applause becomes rhythmic and hypnotic, and nearly hysterical.

That reaction, the queues at the box office when outstanding performances are announced, and the frequent emergence of a black market in tickets, are the answers to those who say that ballet is anachronistic or dying. In fact, as we have seen, it is very much more alive in the United States now than it has ever been before. It is particularly suited to young audiences today, who are inclined to attach more importance to sensation and physical or aesthetic experience than to logical coherence or intellectual content. Both in cinema and the legitimate theater are increasingly inclined to sacrifice continuity and plot to impressionism and the creation of exciting sense experiences. That is, and always has been, ballet's peculiar strength. Ballet, with its mixture of dance, decor and sound, is also particularly well suited to today's obsession with multimedia experiments of all kinds.

Moreover ballet is the most international form of theater. It is now developing and booming in more centers and in more countries than ever before. From being an art for a select elite, it has become truly popular on a gigantic scale. Opera is international, but only because operagoers either learn smatterings of German and Italian or are content to miss some of the drama or comedy which should be allied with opera's musical appeal. Ballet has no such problem; the international barriers are only those of style and taste, which can admittedly be almost as formidable but which with the increase in travel are being quickly broken down. In ballet, as in everything else, the world is rapidly becoming one. The dancers of America, Russia and Western Europe know each other and each other's work; so, increasingly, do their audiences. Exchange visits by companies and individual dancers, festivals, tourism, and ballet magazines are all helping to achieve a situation where dancers can more and more easily fit into a company or class anywhere in the world.

Ballet can easily be more poignant than spoken drama, more exciting than a sporting event, as entertaining as a variety show and as aesthetically satisfying as painting or sculpture. It can give an extra dimension to music, and reveal unsuspected grace and skill in the human body. In doing all this, it lifts the spectator out of his environment, out of time, out of himself. It leaves him feeling enriched or ennobled by the experience. That is the secret of its intense appeal. That is what makes it one of the highest forms of art. That is why it will not die.

Index

ST. MARY'S COLLEGE OF MARYLAND
ST. MARY'S CITY, MARYLAND

44321

ST. MARY'S COLLEGE OF MARYLAND
ST. MARY'S CITY, MARYLAND

7.95